POLICE OFFICER
EXAM
NEW YORK CITY

Prepare for Success!

Angelo Tropea

ISBN-13: 978-1508822776
ISBN-10: 1508822778

Published by Angelo Tropea

Please note that the passages, examples and questions used in this book are for study purposes only and do not reflect official names, codes, policies, rules or procedures of any governmental or public or private business, agency or department.

Unless otherwise clearly indicated, any similarity of names of persons, addresses, places and telephone numbers used in this book to any actual names of persons, addresses and telephone numbers is purely coincidental.

The information and web addresses presented in this book are current as of January 2017, but may change as time passes. Always consult the official NYPD site and other sites for the most up-to-date information.

CONTENTS

HOW TO PREPARE FOR SUCCESS   1

There are probably as many ways to study successfully as there are people. However, in more than thirty years of preparing study materials and conducting classes for civil service exams, I have found that certain methods seem to work better than others with the great majority of students. The following are time tested suggestions that you might want to consider as you incorporate this book in the study plan that is best for you.

SUGGESTIONS

1. First, read the Police Officer Exam Announcement.

As of January 2017, the exam announcement for exam No. 7323 is posted at:
https://www.nyc.gov/html/dcas/downloads/pdf/noes/201707323000.pdf

Future exam announcements will also be posted. For links to those announcements and for exam schedules, visit: http://www.nyc.gov/html/dcas/html/work/exam_monthly.shtml

The exam announcement details the job requirements and provides insights into the exam content and screening procedures. Visit NYPDRECRUIT.COM and their "Exam Center" which provides helpful and informative "Exam Tutorials," online and in PDF printable formats.

2. Briefly "skim" the contents of this book by reading the table of contents and then looking at each section to see the different types of questions, how they correspond to the Police Officer Exam (New York City) announcement, and the NYPD tutorials provided for free at NYPDRECRUIT.COM.

3. Try to study every day for at least half an hour – and longer (1-2 hours) if you can. To get the greatest benefit, try not to have very long sessions. Studies have indicated that frequent, shorter sessions are more effective than fewer, longer ones.

4. Study in a quiet, well-lit area with as few distractions as possible. This will help you to obtain the maximum benefit from each session.

5. Work on sections 3 – 11 in this book. They will introduce you to each type of question and provide practice questions with the answers explained.

The questions are similar to questions which the NYPD provides in their "Test Preparation Kit Sample Questions" at http://nypdrecruit.beta.hodes.com/exam-center/exam-tutorials The NYPD questions and answers are presented in two formats: "Online Tutorials" and in "Adobe Acrobat Reader" printable form.

Do not continue to the two practice exams until you have mastered all the different types of questions. Read all the comments after each answer to reinforce important facts and test-answering techniques. Try to record your answers on a separate sheet of paper and not in the book. This will make it easier for you to come back to the questions and answer them again without being influenced by your prior work.

6. Now tackle the multiple-choice Practice Exam #1. The exam has 86 questions, close to what you may see on the actual Police Officer Exam. Pay careful attention to every question that you don't answer correctly. If necessary, review the section in the book that relates to that type of question.

Try to take the practice exam in a single session (about 2 hours). By doing so, you will gain a valuable understanding of how long your attention span must last during the actual exam.

7. When you think you're ready, take Practice Exam #2. Again, pay careful attention to every question that you don't answer correctly and, if necessary, review the section in the book that relates to that question.

8. Because the test is administered on the computer, make sure that <u>before</u> the test date you're familiar with the computer keyboard and the fundamentals of computer operation. Practice with the "Online Tutorial" provided by the NYPD at

http://nypdrecruit.beta.hodes.com/exam-center/exam-tutorials

At the test site, listen carefully to the directions on how to use the computer, including how to select or change answers. Also, listen carefully to the procedure to follow if there is a computer malfunction. If you're not certain about anything, ask questions.

9. If some questions are hard for you, keep in mind what Thomas Edison once said: "Genius is one percent inspiration and ninety-nine percent perspiration."

Therefore, study every day.
Take this book with you – and make it your friend.

> "That which we persist in doing becomes easier, not that the task itself has become easier, but that our ability to perform it has improved."
>
> - Ralph Waldo Emerson

POLICE OFFICER NEW YORK CITY 2

INTRODUCTION

You must score well on the NYPD Police Officer Entrance Exam to be considered for appointment.

Because of this, the aim of this book is to keep it **simple** and **focused** on the NYPD written exam, instead of complicating it with other information about police officer jobs, tests and benefits in other cities and states which does <u>NOT</u> contribute to attaining a higher score on the NYPD written exam.

SIMPLE  FOCUSED

The NYPD has refined the process of applying and testing for the police officer job. The test is now administered on computer terminals at testing centers.

The application, testing process and subsequent hiring procedures are explained in detail in the official and informative website:

www.nypdrecruit.com

To obtain the most complete and up-to-date information, visit this website.

As of January 2017, the exam announcement for exam No. 7323 is posted at:
https://www.nyc.gov/html/dcas/downloads/pdf/noes/201707323000.pdf

Future exam announcements will also be posted as they become available. For links to those announcements and for exam schedules, visit:
http://www.nyc.gov/html/dcas/html/work/exam_monthly.shtml

POLICE OFFICER EXAM NEW YORK CITY

Among the topics covered on the nypdrecruit.com website are the following:

"Inside the NYPD"

    300 units

    Language Opportunities

    NYPD Sports

    Civilian Opportunities

    NYPD History

    Latest News

"Benefits and Salary"

    Military Benefits

    Promotional Opportunities

    Educational Opportunities

    College Resources

"Exam Center"

    Exam Schedule

    Exam & Employment Requirements

    Exam Tutorials

"The Hiring process"

    Job Standard Test

    JST Training Tips

    Bulletin Board

    Relocation Assistance

"Police Academy"

    Officer Standards

"FAQ"

As we said before, our aim is not to repeat what the NYPD already says well at the above website, but to provide **additional exercises and explanations and hints** about the types of questions that may be asked on the test with the aim of maximizing your score and thereby increasing your chances of being considered for a job.

TYPES OF QUESTIONS ON EXAM

Section	Question Type
3	**Written Comprehension** questions evaluate a candidate's ability to understand written passages, especially details in sentences and paragraphs.
4	**Written Expression** questions evaluate a candidate's ability to express herself clearly.
5	**Memorization** questions evaluate a candidate's ability to remember information that is provided in the form of pictures, numbers, procedures, etc.
6	**Problem Sensitivity** questions evaluate a candidate's ability to see the elements of a problem and the problem in its entirety.
7	**Deductive Reasoning** questions evaluate a candidate's ability to understand general rules and apply them to specific situations.
8	**Inductive Reasoning** questions evaluate a candidate's ability to combine details or separate pieces of information to form general rules.
9	**Information Ordering** questions evaluate a candidate's ability to put in order given rules or actions. The rules or actions can include letters, words, sentences, procedures, pictures, and logical or mathematical operations.
10	**Spatial Orientation** questions evaluate a candidate's ability to determine the candidate's location and the location of an object with respect to the candidate.
11	**Visualization** questions evaluate a candidate's ability to understand how an object would look when it is rotated or unfolded, or moved in any manner. These questions may also include facial recognition.

WRITTEN COMPREHENSION | 3

Written Comprehension

These questions evaluate your ability to understand written passages, especially **details** in sentences and paragraphs.

A written passage is presented and questions are asked that require you to carefully refer back to the passage.

SUGGESTIONS

Read all four choices (A, B, C, and D) and carefully consider each one before deciding which choice is best.

Pay careful attention to the details. Match every detail of each choice to the detail in the passage.

The correct answer choice will be the choice that most nearly matches all the details.

(To double-check your answer, make sure that the other choices are not correct because they contain at least one detail that does not match what is stated in the passage.)

POLICE OFFICER EXAM NEW YORK CITY

<u>Questions 1 - 3</u>

Answer questions 1 - 3 based on the information contained in the following paragraphs.

Police Officers Juan Medina and Cheryl Johnston were on foot patrol on July 4, 2016 when at 10:15 a.m. they came upon the scene of a minor traffic accident (at 5th Avenue and 48th Street in Manhattan) that had occurred 5 minutes earlier. Officer Medina called the Police Dispatcher at 10:20 a.m. and reported that the two drivers, who were the only persons in the vehicles, did not sustain any personal injuries. One of the vehicles, the one driven by a male named William Buxton, did have minor damage to the front bumper, and the other vehicle, driven by a male named Jack Solmer, had extensive damage to the rear bumper.

Officer Juan Medina examined the driver's licenses, vehicle registration certificates and vehicle insurance identification cards. The auto driven by William Buxton, age 39, was a silver 2009 Lexus, N.Y. license plate 9327ZA, owned by the driver, residing at 2932 East 78th Street, New York, N.Y. Mr. Buxton's N.Y. driver's license identification number is D1749 38647 92132 and the expiration date is November 30, 2018.

The driver of the other auto was Jack Solmer, age 41, residing at 9822 East 7th Street, Brooklyn, N.Y. Mr. Solmer's auto was a blue 2007 Infinity, NY license plate 407PMB. Mr. Solmer's driver's license identification number is A214 295 337 and the expiration date is December 31, 2018.

Officers Medina and Johnston completed a Vehicle Accident Report at 10:35 a.m. The report number was 08492647437.

-----

1. Select the best answer: What is the time of the accident?
A. 10:15 a.m.   C. 10:20 a.m.
B. 10:35 a.m.   D. before 10:15 a.m.

----

2. How many persons were injured as a result of the traffic accident?
A. 1   C. 2
B. 0   D. none of the above

----

3. Which car sustained extensive damage to the rear bumper?
A.   NY plate #407PMB, silver 2007 Infinity
B.   NY plate #9327ZA, silver 2009 Lexus
C.   NY plate #9327ZA, blue 2009 Lexus
D.   NY plate #407PMB, blue 2007 Infinity

Answers 1 – 3
(Correct answers are in **bold and underlined**.)

1. Select the best answer: What is the time of the accident?
A. 10:15 a.m.   C. 10:20 a.m.
B. 10:35 a.m.   **D. before 10:15 a.m.**

("Police Officers Juan Medina and Cheryl Johnston were on foot patrol on July 4, 2016 when at 10:15 a.m. they came upon the scene of a minor traffic accident (at 5ᵗʰ Avenue and 48ᵗʰ Street in Manhattan) that had occurred 5 minutes earlier."

The traffic accident happened 5 minutes before 10:15 a.m. (the time that the officers arrived at the scene). Therefore, the accident happened at 10:10 a.m. This 10:10 a.m. time is not listed as one of the choices, and choices "B" and "C" are times after 10:15 a.m. The best choice therefore is **"D. before 10:15 a.m."**)

----

2. How many persons were injured as a result of the traffic accident?
A. 1   C. 2
B. 0   D. none of the above

(In paragraph one it states, "... the two drivers, who were the only persons in the vehicles, did not sustain any personal injuries.")

----

3. Which car sustained extensive damage to the rear bumper?
A.   NY plate #407PMB, silver 2007 Infinity
B.   NY plate #9327ZA, silver 2009 Lexus
C.   NY plate #9327ZA, blue 2009 Lexus
D.   NY plate #407PMB, blue 2007 Infinity

(In paragraph one it states, **"...**the other vehicle, driven by a male named Jack Solmer, had extensive damage to the rear bumper...." In paragraph three it states, Mr. Solmer's auto was a blue 2007 Infinity, NY license plate 407PMB." The answer is choice "**D**" and not choice "A" because in choice "A" the color of the vehicle is stated as silver.)

Questions 4 - 6

Answer questions 4 - 6 based on the information contained in the following paragraphs.

Police Officers Jonathan Spencer and Anita Korich were on patrol in their squad car on May 17, 2016 when at 4:47 p.m. they witnessed a traffic accident at the intersection of 13th Avenue and 39th Street in Brooklyn. Officer Spencer called the Police Dispatcher at 4:55 p.m. and reported that the two drivers and their six passengers (three in each vehicle) did not sustain any personal injuries. One of the vehicles, the one driven by a male, Clark Winston, had damage to the driver's door, and the other vehicle, driven by a female, Beverly Marino, had damage to the front bumper and right side.

Officer Korich examined the driver's licenses, vehicle registration certificates and vehicle insurance identification cards. The auto driven by Clark Winston, age 49, was a red 2010 Ford Fusion, N.Y. license plate 3374BH, owned by the driver, residing at 2532 Cadman Plaza, Brooklyn, N.Y. Mr. Winston's N.Y. driver's license identification number is M3842 48547 62537 and the expiration date is October 31, 2018.

The driver of the other auto was Beverly Marino, age 54, residing at 165 Kings Avenue, Brooklyn, N.Y. Ms. Marino's auto was a black 2008 Ford Taurus, NY license plate 5491HKD. Ms. Marino's driver's license identification number is B315 396 236 and the expiration is December 31, 2018.

Officers Spencer and Korich completed a Vehicle Accident Report at 5:35 p.m. The report number was 04495642441.

-----

4. What is the time of the accident?
A. 4:47 a.m.   C. 5:35 p.m.
B. 5:55 p.m.   D. 4:47 p.m.

----

5. Which car sustained damage to the front bumper and right side?
A. NY plate #5497HDK, black 2008 Ford Taurus
B. NY plate #3374BH, red 2010 Ford Fusion
C. NY plate #5491HKD, black 2008 Ford Taurus
D. NY plate #3374BH, red 2001 Ford Fusion

----

6. What is the total number of persons in the two vehicles?
A. 2   C. 9
B. 6   D. none of the above

<u>Answers 4 - 6</u>
(Correct answers are in **<u>bold and underlined</u>**.)

4. What is the time of the accident?
A. 4:47 a.m.
B. 5:55 p.m.
C. 5:35 p.m.
<u>D. 4:47 p.m.</u>

(In paragraph one it states, "Police Officers Jonathan Spencer and Anita Korich were on patrol in their squad car on May 17, 2016 when at <u>4:47 p.m.</u> they witnessed a traffic accident....")

----

5. Which car sustained damage to the front bumper and right side?
A.   NY plate #5497HDK, black 2008 Ford Taurus
B.   NY plate #3374BH, red 2010 Ford Fusion
<u>C.   NY plate #5491HKD, black 2008 Ford Taurus</u>
D.   NY plate #3374BH, red 2001 Ford Fusion

(In paragraph one it states, "...the other vehicle, driven by a female, <u>Beverly Marino, had damage to the front bumper and right side</u>." Paragraph three states, "<u>Ms. Marino's auto was a black 2008 Ford Taurus, NY license plate 5491HKD.</u>")

----

6. What is the total number of persons in the two vehicles?
A. 2
B. 6
C. 9
<u>D. none of the above</u>

(In paragraph one it states, "...<u>the two drivers and their six passengers</u> did not sustain any personal injuries."
(2 drivers + 6 passengers = 8 persons)
The correct answer (8) is not listed as a choice. Therefore, **"<u>D. none of the above</u>,"** is the correct choice.)

Questions 7 - 10

Answer questions 7 - 10 based on the information contained in the following paragraphs.

Police Officers Albert Dixon and Susan Chin were on patrol in their squad car on June 7, 2016 when at 6:35 p.m. a man approached them. The man pointed to his parked car and stated that a blue Infinity had just sideswiped it. The blue Infinity was now stopped about one hundred feet down the block. Police Officer Albert Dixon called the police dispatcher at 6:40 p.m. and reported the traffic accident (which occurred in front of 745 3rd Avenue, Staten Island). Police Officer Susan Chin questioned the driver of the stopped blue Infinity. Both Police Officers reported to the dispatcher that the driver of the blue Infinity and the owner of the sideswiped car (a 2008 Chevy Malibu) did not sustain any injuries. Also, there were no passengers in the two cars. One of the vehicles, the blue Infinity, was driven and owned by a male, Matthew Fowler. It had damage to the front bumper. The other vehicle, owned by a male, Mark Peterson, had damage to the two doors on the driver's side.

Officer Dixon examined the driver's licenses, vehicle registration certificates and vehicle insurance identification cards. The auto driven by Matthew Fowler, age 42, was a blue 2012 Infinity, N.Y. license plate 45834DK, owned by the driver, residing at 147-49 Ferdinand Road, Brooklyn, N.Y. Mr. Fowler's N.Y. driver's license identification number is P3647 38537 22438 and the expiration date is September 30, 2018.

The owner of the parked auto was Mark Peterson, age 57, residing at 284 West 6th Street, Bronx, N.Y. Mr. Peterson's auto was a silver 2008 Chevy Malibu, NY license plate 2493GKL. Mr. Peterson's driver's license identification number is C615 792 339 and the expiration is November 30, 2018.

Officers Dixon and Chin completed a Vehicle Accident Report at 7:05 p.m. The report number was 024976454324.

-----

7. Select the best answer: The time of the accident is approximately:
A. 6:35 a.m.   C. 9:40 p.m.
B. 6:53 p.m.   D. 6:35 p.m.

----

8. Which car sustained damage to the two doors on the driver's side?
A.   NY plate #45834DK, blue 2012 Infinity
B.   NY plate #2493GKL, silver 2008 Chevy Malibu
C.   NY plate #45834DK, silver 2012 Infinity
D.   NY plate #2493GKL, blue 2008 Chevy Malibu

9. What is the total number of persons (passengers and drivers) involved?
A. 1
B. 2
C. 3
D. none of the above

----

10. The owner of the parked vehicle resides at:
A. 284 West 6th Street, Brooklyn, NY
B. 745 3rd Avenue, Staten Island
C. 147-49 Ferdinand Road, Brooklyn, N.Y.
D. 284 West 6th Street, Bronx, N.Y.

Answers 7 – 10
(Correct answers are in **bold and underlined**.)

7. Select the best answer: The time of the accident is approximately:
A. 6:35 a.m.
B. 6:53 p.m.
C. 9:40 p.m.
D. 6:35 p.m.

(In paragraph one it states, "Police Officers Albert Dixon and Susan Chin were on patrol in their squad car on June 7, 2016 when at 6:35 p.m. a man approached them. The man pointed to his parked car and stated that a blue Infinity had just sideswiped it.")

----

8. Which car sustained damage to the two doors on the driver's side?
A.   NY plate #45834DK, blue 2012 Infinity
B.   NY plate #2493GKL, silver 2008 Chevy Malibu
C.   NY plate #45834DK, silver 2012 Infinity
D.   NY plate #2493GKL, blue 2008 Chevy Malibu

(In paragraph two it states, "The owner of the parked auto was Mark Peterson, age 57, residing at 284 West 6th Street, Bronx, N.Y. Mr. Peterson's auto was a silver 2008 Chevy Malibu, NY license plate 2493GKL.)

----

9. What is the total number of persons (passengers and drivers) involved?
A. 1
B. 2
C. 3
D. none of the above

(Only the two drivers were involved. "Both Police Officers reported to the dispatcher that the driver of the blue Infinity and the owner of the sideswiped car (a 2008 Chevy Malibu) did not sustain any injuries. Also, "…there were no passengers in the two cars.")

----

10. The owner of the parked vehicle resides at:
A. 284 West 6th Street, Brooklyn, NY
B. 745 3rd Avenue, Staten Island
C. 147-49 Ferdinand Road, Brooklyn, N.Y.
D. 284 West 6th Street, Bronx, N.Y.

(Paragraph 3: "The owner of the parked auto was Mark Peterson, age 57, residing at 284 West 6th Street, Bronx, NY.")

"Practice even the things you despair in, for even the left hand, ineffectual for things for want of practice, holds the bridle more vigorously than the right hand; for it has been practiced in this."

\- Marcus Aurelius

WRITTEN EXPRESSION

4

These questions evaluate your ability to express yourself clearly enough so that others will understand.

Two or more versions of a written sample are provided.

You are asked to decide which version(s) are clear, accurate, complete, and grammatically correct.

In deciding which versions are correct, consider the following (one at a time):

Is the **grammar correct**?

Is the **passage clear**?

Is the **information accurate**?

Is the **information complete**?

Example

An officer is reviewing a report she is preparing. It contains the following two rough drafts. Which of the two sentences are grammatically correct?

1. Proper training and attitude proper grooming and proper wearing of a well maintained uniform are important in conveying a confident and professional appearance

2. In addition to proper training and attitude, proper grooming and the wearing of a well maintained uniform are important in conveying a confident and professional appearance.

A. Only sentence 1 is grammatically correct.
B. Only sentence 2 is grammatically correct.
C. Both sentences 1 and 2 are grammatically correct.
D. Neither sentence 1 nor sentence 2 is grammatically correct.

Before we attempt to answer, let's develop an approach to this type of question and do a quick review of some basic rules of grammar, usage, punctuation and sentence structure.

FIRST, READ EACH SENTENCE CAREFULLY TO SEE IF IT HAS ANY OF THE FOLLOWING FLAWS:

1. DOES IT SOUND LIKE ENGLISH - OR DOES IT SOUND LIKE STREET TALK?
Some obvious examples: (Underlining is for emphasis of correct/incorrect English usage.)
>   **Correct:** I go to the store every day.
>   **Not Correct:** I goes to the store every day.

>   **Correct:** It doesn't matter how much it costs.
>   **Not Correct:** It don't matter how much it costs.

2. IS THE SENTENCE IN A LOGICAL SEQUENCE? ARE THE MAIN IDEAS PROPERLY CONNECTED?
Example: Which of the following three choices is/are correct?
>   (1) The boy who dropped out of high school didn't like to study.
>   (2) The boy didn't like to study dropped out of high school.
>   (3) The boy dropped out didn't like to study.
Answer: (1) is the most logical and grammatically correct.

3. ARE THERE ANY MISSPELLED WORDS?
Example:

    assistant and NOT asistant
    court facility and NOT court fasility
    believe and NOT beleive
    precinct and NOT precint

(For a list of important spelling and vocabulary words, see page 292.)

4. ARE WORDS USED CORRECTLY?
    The principal (NOT principle) of the school was Mr. Kane.
    The advice (NOT advise) was very welcomed.
    They complimented (NOT complemented) her for her hard work.
    Their (NOT there) car needed repair.
    He picked up the stationery (NOT stationary) for the captain in room 605.
    He was too (NOT "to" or "two") happy to speak.
    The Police Officer accepted (NOT excepted) the medal.
    The work site (NOT cite) was very clean.
    Someone who is not moving is stationary (NOT stationery).
    The capital city (NOT capitol) of New York State is Albany.

5. ARE APOSTROPHES USED CORRECTLY?
    The boy's (NOT boys) hat was yellow.

IF YOU CANNOT ELIMINATE THE SENTENCE AS BEING BAD AFTER APPLYING THE ABOVE GENERAL RULES, REVIEW THE SENTENCE FOR THE FOLLOWING GRAMMATICAL ERRORS. (REMEMBER THAT FOR ALL OF THE FOLLOWING RULES, THERE ARE EXCEPTIONS.)

---

1. EVERY SENTENCE BEGINS WITH A CAPITAL LETTER AND ENDS WITH A PERIOD.

2. FOR A SENTENCE TO BE COMPLETE, IT MUST HAVE AT MINIMUM A SUBJECT AND A PREDICATE. OTHERWISE, IT IS JUST A SENTENCE FRAGMENT.

A **subject** is usually a noun (person, place, or thing) about which something is asked or stated. Example: The police officer (subject) speaks softly.

A **predicate** contains a verb (an "action" word) and is the part of the sentence about what is said about the subject. In the above example, the predicate is "speaks."

3. A VERB AND ITS SUBJECT MUST AGREE IN NUMBER.
The Police Officers <u>looks</u> tall. (NOT CORRECT)
The Police Officers <u>look</u> tall. (CORRECT)

Police Officers is plural (more than one). "Police Officers" and "look" agree in number.

Another example:
The men and the woman <u>works</u> in the same precinct. (NOT CORRECT)
The men and the woman <u>work</u> in the same precinct. (CORRECT)

The men and the woman is a plural subject and takes a plural verb <u>work</u>.

The boy <u>works</u> (singular verb). The boy and girl <u>work</u> (plural verb).

4. A COMMA USUALLY GOES BEFORE THE FOLLOWING WORDS - but, for, or, nor, so, yet - WHEN THE WORD CONNECTS TWO MAIN CLAUSES.
Examples:
He didn't like to study, but he liked to play.
He scored a high mark, for he had received good training.
You can try hard and succeed, or you can make a feeble attempt and fail.
He didn't try hard, nor did he try for long.
He studied long and hard, so he passed.
He was sick when he took the test, yet he did very well.

5. A COMMA USUALLY GOES AFTER AN INTRODUCTORY PHRASE.
Examples:
When you study, you build up the neural connections in your brain.
Because of hard work and a little good luck, he succeeded in life.

6. A COMMA USUALLY GOES BETWEEN SEPARATE ITEMS IN A LIST OR SERIES OF ADJECTIVES.
Examples:
The boy was young, proud, and happy.
The tall, young, proud boy walked up to the front of the room.

7. COMMAS USUALLY SET OFF <u>PARENTHETICAL ELEMENTS</u>.
Examples:
Young boys, <u>as Abraham Lincoln once observed</u>, should not be afraid to work hard.
American soldiers, <u>generally speaking,</u> are very well trained.

8. A SEMICOLON IS USUALLY USED BETWEEN MAIN CLAUSES NOT LINKED BY and, but, for, or, nor, so, yet.
Examples:
The young boys played basketball; the older men sat on the bleachers.
The war had many battles; few were as fierce as this one.

Notice that the letter after the semicolon is NOT capitalized.

9. THE COLON IS USUALLY USED TO DIRECT ATTENTION TO A SERIES.
Example: The ingredients of success are as follows: hard work, commitment, and luck.

If grammar is not your strong point, or if you feel you need to concentrate more on it, there are many "rules of grammar" books available. For free online resources, search "rules of grammar" for an almost endless number of informative websites.

For a list of important spelling and vocabulary words, see section 17.

Question 1

1. An officer is reviewing a report she is preparing. It contains the following two rough drafts. Which of the two sentences are grammatically correct?

1. Proper training and attitude proper grooming and proper wearing of a well maintained uniform are important in conveying a confident and professional appearance

2. In addition to proper training and attitude, proper grooming and the wearing of a well maintained uniform are important in conveying a confident and professional appearance.

A. Only sentence 1 is grammatically correct.
B. Only sentence 2 is grammatically correct.
C. Both sentences 1 and 2 are grammatically correct.
D. Neither sentence 1 nor sentence 2 is grammatically correct.

Answer 1

ANSWER IS "B. Only sentence 2 is grammatically correct."
(Sentence 1 needs a comma after "attitude" and a period at the end of the sentence.)

Applicable rules:
"A comma usually goes between separate items on a list or series of adjectives."
"Every sentence begins with a capital letter and ends with a period."

Questions 2 – 3

2. An officer is asked by his partner to review a report that the officer is preparing. It contains the following two versions of one part of the report. Which are grammatically correct?

1. Mr Jones stated that although he would accept the speeding ticket, he would not pay it on principal and that he would immediately tear it up.

2. Mr Jones said that he would accept the speeding ticket, but on principle he would not pay it and would immediately tear it up.

A. Only sentence 1 is grammatically correct.
B. Only sentence 2 is grammatically correct.
C. Both sentences 1 and 2 are grammatically correct.
D. Neither sentence 1 nor sentence 2 is grammatically correct.

----

3. An officer is preparing a report and has not decided which of two versions of a specific section he wishes to use. Which of the following two versions are grammatically correct?

1. Mr. Kim Jones and Mr. David Alsbury has not decided whether to testify. Both believe that the complaint is not merited.

2. Mr. Kim Jones and Mr. David Alsbury have not decided whether to testify. Both beleive that the complaint is not merited.

A. Only sentence 1 is grammatically correct.
B. Only sentence 2 is grammatically correct.
C. Both sentences 1 and 2 are grammatically correct.
D. Neither sentence 1 nor sentence 2 is grammatically correct.

Answers 2 – 3

2. An officer is asked by his partner to review a report that the officer is preparing. It contains the following two versions of one part of the report. Which are grammatically correct?

1. Mr Jones stated that although he would accept the speeding ticket, he would not pay it on principal and that he would immediately tear it up.

2. Mr Jones said that he would accept the speeding ticket, but on principle he would not pay it and would immediately tear it up.

D. Neither sentence 1 nor sentence 2 is grammatically correct.
(Both sentences need a period at the end of "Mr." Also, "principal" in sentence 1 should be "principle.")

----

3. An officer is preparing a report and has not decided which of two versions of a specific section he wishes to use. Which of the following two versions are grammatically correct?

    1. Mr. Kim Jones and Mr. David Alsbury <u>has</u> not decided whether to testify. Both believe that the complaint is not merited.

    2. Mr. Kim Jones and Mr. David Alsbury have not decided whether to testify. Both <u>beleive</u> that the complaint is not merited.

D. Neither sentence 1 nor sentence 2 is grammatically correct.
(The "has" in sentence 1 should be "have" and "beleive" in sentence two should be "believe.")

Questions 4 - 6

4. Police Officer Charles Pinto is preparing a speech that he will give at a Community Board meeting. Which of the following two versions are correct?

    1. Persons should call 911 to report emergencies they will receive a fast response.

    2. Persons should call 911 to report emergencies. They will receive a fast response.

A. 1 only is correct.

B. 2 only is correct.

C. Neither 1 nor 2 is correct.

D. Both 1 and 2 are correct.

----

5. Police Officer Janet Ryker is preparing an instruction sheet on how to process reports. Which of the following two versions are correct?

    1. Properly preparing reports is an important part of a Police Officers duties. This is especially true when filling out reports of aided cases or unusual occurrences.

    2. Properly preparing reports is an important part of a Police Officer's duties this is especially true when filling out reports of aided cases or unusual occurrences.

A. 1 only is correct.

B. 2 only is correct.

C. Neither 1 nor 2 is correct.

D. Both 1 and 2 are correct.

----

6. Police Officer Kim Gallon is checking the correctness of sentences in one of her reports. Which of the following two sentences are correct?

1. Because rules and reggulations must be clearly understood and correctly applied, your ability to understand and apply facts and information to given situations is vital for the proper performance of your duties.

2. Because rules and regulations must be clearly understood and correctly applied, your ability to understand and apply facts and information to given situations is vital for the proper performence of your duties.

A. 1 only is correct.

C. Neither 1 nor 2 is correct.

B. 2 only is correct.

D. Both 1 and 2 are correct.

Answers 4 – 6

4. Police Officer Charles Pinto is preparing a speech that he will give at a Community Board meeting. Which of the following two sentences are correct?

1. Persons should call 911 to report <u>emergencies they</u> will receive a fast response.

2. Persons should call 911 to report emergencies. They will receive a fast response.

B. 2 only is correct.

(Sentence one is a run-on sentence. It needs a period after "emergencies" and a capital "T" for the word "they.")

----

5. Police Officer Janet Ryker is preparing an instruction sheet on how to process reports. Which of the following two versions are correct?

1. Properly preparing reports is an important part of a <u>Police Officers</u> duties. This is especially true when filling out reports of aided cases or unusual occurrences.

2. Properly preparing reports is an important part of a Police Officer's <u>duties this</u> is especially true when filling out reports of aided cases or unusual occurrences.

C. Neither 1 nor 2 is correct.

(One is not correct because "a Police Officers" should be "a Police Officer's" – <u>singular possessive</u>. Two is not correct because it is a run-on sentence. It should have a period after "duties" and a capital "T" for the word "this.")

6. Police Officer Kim Gallon is checking the correctness of sentences in one of her reports. Which of the following two sentences are correct?

1. Because rules and <u>reggulations</u> must be clearly understood and correctly applied, your ability to understand and apply facts and information to given situations is vital for the proper performance of your duties.

2. Because rules and regulations must be clearly understood and correctly applied, your ability to understand and apply facts and information to given situations is vital for the proper <u>performence</u> of your duties.

C. Neither 1 nor 2 is correct.

(One is not correct because the word "regulations" is misspelled "reggulations." Two is not correct because the word "performance" is misspelled "performence.")

Another type of WRITTEN EXPRESSION question may ask you to select the best summary of the information that is provided.

The best summary is the one that expresses the information in the most <u>clear, accurate and complete manner.</u>

Before we try to answer a question of this type, let's consider the following simple example:

Information provided:

A 16 year old boy was struck by a 2002 Buick on August 17, 2016.

Not clear:

2002 Buick on August 17, 2016, a 16 year old boy.

Clear:

A 2002 Buick, on August 17, 2016, struck a 16 year old boy.

Not accurate:

A 16 year old boy was struck by a 2012 Buick on August 17, 2016.

(Year of vehicle is not correct. It should be <u>2002</u> and not 2012.)

Accurate:

A 16 year old boy was struck by a <u>2002</u> Buick on August 17, 2016.

Not complete:

A boy was struck by a 2002 Buick on August 17, 2016.

(Age of the boy is missing.)

Complete:

A <u>16 year old boy</u> was struck by a 2002 Buick on August 17, 2016.

Question 7

Officer Ahren is asked to select the best summary (A, B, C, or D) of the following information: (The best summary is the one that expresses the information in the **most clear, accurate and complete manner**).

Place of accident: in front of 1726 West 8th Street, Brooklyn

Time of accident: 12:25 P.M.

Date of accident: September 11, 2016

Vehicle involved: 2006 Toyota

Driver: Cecilia Langer

Damage: cracked windshield

Details: A small branch fell from a tree and cracked the windshield of a 2006 Toyota.

-----

7. A. On September 11, 2016, in front of 1726 West 8th Street, Brooklyn, a small branch fell from a tree and cracked the windshield of a 2006 Toyota, owned by Cecilia Langer.

B. On September 11, 2016, in front of 1726 West 8th Street, Brooklyn, a small branch fell from a tree and cracked the windshield of a 2006 Toyota, driven by Cecilia Langer.

C. On September 11, 2016, at 12:52 P.M., in front of 1726 West 8th Street, Brooklyn, a small branch fell from a tree and cracked the windshield of a 2006 Toyota, driven by Cecilia Langer.

D. On September 11, 2016, at 12:25 P.M., in front of 1726 West 8th Street, Brooklyn, a small branch fell from a tree and cracked the windshield of a 2006 Toyota, driven by Cecilia Langer.

Answer 7

Officer Ahren is asked to select the best summary (A, B, C, or D) of the following information: (The best summary is the one that expresses the information in the **most clear, accurate and complete manner).**

Place of accident: in front of 1726 West 8th Street, Brooklyn

Time of accident: 12:25 P.M.

Date of accident: September 11, 2016

Vehicle involved: 2006 Toyota

Driver: Cecilia Langer

Damage: cracked windshield

Details: A small branch fell from a tree and cracked the windshield of a 2006 Toyota.

-----

7. A. On September 11, 2016, in front of 1726 West 8th Street, Brooklyn, a small branch fell from a tree and cracked the windshield of a 2006 Toyota, owned by Cecilia Langer.

(WRONG because it states the car was "owned" by Cecilia Langer. The information says that Cecilia Langer was the "driver." Also, the time of the accident, 12:25 P.M., is not stated.)

B. On September 11, 2016, in front of 1726 West 8th Street, Brooklyn, a small branch fell from a tree and cracked the windshield of a 2006 Toyota, driven by Cecilia Langer.

(WRONG because the time of the accident, 12:25 P.M. is not stated.)

C. On September 11, 2016, at 12:52 P.M., in front of 1726 West 8th Street, Brooklyn, a small branch fell from a tree and cracked the windshield of a 2006 Toyota, driven by Cecilia Langer.

(WRONG because the time of the accident is wrong. The correct time is 12:25 P.M. and not 12:52 P.M.)

D. On September 11, 2016, at 12:25 P.M., in front of 1726 West 8th Street, Brooklyn, a small branch fell from a tree and cracked the windshield of a 2006 Toyota, driven by Cecilia Langer.

(CORRECT ANSWER. This is the only choice that contains all the information and does not contain any factual errors.)

Question 8

Police Officer Slavik obtains the following information at the scene of a traffic accident:

Date of accident: July 4, 2016
Time of accident: 2:25 P.M.
Place of accident: intersection of 5th Avenue and 48th Street, Staten Island
Vehicles involved: 2007 Nissan and 2011 Buick
Drivers: Abe Molson (2007 Nissan) and Carol Soto (2011 Buick)
Damage: dent on driver's door of 2011 Buick

-----

8. Police Officer Slavik drafts four versions to express the above information. Which of the following four versions is most clear, accurate and complete?

A. On July 4, 2016, at 2:25 P.M., at the intersection of 5th Avenue and 48th Street, Staten Island, a 2007 Nissan and a 2011 Buick were involved in a traffic accident. The 2011 Buick, owned by Carol Soto, sustained a dent on the driver's door. The 2007 Nissan, driven by Abe Molson, did not sustain any damage.

B. At the intersection of 5th Avenue and 48th Street, Staten Island, a 2007 Nissan, owned by Abe Molson, and a 2011 Buick owned by Carol Soto, were involved in a car accident. The driver's door of the 2007 Nissan was dented. The accident occurred on July 4, 2016, at 2:25 P.M.

C. At the intersection of 5th Avenue and 48th Street, a 2007 Buick, owned by Abe Molson, and a 2011 Buick owned by Carol Soto, were involved in a car accident. The driver's door of the 2007 Nissan was dented. The accident occurred on July 4, 2016.

D. On July 4, 2016, at 2:25 P.M., at the intersection of 5th Avenue and 48th Street, Staten Island, a 2007 Nissan and a 2011 Buick were involved in a traffic accident. The 2011 Buick, driven by Carol Soto, sustained a dent on the driver's door. The 2007 Nissan, driven by Abe Molson, did not sustain any damage.

Answer 8

Police Officer Slavik obtains the following information at the scene of a traffic accident:

Date of accident: July 4, 2016
Time of accident: 2:25 P.M.
Place of accident: intersection of 5ᵗʰ Avenue and 48ᵗʰ Street, Staten Island
Vehicles involved: 2007 Nissan and 2011 Buick
Drivers: Abe Molson (2007 Nissan) and Carol Soto (2011 Buick)
Damage: dent on driver's door of 2011 Buick

-----

8. Police Officer Slavik drafts four versions to express the above information. Which of the following four versions is most clear, accurate and complete?

A. On July 4, 2016, at 2:25 P.M., at the intersection of 5ᵗʰ Avenue and 48ᵗʰ Street, Staten Island, a 2007 Nissan and a 2011 Buick were involved in a traffic accident. The 2011 Buick, owned by Carol Soto, sustained a dent on the driver's door. The 2007 Nissan, driven by Abe Molson, did not sustain any damage.
(WRONG. This summary is not accurate. The 2011 Buick was driven by Carol Soto, not owned by her.)

B. At the intersection of 5ᵗʰ Avenue and 48ᵗʰ Street, Staten Island, a 2007 Nissan, owned by Abe Molson, and a 2011 Buick owned by Carol Soto, were involved in a car accident. The driver's door of the 2007 Nissan was dented. The accident occurred on July 4, 2016, at 2:25 P.M.
(WRONG. This summary is not accurate. The damage was to the 2011 Buick, not the 2007 Nissan. Also, the 2011 Buick was driven by Carol Soto, not owned by her, and the 2007 Nissan was driven by Abe Molson and not owned by him.)

C. At the intersection of 5ᵗʰ Avenue and 48ᵗʰ Street, a 2007 Buick, owned by Abe Molson, and a 2011 Buick owned by Carol Soto, were involved in a car accident. The driver's door of the 2007 Nissan was dented. The accident occurred on July 4, 2016.
(WRONG. This summary is incomplete and not accurate. The time of the accident, 2:25 P.M., is not stated. Also, the cars were "driven by" and not "owned" by the persons named.)

D. On July 4, 2016, at 2:25 P.M., at the intersection of 5ᵗʰ Avenue and 48ᵗʰ Street, Staten Island, a 2007 Nissan and a 2011 Buick were involved in a traffic accident. The 2011 Buick, driven by Carol Soto, sustained a dent on the driver's door. The 2007 Nissan, driven by Abe Molson, did not sustain any damage.
(CORRECT ANSWER. It contains all the information and has no errors.)

MEMORIZATION 5

These questions evaluate your ability to remember information that is provided in the form of pictures, numbers, procedures, etc.

You may be shown a picture and asked to examine it for a specified number of minutes (5 – 10 minutes). You will then be instructed not to look at the picture any longer and to answer 10-15 questions relating to details in the picture (Example: words, numbers, and images).

This question is probably not a type of question that you encountered during your school years. Because it may be different and new to you, it may be very helpful to practice answering such questions.

MEMORIZATION

The methods of remembering details from a written passage or a picture are similar. In both cases, we can remember more if we concentrate on the details and organize the information into logical categories.

ORGANIZING INFORMATION INTO 5 CATEGORIES

1. WHO?

Names or Titles of Persons

(Police Officers, pedestrians, children, drivers, perpetrators, ethnicity, race, etc.)

2. WHAT?

(a scheduled event, accident, parade, protest, daily scene, store sales, etc.)

3. WHERE?

(address, in front of, place, room, specific area....)

4. WHEN?

(date, event, special occasion; before/after)

5. WHY?

(reason for scene, motivation of persons depicted, etc.)

HOW CAN I PRACTICE MEMORY QUESTIONS?

Every day we are bombarded with a variety of pictures, including in newspapers, magazines and on the web.

Choose any picture from one of these sources and concentrate on it for ten minutes. Try to memorize as much detail as you can by using the organizing technique described above (or by any other method that helps you remember). Put the picture aside and do something else for another ten minutes. Then, without looking back at the picture, write down as much detail as you can remember – no matter how trivial. (Waiting for 10 minutes will help you reinforce your memory technique.)

Do at least one exercise each day. Choose different types of images. You will be surprised at how much your memory technique (and comfort level with this type of question) will improve.

Memorization

Memory is <u>not</u> dependent on intelligence.

Memorization is a <u>skill</u> and it can be improved with practice!

The following pages contain memory exercises. While doing the exercises, consider the following suggestions:

-----

1. Study the picture carefully for the entire time that you are allowed to look at it.

2. Try to remember as much detail as you can. The more detail you can remember, the greater will be your chances of obtaining a higher score. Keep in mind that details that are relevant to the job probably have a greater possibility of being the subject of memory questions.

3. Some memory experts suggest that you mentally divide the picture into 4 quarters and examine each quarter individually. They also suggest that after you finish examining each quarter, you quickly try to remember the details in the preceding quarters that you have memorized. During the memorization periods, try to repeat in your mind important details.

4. While you are trying to memorize the entire picture (or a quarter at a time) keep in mind the Who? What? Where? When? and Why?

5. As much as possible, arrange or group things and events in your mind.

6. If you find it helpful, close your eyes briefly and form a mental picture of the image.

7. If you feel that you have finished memorizing as much detail as possible and you still have more time to memorize, go back to the picture and memorize some more.

8. If appropriate and time permits, imagine yourself "walking through the scene." Many agree that after walking to a new place they have little trouble remembering the route.

_____

Memory Exercise #1

Study the picture below for the next ten minutes. Try to remember as many details about the people and objects as you can. During the ten minutes, you are not permitted to take any notes or write anything.

At the end of ten minutes you will be asked to answer questions 1 – 10 (<u>without</u> looking back at the picture).

(After ten minutes)

Instructions for questions 1 – 10:

<u>Without</u> looking back at the picture, answer questions 1 – 10 on the following page.

(Note: These questions are intentionally difficult – probably harder than on the test.)

1. The number of people in the picture is:

A. 4   B. 5   C. 6   D. 7

2. How many of the males are wearing a hat?

A. 1   B. 2   C. 3   D. 4

3. Choose the best answer. The male wearing black sneakers is:

A. wearing white pants.

B. not wearing sunglasses.

C. black.

D. wearing a mostly white cap with a dark circle on it.

4. How many females are there in the picture?

A. 1

B. 2

C. 3

D. 4

5. With regard to the females:

A. Only one is wearing a necklace.

B. Neither one is wearing a necklace.

C. Both are wearing sunglasses.

D. none of the above

6. How many of the males are wearing sunglasses?

A. none   B. one   C. two   D. three

7. How many people are wearing sneakers?

A. 2   B. 3   C. 4   D. 5

8. How many of the females are wearing white blouses?

A. none   B. one   C. two   D. three

9. How many males are wearing white T-shirts?

A. none   B. one   C. two   D. three

10. How many openings are there in the walls behind the people?

A. one

B. two

C. three

D. four

_____

Memory Exercise #1

How did you try to notice and remember the details in the picture?

As you looked at the picture, you may have been asking -

- What am I looking at?

    5 young people, 3 males and 2 females in front of brick walls

- What kind of brick walls?

    old and worn, with 2 "window-like" openings

-What do the 5 people have in common?

    All are wearing sunglasses.

    All are wearing sneakers.

    All are wearing dark colored clothes.

- What do the 3 males have in common?

    All are wearing caps, dark sunglasses, and sneakers.

    The caps have symbols on them (circle, rectangle, etc.).

- What do the 2 females have in common?

    Both are wearing sunglasses and necklaces (and shortened, black T-shirts).

> "The true art of memory is the art of attention."
>
> - Samuel Johnson (1709-1784)

1. The number of people in the picture is:

A. 4   **B. 5**   C. 6   D. 7

2. How many of the males are wearing a hat?

A. 1   B. 2   **C. 3**   D. 4

3. Choose the best answer. The male wearing black sneakers is:

A. wearing white pants.

B. not wearing sunglasses.

C. black.

D. wearing a mostly white cap with a dark circle on it.

4. How many females are there in the picture?

A. 1   **B. 2**   C. 3   D. 4

5. With regard to the females:

A. Only one is wearing a necklace.

B. Neither one is wearing a necklace.

C. Both are wearing sunglasses.

D. none of the above

6. How many of the males are wearing sunglasses?

A. None   B. one   C. two   **D. three**

7. How many people are wearing sneakers?

A. 2   B. 3   C. 4   **D. 5**

8. How many of the females are wearing white blouses?

A. none   B. one   C. two   D. three

9. How many males are wearing white T-shirts?

A. none   B. one   C. two   D. three

10. How many openings are there in the walls behind the people?

A. one   **B. two**   C. three   D. four

Memory Exercise #2

Study the picture below for the next ten minutes. Try to remember as many details about the people and objects as you can. During the ten minutes, you are not permitted to take any notes or write anything.

At the end of ten minutes you will be asked to answer questions 1 – 10 (<u>without</u> looking back at the picture).

(After ten minutes)

Instructions for questions 1 – 10:

<u>Without</u> looking back at the picture, answer questions 1 – 10 on the following page.

(Note: These questions are intentionally difficult – probably harder than on the test.)

1. Choose the best answer: The mini-van (closest to you, the viewer) that is making a right turn is:

A. white with a checkered passenger door

B. all black

C. black with a checkered passenger door

D. all white

2. The man in the front who is carrying a white object is wearing:

A. a white jumpsuit

B. overalls

C. a black suit

D. none of the above

3 The woman closest to the front is:

A. carrying a black handbag.

B. carrying a white handbag.

C. carrying a black attaché case.

D. wearing long, black slacks

4. Above the head of the man with the dark suit who is carrying a white bag:

A. there is a street sign with the text "W 141 Street."

B. there is a street sign with the text "E 141 Street."

C. there is a street sign with the text "W 41 Street."

D. there is no street sign with visible text.

5. The vehicle between the two white vehicles in the front is:

A. a truck

B. a bus

C. a Ford convertible

D. none of the above

6. Choose the best answer: The approximate number of people on the left side of the picture is:

A. 3   B. 4   C. 5 or more, but less than 10   D. more than 20

7. What is correct about the three white minivans in the front of the picture?

A. All are making left turns.

B. All are making right turns.

C. They are all taxis.

D. none of the above

8. The number displayed on one of the buildings is:

A. 671

B. 761

B. 6717

D. none of the above

9. With regard to the sky:

A. It cannot be seen in the image.

B. It seems clear.

C. It is extremely cloudy.

D. none of the above.

10. On the sidewalk surface there is drawn:

A. An arrow pointing left (←——).

B. An arrow pointing right (——→).

C. A double arrow (←——→).

D. none of the above

———————————

Answers for Memory Exercise #2

How did you try to notice and remember the details in the picture?

As you looked at the picture, you may have been asking –

- What am I looking at?

    city scene, large buildings, wide streets, vehicles, and pedestrians

- How many pedestrians are clearly visible?

    about 6 (4 males and 2 females)

- What is common about some pedestrians?

    dark clothes

    white shirts (men); some men with dark suits

    men with white shirts

- Anything different or unusual?

    a male is carrying a white bag, same color as a woman's pocketbook

- What are the cars doing?

    most are making turns

- What type of autos are they?

    3-4 mini-vans, several sedans

- Anything else in the picture?

    lamp posts, no street signs

    pavement is etched with rectangle designs

    some trees in the background

-----

1. Choose the best answer: The mini-van (closest to you, the viewer) that is making a right turn is:

A. white with a checkered passenger door

B. all black

C. black with a checkered passenger door

D. all white

2. The man in the front who is carrying a white object is wearing:

A. a white jumpsuit

B. overalls

C. a black suit

D. none of the above

3. The woman closest to the front is:

A. carrying a black handbag.

B. carrying a white handbag.

C. carrying a black attaché case.

D. wearing long, black slacks

4. Above the head of the man with the dark suit who is carrying a white bag:

A. there is a street sign with the text "W 141 Street."

B. there is a street sign with the text "E 141 Street."

C. there is a street sign with the text "W 41 Street."

D. there is no street sign with visible text.

5. The vehicle between the two white vehicles in the front is:

A. a truck

B. a bus

C. a Ford convertible

D. none of the above (a sedan)

6. Choose the best answer: The approximate number of people on the left side of the picture is:

A. 3

B. 4

C. 5 or more, but less than 10

D. more than 20

7. What is correct about the three white minivans in the front of the picture?

A. All are making left turns.

B. All are making right turns.

C. They are all taxis.

D. none of the above (Two are making right turns. One is making a left turn. None of them are taxis.)

8. The number displayed on one of the buildings is:

A. 671

B. 761

B. 6717

D. none of the above (No numbers are displayed.)

9. With regard to the sky:

A. It cannot be seen in the image.

B. It seems clear.

C. It is extremely cloudy.

D. none of the above.

10. On the sidewalk surface there is drawn:

A. An arrow pointing left (◄───).

B. An arrow pointing right (───►).

C. A double arrow (◄───►).

D. none of the above (No arrows are drawn on the sidewalk.)

───────────

"Genius is one percent inspiration and ninety-nine percent perspiration."

- Thomas Edison

Memory Exercise #3

Study the picture below for the next ten minutes. Try to remember as many details about the people and objects as you can. During the ten minutes, you are not permitted to take any notes or write anything.

At the end of ten minutes you will be asked to answer questions 1 – 10 (<u>without</u> looking back at the picture).

(After ten minutes)

Instructions for questions 1 – 10:

<u>Without</u> looking back at the picture, answer questions 1 – 10 on the following page.

1. The number of people very close to the drum of the cement truck is:

A. 4   B. 1   C. 2   D. 3

2. How many cranes are displayed in the picture?

A. 0   B. 1   C. 2   D. 3

3. The drum of the cement truck is:

A. white and with a dark stripe.   C. all black.

B. all white.   D. none of the above.

4. The building that is being worked on:

A. is fully scaffolded.   C. is 6 stories high.

B. is only partially scaffolded.   D. none of the above

5. Behind the building under construction, there is:

A. a parks scene.   C. a city skyline.

B. an airport.   D. none of the above.

6. The number of people on the ground is approximately:

A. 5 - 9   C. 13 - 15

B. 10 - 12   D. 16 - 20

7. In the sky there is clearly visible:

A. an airplane.   B. a helicopter.

C. a large bird.   D. none of the above.

8. How many cranes on the roof are lifting a horizontal object?

A. 0   C. 2

B. 1   D. 3

9. The excavator with a scoop full of dirt:

A. is near the middle of the picture.   B. is on the extreme left side of the picture.

C. has eight wheels.   D. being pulled by a tow truck.

10. Which of the following is in the picture?

A. a large advertising poster on the building's left side

B. a snack truck with a striped canopy

C. a camp trailer

D. none of the above

Answers for Memory Exercise #3

1. The number of people very close to the drum of the cement truck is:
A. 4
B. 1
C. 2
D. 3

2. How many cranes are displayed in the picture?
A. 0
B. 1
C. 2
D. 3

3. The drum of the cement truck is:
A. white and with a dark stripe.
B. all white.
C. all black.
D. none of the above.

4. The building that is being worked on:
A. is fully scaffolded.
B. is only partially scaffolded.
C. is 6 stories high.
D. none of the above

5. Behind the building under construction, there is:
A. a parks scene.
B. an airport.
C. a city skyline.
D. none of the above.

6. The number of people on the ground is approximately:
A. 5 - 9
B. 10 - 12
C. 13 - 15
D. 16 - 20

7. In the sky there is clearly visible:
A. an airplane.
B. a helicopter
C. a large bird.
D. none of the above.

8. How many cranes on the roof are lifting a horizontal object?
A. 0
B. 1
C. 2
D. 3

9. The excavator with a scoop full of dirt:
A. is near the middle of the picture.
B. is on the extreme left side of the picture.
C. has eight wheels.
D. is being pulled by a tow truck.

10. Which of the following is in the picture?
A. a large advertising poster on the building's left side
B. a snack truck with a striped canopy
C. a camp trailer
D. none of the above

_____

Memory Exercise #4

Study the picture below for the next ten minutes. Try to remember as many details about the people and objects as you can. During the ten minutes, you are not permitted to take any notes or write anything.

At the end of ten minutes you will be asked to answer questions 1 – 10 (<u>without</u> looking back at the picture).

(After ten minutes)

Instructions for questions 1 – 10:

<u>Without</u> looking back at the picture, answer questions 1 – 10 on the following page.

1. The number of buildings whose fronts are fully in the picture is:

A. 2   B. 3   C. 4   D. 5

2 The building with a sign that reads "ANTIQUES":

A. is in the center of the picture.   B. is the tallest building in the picture.

C. is a two-story building.   D. does not have an awning.

3. The building with the widest awning:

A. has two windows on the second floor.   B. has three windows on the second floor.

C. has four windows on the second floor.   D. has five windows on the second floor.

4. The American flag is attached to:

A. a window.   B. a lamppost

C. a garbage can   D. none of the above

5. How many outdoor garbage cans are there in the picture?

A. 1   B. 2   C. 3   D. 5

6. How many outdoor sitting benches are in the picture?

A. 1   B. 2   C. 3   D. 5

7. The sky can best be described as:

A. completely clear of clouds.   B. dark with lightning.

C. partly cloudy.   D. filled with rain.

8. The three buildings that are fully in the picture each have how many windows on the second floor?

A. 5   B. 2   C. 3   D. 1

9. How many buildings have fronts that are only partially in the picture?

A. 0   B. 1

C. 2   D. 3

10. How many lampposts are there in the picture?

A. 1   B. 2   C. 3   D. 5

Answers for Memory Exercise #4

1. The number of buildings whose fronts are fully in the picture is:

A. 2　　　　　　　**B. 3**　　　　　　　C. 4　　　　　　　D. 5

2 The building with a sign that reads "ANTIQUES":

A. is in the center of the picture.　　　　　B. is the tallest building in the picture.

C. is a two-story building.　　　　　　　D. does not have an awning.

3. The building with the widest awning:

A. has two windows on the second floor.　　　**B. has three windows on the second floor.**

C. has four windows on the second floor.　　　D. has five windows on the second floor.

4. The American flag is attached to:

A. a window.　　　　　　　　　　　　　**B. a lamppost**

C. a garbage can　　　　　　　　　　　D. none of the above

5. How many outdoor garbage cans are there in the picture?

A. 1　　　　　　　B. 2　　　　　　　C. 3　　　　　　　D. 5

6. How many outdoor sitting benches are in the picture?

A. 1　　　　　　　B. 2　　　　　　　C. 3　　　　　　　D. 5

7. The sky can best be described as:

A. completely clear of clouds.　　　　　　B. dark with lightning.

C. partly cloudy.　　　　　　　　　　　D. filled with rain.

8. The three buildings that are fully in the picture each have how many windows on the second floor?

A. 5　　　　　　　B. 2　　　　　　　**C. 3**　　　　　　　D. 1

9. How many buildings have fronts that are only partially in the picture?

A. 0　　　　　　　　　　　　　　　　B. 1

C. 2　　　　　　　　　　　　　　　D. 3

10. How many lampposts are there in the picture?

A. 1　　　　　　　B. 2　　　　　　　C. 3　　　　　　　D. 5

PROBLEM SENSITIVITY

6

These questions evaluate your ability to see the elements of a problem and also the problem in its entirety.

Problem sensitivity is important in a Police Officer's daily work. Spotting a possible problem developing during a patrol may aid the officer in preventing an incident or being ready if one does occur.

This type of question evaluates your ability to analyze different situations using personal experience, problem sensitivity and maturity of thought.

In one version of this type of question, rules or procedures may be presented along with a situation or incident in which the stated rules or procedures should be applied.

Another version of this type of question may present a number of "facts" (some conflicting), as stated by witnesses, victims or suspects. The candidate may be asked which description or account is not reliable, or which description or account is the most correct.

Questions 1 - 6

1. Police Officer Silvers is informed by a person who has just been mugged on the sidewalk that the perpetrator was a male with a pale complexion, about five feet ten inches tall and wearing a red T-shirt.

Officer Silvers looks down the street in an attempt to spot the perpetrator. According to the information provided by the victim, Police Officer Silvers should:

A. question all males and females on the street.

B. question all females wearing a red T-shirt.

C. question all persons of about the height of five feet ten inches.

D. question all light skinned males on the street who are wearing a red T-shirt and are about five feet ten inches tall.

----

2. Police Officer Horowitz notices that a heavy tree branch has fallen on lane 1 and lane 2 of a busy, four-lane highway. He has several traffic cones with him. Police Officer Horowitz should:

A. immediately barricade the four lanes to stop all traffic and thereby decrease the possibility of an accident.

B. immediately barricade three lanes with the cones and keep one lane open.

C. immediately barricade lanes three and four with the cones.

D. immediately barricade lanes one and two with the cones.

----

3. During his patrol, Police Officer David Swanson notices that a metal store sign approximately three feet wide and ten feet long has partially detached from the building and is dangerously close to crashing down to the crowded sidewalk, about twenty feet below.

Based on the preceding information, what is the first step that Police Officer Swanson should take?

A. Call for backup since he is on patrol alone.

B. Quickly get all persons away from the front of building.

C. Look at the sign for at least five minutes to determine when it will fall.

D. Go inside the store and notify the store owner.

4. Before you leave for patrol, your sergeant gives you written instructions which direct you to interview a Mr. Mary Boggs, owner of a bar and grill, regarding a complaint from the bar that youths from the neighborhood are breaking the bar windows when the bar is closed. You are confused about the identity (name and gender) of Mr. Mary Boggs. What is the first step you should take in this situation?

A. At the bar interview anyone named Boggs (male or female).

B. Disregard the sergeant's instructions as they are clearly confused.

C. Do not ask questions of the sergeant, as he might get upset.

D. Ask the sergeant for clarification of the name and gender of the owner of the bar.

----

5. Police Officer Susan Demitros is on patrol when she notices a man walking in an apparent daze in front of a liquor store. Because the man seems like he might collapse, Police Officer Demitros asks him if there is any problem. The man is clearly startled at being asked a question and hurriedly says, "I have no gun!" and quickly empties his pants pockets, which contained only a bottle of prescription pills which Officer Demitros knows are for anxiety. At that point the man loses consciousness and collapses, but Officer Demitros is able to catch him before he falls on the sidewalk.

Based on the preceding information, what should Police Officer Demitros do first?

A. Take the man into the liquor store and ask the owner if the man had just bought liquor.

B. Interview all nearby persons to determine if any are aware of this person ever having a gun.

C. Call for medical assistance.

D. Call the precinct to determine if the man has an arrest record, including DWI.

----

6. Prior to the start of your patrol, your sergeant gives you instructions which due to your distance from him, you do not hear part of the instructions. What should you do first?

A. Quickly carry out as many instructions as you can remember.

B. Ask your sergeant to repeat the instructions.

C. After you leave the precinct, ask a senior officer if he heard the instructions.

D. Carry out all instructions that you heard and then call the sergeant to ask him if you have completed all his instructions.

Answers 1 - 6

1. Police Officer Silvers is informed by a person who has just been mugged on the sidewalk that the perpetrator was a <u>male with a pale complexion</u>, about five feet ten inches tall and wearing a red T-shirt.

Officer Silvers looks down the street in an attempt to spot the perpetrator. According to the information provided by the victim, Police Officer Silvers should:

A. question all males and females on the street.

(WRONG. The description of a <u>male</u> with a pale complexion is specific. Questioning everyone is not called for and would likely result in wasted time and effort.)

B. question all females wearing a red T-shirt.

(WRONG. The description is of a <u>male</u>. Questioning females is not called for.)

C. question all persons of about the height of five feet ten inches.

(WRONG. The other details, "male" and "pale complexion," should be taken into consideration when deciding whom to question.)

D. question all light skinned males on the street who are wearing a red T-shirt and are about five feet ten inches tall.

(CORRECT. The description of these males matches the description of the alleged mugger.)

----

2. Police Officer Horowitz notices that a heavy tree branch has fallen on <u>lane 1 and lane 2</u> of a busy, four-lane highway. He has several traffic cones with him. Police Officer Horowitz should:

A. immediately barricade the four lanes to stop all traffic and thereby decrease the possibility of an accident.

(WRONG. The tree branch fell on lanes 1 and 2. Barricading the other two lanes is not necessary and could cause delays on the busy highway.)

B. immediately barricade three lanes with the cones and keep one lane open.

(WRONG. There is no apparent need to close the third lane.)

C. immediately barricade lanes three and four with the cones.

(WRONG. Lanes 1 and 2 (where the branch fell) should be barricaded, not the two lanes that are clear, lanes 3 and 4).

D. immediately barricade lanes one and two with the cones.

(CORRECT. These are the two lanes on which the branch has fallen and which need to be barricaded to reduce the possibility of accidents.)

----

3. During his patrol, Police Officer David Swanson notices that a metal store sign approximately three feet wide and ten feet long has partially detached from the building and is dangerously close to crashing down to the crowded sidewalk, about twenty feet below.

Based on the preceding information, what is the first step that Police Officer Swanson should take?

A. Call for backup since he is on patrol alone.

(WRONG. This is an emergency situation where the presence of additional officers will not address the immediate dangerous situation.)

B. Quickly get all persons away from the front of the building.

(CORRECT. The sign is "dangerously close to crashing to the crowded sidewalk, about twenty feet below." To prevent the possibility of injury, the officer should first concentrate on getting all persons away from the front of the building.)

C. Look at the sign for at least five minutes to determine when it will fall.

(WRONG. This is an emergency situation (people under the sign) that requires immediate action.)

D. Go inside the store and notify the store owner.

(WRONG. Officer Swanson should first warn the people who are in immediate danger.)

----

4. Before you leave for patrol, your sergeant gives you written instructions which direct you to interview a Mr. Mary Boggs, owner of a bar and grill, regarding a complaint from the bar that youths from the neighborhood are breaking the bar windows when the bar is closed. You are confused about the identity (name and gender) of Mr. Mary Boggs. What is the first step you should take in this situation?

A. At the bar interview anyone named Boggs (male or female).

(WRONG. You should get clarification from the sergeant of the correct name before going to the bar.)

B. Disregard the sergeant's instructions as they are clearly confused.

(WRONG. Orders from a superior should not be disregarded. You should ask for clarification.)

C. Do not ask questions of the sergeant, as he might get upset.

(WRONG. Questions should be asked if clarification is needed.)

D. Ask the sergeant for clarification of the name and gender of the owner of the bar.

(CORRECT. An officer should ask questions of a superior whenever clarification or additional relevant information is needed.)

----

5. Police Officer Susan Demitros is on patrol when she notices a man walking in an apparent daze in front of a liquor store. Because the man seems like he might collapse, Police Officer Demitros asks him if there is any problem. The man is clearly startled at being asked a question and hurriedly says, "I have no gun!" and quickly empties his pants pockets, which contained only a bottle of prescription pills which Officer Demitros knows are for anxiety. At that point the man loses consciousness and collapses, but Officer Demitros is able to catch him before he falls on the sidewalk.

Based on the preceding information, what should Police Officer Demitros do first?

A. Take the man into the liquor store and ask the owner if the man had just bought liquor.

(WRONG. Medical assistance is first required because the man lost consciousness.)

B. Interview all nearby persons to determine if any are aware of this person ever having a gun.

(WRONG. Medical assistance is first required. Any investigation should come after.)

C. Call for medical assistance.

(CORRECT. The man lost consciousness. This is a medical emergency. The correct action is to call for medical assistance.)

D. Call the precinct to determine if the man has an arrest record, including DWI.

(WRONG. Medical assistance is first required. Any investigation should come after.)

6. Prior to the start of your patrol, your sergeant gives you instructions which due to your distance from him, you do not hear part of the instructions. What should you do first?

A. Quickly carry out as many instructions as you can remember.

(WRONG. You should try to carry out all instructions from the sergeant, and not just those that you remember.)

B. Ask your sergeant to repeat the instructions.

(CORRECT. Asking for clarification is correct because this will help you understand all the instructions which you must follow.)

C. After you leave the precinct, ask a senior officer if he heard the instructions.

(WRONG. Any clarification should first come from the sergeant.)

D. Carry out all instructions that you heard and then call the sergeant to ask him if you have completed all his instructions.

(WRONG. You should get clarification as soon as possible, in this instance at the time that the sergeant gave the instructions.)

———————————

"There are no easy methods of learning difficult things; the method is to close your door, give out that you are not at home, and work."

– Joseph de Maistre

DEDUCTIVE REASONING

7

Deductive Reasoning

These questions evaluate your ability to understand general rules and apply them to specific situations.

Sometimes a question of this type may be difficult to answer, especially when the question involves a detailed procedure or complex section of law.

When answering a question of this type, try to understand fully the procedure or law. More than one reading may be necessary. As you read, try to see the relationships among the details provided.

Keep in mind that although it may be possible to answer very quickly some questions in other sections of the exam, the questions in this section may require more concentration and time.

Questions 1 - 3

Answer question 1 based on the information provided in the following section of PL 120.60.

PL § 120.60 Stalking in the first degree

A person is guilty of stalking in the first degree when he or she commits the crime of stalking in the third degree as defined in subdivision three of section 120.50 or stalking in the second degree as defined in section 120.55 of this article and, in the course and furtherance thereof, he or she:

1. intentionally or recklessly causes physical injury to the victim of such crime, or

2. commits a class A misdemeanor defined in article one hundred thirty of this chapter, or a class E felony defined in section 130.25, 130.40 or 130.85 of this chapter, or a class D felony defined in section 130.30 or 130.45 of this chapter.

Stalking in the first degree is a class D felony.

-----

1. According to the preceding definition of stalking in the first degree, which of the following choices is an example of stalking in the first degree?

A. A male intentionally or recklessly causes physical injury to the victim of any crime.

B. A male or female commits a class A misdemeanor defined in article one hundred thirty of this chapter, or a class E felony defined in section 130.25, 130.40 or 130.85 of this chapter, or a class D felony defined in section 130.30 or 130.45 of this chapter (PL).

C. An adult intentionally or recklessly causes physical injury to the victim of a crime; or commits a class A misdemeanor defined in article one hundred thirty of this chapter, or a class E felony defined in section 130.25, 130.40 or 130.85 of this chapter, or a class D felony defined in section 130.30 or 130.45 of this chapter (PL).

D. none of the above

Answer question 2 based on the information provided in the following example of a Miranda Warning.

The following is an example of a Miranda Warning:

"You have the right to remain silent when questioned.

Anything you say or do may be used against you in a court of law.

You have the right to consult an attorney before speaking to the police and to have an attorney present during questioning now or in the future.

If you cannot afford an attorney, one will be appointed for you before any questioning, if you wish.

If you decide to answer any questions now, without an attorney present, you will still have the right to stop answering at any time until you talk to an attorney.

Knowing and understanding your rights as I have explained them to you, are you willing to answer my questions without an attorney present?"

-----

2. According to this version of the Miranda Warning, which of the following four choices is incorrect?

A. The person warned must be asked if he/she is willing to answer any questions without an attorney present after the person knows and understands his/her rights as explained.

B. The person must be informed that anything the person says or does may be used against the person in a court of law.

C. If the person cannot afford an attorney, one will be appointed only at the time of trial.

D. A person without an attorney present has the right to stop answering at any time until the person talks to an attorney.

Answer question 3 based on the information provided in the following section of CPL 720.10.

CPL § 720.10 Youthful offender procedure; definition of terms

As used in this article, the following terms have the following meanings:

1. "Youth" means a person charged with a crime alleged to have been committed when he was at least sixteen years old and less than nineteen years old or a person charged with being a juvenile offender (ages 13, 14 or 15) as defined in subdivision forty-two of section 1.20 of this chapter.

2. "Eligible youth" means a youth who is eligible to be found a youthful offender. Every youth is so eligible unless:

(a) the conviction to be replaced by a youthful offender finding is for (i) a class A-I or class A-II felony, or (ii) an armed felony as defined in subdivision forty-one of section 1.20, except as provided in subdivision three, or (iii) rape in the first degree, criminal sexual act in the first degree, or aggravated sexual abuse, except as provided in subdivision three, or

(b) such youth has previously been convicted and sentenced for a felony, or

(c) such youth has previously been adjudicated a youthful offender following conviction of a felony or has been adjudicated on or after September first, nineteen hundred seventy-eight a juvenile delinquent who committed a designated felony act as defined in the family court act.

-----

3. According to the preceding, which one of the following persons qualifies as an "eligible youth"?

A. Bernard Cranson, male, 20 years old, is arrested and charged with a crime. He was never found to be a juvenile offender.

B. Martin Frieds, male, 20 years old, is arrested and charged with a crime. He has previously been adjudicated a youthful offender following conviction of a felony.

C. Cecilia Norwin, a female, 17 years old, is arrested and charged with a crime. She had previously been adjudicated a youthful offender following a conviction and sentencing for a felony.

D. none of the above

Answers 1 - 3

Answer question 1 based on the information provided in the following section of PL 120.60.

PL § 120.60 Stalking in the first degree

A person is guilty of stalking in the first degree when he or she commits the crime of stalking in the third degree as defined in subdivision three of section 120.50 or stalking in the second degree as defined in section 120.55 of this article <u>and, in the course and furtherance thereof, he or she:</u>

1. intentionally or recklessly causes physical injury to the victim of such crime, or

2. commits a class A misdemeanor defined in article one hundred thirty of this chapter, or a class E felony defined in section 130.25, 130.40 or 130.85 of this chapter, or a class D felony defined in section 130.30 or 130.45 of this chapter.

Stalking in the first degree is a class D felony.

A couple of careful readings of the preceding section of law can help us to summarize it as follows:

A person is guilty of stalking in the first degree IF the person in the process of committing the crime of stalking in the second degree or stalking in the third degree ALSO does at least one of the following:

1. intentionally or recklessly causes physical injury to the victim of the second or third degree stalking, OR

2. commits one of the specific A misdemeanors or E felonies listed in PL 120.60.

Stalking in the first degree is a class D felony.

1. According to the preceding definition of stalking in the first degree, which of the following choices is an example of stalking in the first degree?

A. A male intentionally or recklessly causes physical injury to the victim of any crime.

(WRONG. According to our summary, the physical injury must be in the course of committing stalking in the second degree or stalking in the third degree and other specified offense.)

B. A male or female commits a class A misdemeanor defined in article one hundred thirty of this chapter, or a class E felony defined in section 130.25, 130.40 or 130.85 of this chapter, or a class D felony defined in section 130.30 or 130.45 of this chapter (PL).

(WRONG. According to our summary, the offense must be in the course of committing stalking in the second degree or stalking in the third degree.)

C. An adult intentionally or recklessly causes physical injury to the victim of a crime; or commits a class A misdemeanor defined in article one hundred thirty of this chapter, or a class E felony defined in section 130.25, 130.40 or 130.85 of this chapter, or a class D felony defined in section 130.30 or 130.45 of this chapter (PL).

(WRONG. According to our summary, the physical injury must be in the course of committing stalking in the second degree or stalking in the third degree.)

D. none of the above

(THIS IS THE RIGHT CHOICE. All the other choices ("A", "B," and "C") do not consider that the physical injury or commission of any of the specified crimes <u>must</u> be during the commission of stalking in the second degree or stalking in the third degree.)

Answer question 2 based on the information provided in the following example of a Miranda Warning.

The following is an example of a Miranda Warning:

"You have the right to remain silent when questioned.

Anything you say or do may be used against you in a court of law.

You have the right to consult an attorney before speaking to the police and to have an attorney present during questioning now or in the future.

If you cannot afford an attorney, one will be appointed for you before any questioning, if you wish.

If you decide to answer any questions now, without an attorney present, you will still have the right to stop answering at any time until you talk to an attorney.

Knowing and understanding your rights as I have explained them to you, are you willing to answer my questions without an attorney present?"

-----

2. According to this version of the Miranda Warning, which of the following four choices is <u>incorrect?</u>

A. The person warned must be asked if he/she is willing to answer any questions without an attorney present after the person knows and understands his/her rights as explained.

(CORRECT STATEMENT. The last sentence states, "Knowing and understanding your rights as I have explained them to you, are you willing to answer my questions without an attorney present?" Statement "A" is therefore a correct statement and not the incorrect statement that we are looking for.)

B. The person must be informed that anything the person says or does may be used against the person in a court of law.

(CORRECT STATEMENT. Sentence two states, "Anything you say or do may be used against you in a court of law." Statement "B" is therefore a correct statement and not the incorrect statement that we are looking for.)

C. If the person cannot afford an attorney, one will be appointed only at the time of trial.

(INCORRECT STATEMENT. Therefore, "C" is the answer. Sentence four states, "If you cannot afford an attorney, one will be appointed for you <u>before any questioning</u>, if you wish.")

D. A person without an attorney present has the right to stop answering at any time until the person talks to an attorney.

(**CORRECT STATEMENT.** Sentence five states, "If you decide to answer any questions now, without an attorney present, you will still have the right to stop answering at any time until you talk to an attorney." Statement "D" is therefore a correct statement and not the incorrect statement that we are looking for.)

Answer question 3 based on the information provided in the following section of CPL 720.10.

CPL § 720.10 Youthful offender procedure; definition of terms

As used in this article, the following terms have the following meanings:

1. "Youth" means a person charged with a crime alleged to have been committed when he was at least sixteen years old and less than nineteen years old or a person charged with being a juvenile offender (ages 13, 14 or 15) as defined in subdivision forty-two of section 1.20 of this chapter.

2. "Eligible youth" means a youth who is eligible to be found a youthful offender. Every youth is so eligible unless:

(a) the conviction to be replaced by a youthful offender finding is for (i) a class A-I or class A-II felony, or (ii) an armed felony as defined in subdivision forty-one of section 1.20, except as provided in subdivision three, or (iii) rape in the first degree, criminal sexual act in the first degree, or aggravated sexual abuse, except as provided in subdivision three, or

(b) such youth has previously been convicted and sentenced for a felony, or

(c) such youth has previously been adjudicated a youthful offender following conviction of a felony or has been adjudicated on or after September first, nineteen hundred seventy-eight a juvenile delinquent who committed a designated felony act as defined in the family court act.

3, According to the preceding, which one of the following persons qualifies as an "eligible youth"?

A. Bernard Cranson, male, 20 years old, is arrested and charged with a crime. He was never found to be a juvenile offender.

(**DOES NOT QUALIFY.** The youth must be less than 19 years old (See "1" in section 720.10)

B. Martin Frieds, male, 20 years old, is arrested and charged with a crime. He has previously been adjudicated a youthful offender following conviction of a felony.

(DOES NOT QUALIFY. The youth must be less than 19 years old (See "1" in section 720.10).

C. Cecilia Norwin, a female, 17 years old, is arrested and charged with a crime. She had previously been convicted and sentenced for a felony.

(DOES NOT QUALIFY. The section states, "2. Eligible youth means a youth who is eligible to be found a youthful offender. <u>Every youth is so eligible **unless**... (b) such youth has previously been adjudicated a youthful offender following a conviction and sentencing for a felony</u>." Ms. Norwin was previously convicted and sentenced for a felony.)

D. none of the above

(THIS IS THE ANSWER because none of the preceding three persons qualify as a youthful offender.)

"In a major matter, no details are small."

- Paul De Gondi

The next question tests our ability to pay attention to detail.

Question 4

Below is a drawing of a "Revolver" and 4 more drawings of revolvers (A, B, C, and D). Which of the four drawings (A, B, C, D) best matches the drawing of the "Revolver"?

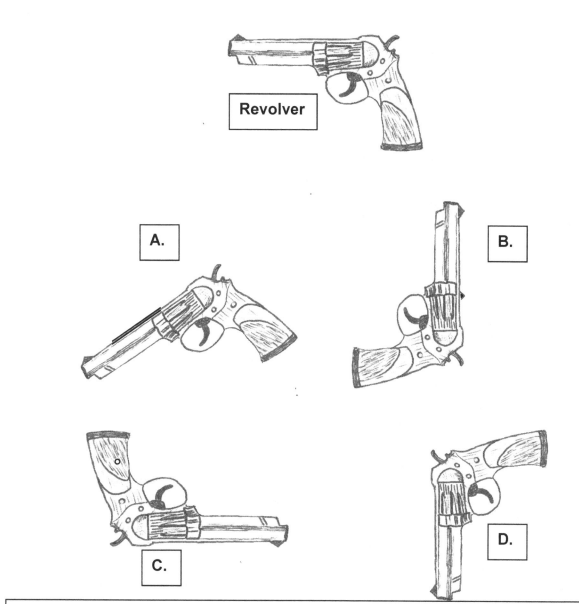

Revolver

A.

B.

C.

D.

4. The drawing which best matches the drawing of the "Revolver" is:

A. Drawing A   B. Drawing B

C. Drawing C   D. Drawing D

Answer 4

Below is a drawing of a "Revolver" and 4 more drawings of revolvers (A, B, C, and D). Which of the four drawings (A, B, C, D) best matches the drawing of the "Revolver"?

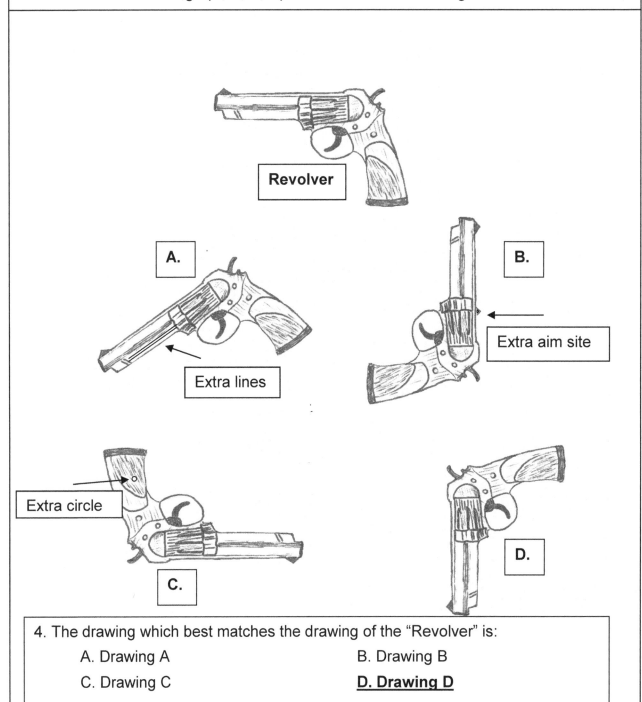

Revolver

A.

Extra lines

B.

Extra aim site

Extra circle

C.

D.

4. The drawing which best matches the drawing of the "Revolver" is:

A. Drawing A   B. Drawing B

C. Drawing C   **D. Drawing D**

Questions 5 - 6

Answer questions 5 - 6 based on the information provided in the following summaries of two Penal Law and Criminal Procedure Law sections.

Penal Law (PL) S 240.40 Appearance in public under the influence of narcotics or a drug other than alcohol.

A person is guilty of appearance in public under the influence of narcotics or a drug other than alcohol when he appears in a public place under the influence of narcotics or a drug other than alcohol to the degree that he may endanger himself or other persons or property, or annoy persons in his vicinity. Appearance in public under the influence of narcotics or a drug other than alcohol is a violation.

Criminal Procedure Law (CPL) S 160.10 When fingerprints may or must be taken

Following an arrest, or following arraignment upon a local criminal court accusatory instrument, a defendant must be fingerprinted where the accusatory instrument charges:

(a) a felony

(b) a misdemeanor defined in the Penal Law

(c) a misdemeanor defined outside of the Penal Law which would constitute a felony if such person had a previous judgment of conviction for a crime

(d) loitering for the purposes of engaging in a prostitution offense (Penal Law 240.37)

After an arrest for any offense, fingerprints may be taken where:

(a) law enforcement is unable to ascertain the person's identity.

(b) identification given by such person may not be accurate.

(c) there is reasonable cause to believe the person might be sought by law enforcement officials for the commission of some other offense.

When fingerprints are required to be taken, photographs and palm prints may be taken.

-----

5. Police Officer Marino arrests a person whom he reasonably believes is appearing in public under the influence of narcotics or a drug other than alcohol and who is annoying persons in his vicinity. The person provides acceptable I.D. (NYS issued driver's license with photo).

Which of the following choices is correct with respect to requiring fingerprints from the person arrested?

A. Fingerprints must be taken because the person was arrested for an offense.

B. Because fingerprints are required for any arrest as per PL S 240.0, photographs and palm prints may be taken.

C. Fingerprints must be taken because all drug offenses are felonies.

D. CPL S 160.10 does not authorize the taking of fingerprints in this particular instance.

----

6. Police Officer Janet Yaeger arrests a person for loitering for the purposes of engaging in a prostitution offense (Penal Law 240.37). Which of the following four statements is correct?

A. Fingerprints must be taken only if the person is of the age of 18 or over.

B. Fingerprints can only be taken if photographs and palm prints are also taken.

C. Fingerprints must be taken, even if Officer Yaeger personally knows the identity of the person arrested.

D. Photographs and palm prints must be taken.

Answers 5 - 6

5. Police Officer Marino arrests a person whom he reasonably believes is appearing in public under the influence of narcotics or a drug other than alcohol and who is annoying persons in his vicinity. The person provides acceptable I.D. (NYS issued driver's license with photo).

Which of the following choices is correct with respect to requiring fingerprints from the person arrested?

A. Fingerprints must be taken because the person was arrested for an offense.

(WRONG. Fingerprints must be taken when the arrest is for <u>specified</u> offenses ((a)-(d)) and not for just any offense.)

B. Because fingerprints are required for an arrest as per PL S 240.40, photographs and palm prints may be taken.

(WRONG. PL 240.40 is for a <u>violation</u> (and is not an offense listed in CPL 160.10 ((a)-(d))

C. Fingerprints must be taken because all drug offenses are felonies.

(WRONG. All drug offenses are not felonies. One example is PL S 240, a violation.)

D. CPL S 160.10 does not authorize the taking of fingerprints in this particular instance.

(CORRECT. The offense is a violation, and not an offense specified in CPL 160.10 ((a)-(d)).

6. Police Officer Janet Yaeger arrests a person for loitering for the purposes of engaging in a prostitution offense (Penal Law 240.37). Which of the following four statements is correct?

A. Fingerprints must be taken only if the person is of the age of 18 or over.

(WRONG. CPL 160.10 does not specify any minimum age.)

B. Fingerprints can only be taken if photographs and palm prints are also taken.

(WRONG. CPL 160.10 states, "When fingerprints are required to be taken, photographs and palm prints <u>may</u> be taken" – the reverse meaning of answer B.)

<u>C. Fingerprints must be taken, even if Officer Yaeger personally knows the identity of the person arrested.</u>

(CORRECT. CPL 160.10 states "Following an arrest, or following arraignment upon a local criminal court accusatory instrument, a defendant <u>must</u> be fingerprinted where the accusatory instrument charges...<u>loitering for purposes of engaging in a prostitution offense</u>....")

D. Photographs and palm prints must be taken.

(WRONG. CPL 160.10 states, "When fingerprints are required to be taken, photographs and palm prints <u>may</u> be taken.")

"I know the price of success: dedication, hard work and an unremitting devotion to the things you want to see happen."

- Frank Lloyd Wright

Answer Questions 7 - 8 based on the following map.

In answering the questions, follow the flow of traffic, as indicated by the arrows. Names of streets, buildings, public areas, and points 1-9 are indicated on the map.

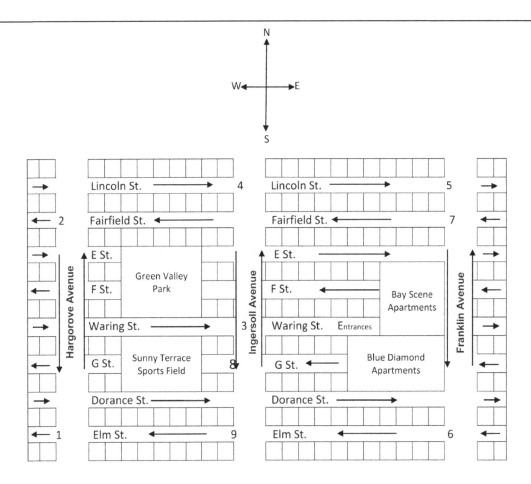

7. Imagine that you are at Elm Street and Ingersoll Avenue and then drive west to Hargrove Avenue, then turn north to Dorance St., then travel east to Ingersoll Avenue, then travel north to Lincoln St. You will be closest to which one of the following points?

A. 2   B. 4   C. 5   D. 7

8. If you start your drive at point number 6, then drive west to Ingersoll Avenue, then drive north to Dorance St., then east to Franklin Avenue, then drive north to Fairfield St., you will be closest to which one of the following points?

A. 4   B. 5   C. 7   D. 2

Answer for Question 7

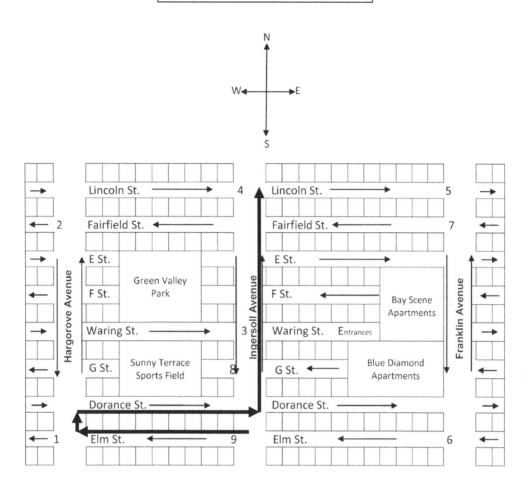

7. Imagine that you are at Elm Street and Ingersoll Avenue and then drive west to Hargrove Avenue, then turn north to Dorance St., then travel east to Ingersoll Avenue, then travel north to Lincoln St. You will be closest to which one of the following points?

A. 2   **B. 4**   C. 5   D. 7

(The route is indicated by dark arrows.)

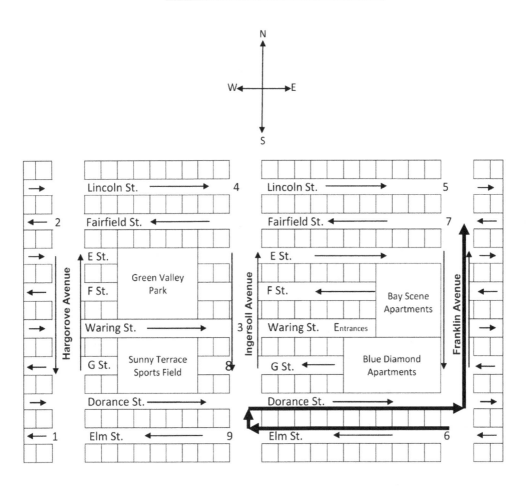

Answer for Question 8

8. If you start your drive at point number 6, then drive west to Ingersoll Avenue, then drive north to Dorance St., then east to Franklin Avenue, then drive north to Fairfield St., you will be closest to which one of the following points?

A. 4   B. 5   **C. 7**   D. 2

(The route is indicated by dark arrows.)

Questions 9 - 14

Answer questions 9 and 10 based on the preceding map.

---

9. You are driving south in your patrol car and you are at the intersection of Lincoln St. and Ingersoll Avenue. You are informed that an auto accident has just occurred at the intersection of Lincoln St. and Hargrove Avenue. Assuming that you must obey all traffic signs, which one of the following four choices describes the most direct route?

A. Drive straight west to the intersection of Lincoln St. and Hargrove Avenue, one block away.

B. Drive east to Franklin Avenue, then south on Franklin Avenue to Fairfield Street, then west on Fairfield St. to Hargrove Avenue, then north on Hargrove Avenue to the intersection of Lincoln St. and Hargrove Avenue.

C. Drive straight east to the intersection of Lincoln St. and Hargrove Avenue, one block away.

D. Drive south on Ingersoll Avenue to Fairfield St, then drive west on Fairfield St. to Hargrove Avenue, then north to the intersection of Lincoln St. and Hargrove Avenue.

----

10. You are driving north in your patrol car and you are at Hargrove Avenue and E St. You are informed that a building is on the verge of collapsing at the corner of Lincoln St. and Franklin Avenue. Which one of the following four choices describes the most direct route?

A. Drive east on Lincoln St. to the corner of Lincoln St. and Franklin Avenue.

B. Drive south to Lincoln St., then right on Lincoln St. to the corner of Lincoln St. and Franklin Avenue.

C. Drive south to Lincoln St., then right on Lincoln St. to the corner of Lincoln St. and Franklin Avenue.

D. Drive north to Lincoln St., then right on Lincoln St. and continue to the corner of Lincoln St. and Franklin Avenue.

Answer question 11 based on the following information:

During the month of July 2016 there were 9 burglaries reported in Police Officer Callion's precinct. In two of the burglaries, neighbors reported that at the approximate time of the burglaries they witnessed a male white, average height, shoulder length, dark hair, "with about a one inch scar on his left cheek." Both times the man was carrying a large brown carton out of the residence that had been burglarized. They also reported that at both times he had been wearing a blue T-shirt, dark blue, dirty dungarees, and white sneakers.

-----

11. During his patrol, Officer Callion stops four white males for questioning. He had recorded in his memo book the description given by the two witnesses. Which piece of information should Officer Callion consider the most important and pay careful attention to in identifying the suspected burglar?

A. the dark blue, dirty dungarees

B. the shoulder length, dark hair

C. the approximately one inch scar on his left cheek

D. the blue T-shirt

Answer question 12 based on the following information:

Prior to the start of his patrol, Officer Kevin Johnson learns at the precinct that a female, about 65 years old, had been mugged one hour earlier by a person who the victim described as a "white young man, about twenty years old, with dark hair tied in a shoulder length ponytail, and with severe acne on his face." She also described him as wearing black pants, a yellow T-shirt, and black sneakers.

-----

12. During his patrol, Officer Johnson sees a group of six white males, about 20-25 years old, standing in front of Ernie's Bar. Officer Johnson stops his patrol car about twenty feet away to get a better look at the six males. Which of the following parts of the description provided by the victim is most important for Officer Johnson to consider in his attempt to identify the possible suspect?

A. the yellow T-shirt

B. the shoulder length pony tail

C. the black sneakers

D. the acne on the alleged mugger

Answer questions 13 - 14 based on the following information:

Police Officer Gravitz is assigned to patrol an area which includes four Housing Developments. During the prior four weeks, crime statistics show that four burglaries were reported at the Bellman Housing Development, all between the hours of 10:00 a.m. and 4:00 p.m. At the Diamond Housing Development ten robberies were reported. At the Adrian Housing Development seven mailboxes were broken into. At the Garnacy Housing Development four bicycles were stolen. The robberies all occurred between 9:30 a.m. and 4:30 p.m. The mailboxes were broken into between 9:30 a.m. and 10:30 a.m. The bicycles were all reported stolen in the afternoon and before 5:00 p.m.

13. Officer Gravitz works the 9:00 a.m. to 5:00 p.m. tour. On Monday, his sergeant instructs him to pay careful attention to robberies. To try to reduce the number of robberies, Office Gravitz should patrol the:

A. Garnacy Housing Development

B. Bellman Housing Development

C. Adrian Housing Development

D. Diamond Housing Development

-----

14. On Tuesday Officer Gravitz also works the 9:00 a.m. to 5:00 p.m. tour. On Tuesday, his sergeant tells him that three more mailboxes have been broken into at the same housing development that reported the prior break-ins and instructs him to pay careful attention to mailbox break-ins. To try to reduce the number of break-ins of mailboxes, Office Gravitz should patrol the:

A. Garnacy Housing Development

B. Bellman Housing Development

C. Adrian Housing Development

D. Diamond Housing Development

"An investment in knowledge always pays the best interest."

- Benjamin Franklin

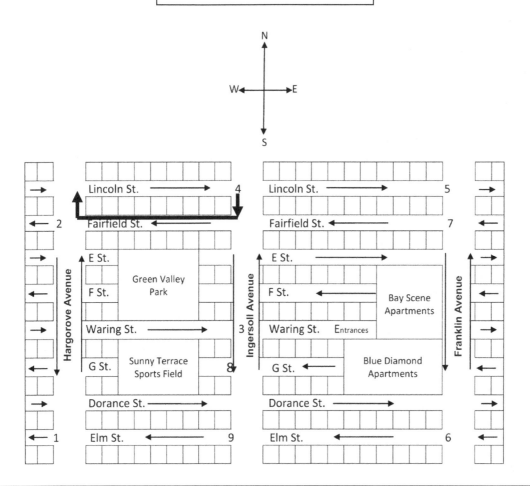

Answer for Question 9

9. You are driving south in your patrol car and you are at the intersection of Lincoln St. and Ingersoll Avenue. You are informed that an auto accident has just occurred at the intersection of Lincoln St. and Hargrove Avenue. Assuming that you must obey all traffic signs, which one of the following four choices describes the most direct route?

A. Drive straight west to the intersection of Lincoln St. and Hargrove Avenue, one block away.

B. Drive east to Franklin Avenue, then south on Franklin Avenue to Fairfield Street, then west on Fairfield St. to Hargrove Avenue, then north on Hargrove Avenue to the intersection of Lincoln St. and Hargrove Avenue.

C. Drive straight east to the intersection of Lincoln St. and Hargrove Avenue, one block away.

D. Drive south on Ingersoll Avenue to Fairfield St, then drive west on Fairfield St. to Hargrove Avenue, then north to the intersection of Lincoln St. and Hargrove Avenue.

Answer for Question 10

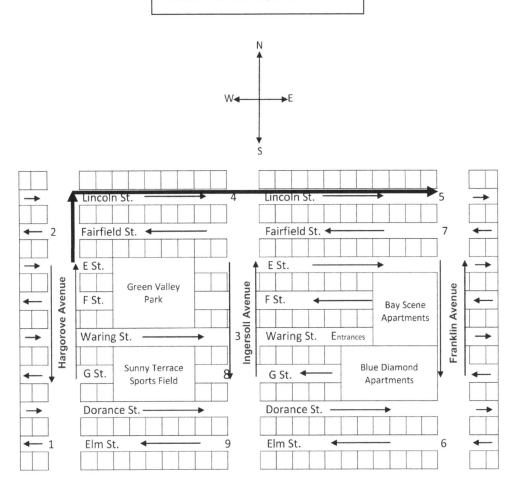

10. You are driving north in your patrol car and you are at Hargrove Avenue and E St. You are informed that a building is on the verge of collapsing at the corner of Lincoln St. and Franklin Avenue. Which one of the following four choices describes the most direct route?

A. Drive east on Lincoln St. to the corner of Lincoln St. and Franklin Avenue.

B. Drive south to Lincoln St., then right on Lincoln St. to the corner of Lincoln St. and Franklin Avenue.

C. Drive south to Lincoln St., then right on Lincoln St. to the corner of Lincoln St. and Franklin Avenue.

D. Drive north to Lincoln St., then right on Lincoln St. and continue to the corner of Lincoln St. and Franklin Avenue.

Answers 11 - 14

Answer question 11 based on the following information:

During the month of July 2016 there were 9 burglaries reported in Police Officer Callion's precinct. In two of the burglaries, neighbors reported that at the approximate time of the burglaries they witnessed a male white, average height, shoulder length, dark hair, "with about a one inch scar on his left cheek." Both times the man was carrying a large brown carton out of the residence that had been burglarized. They also reported that at both times he had been wearing a blue T-shirt, dark blue, dirty dungarees, and white sneakers.

-----

11. During his patrol, Officer Callion stops four white males for questioning. He had recorded in his memo book the description given by the two witnesses. Which piece of information should Officer Callion consider the most important and pay careful attention to in identifying the suspected burglar?

A. the dark blue, dirty dungarees

(WRONG. A suspect can easily change dungarees. Also, many men wear blue, and sometimes dirty, dungarees.)

B. the shoulder length, dark hair

(WRONG. Although the length of the hair may be useful, a suspect can easily change the length of the hair or the hair style.)

C. the approximately one inch scar on his left cheek

(CORRECT. This is the best answer because a scar cannot easily be changed or hidden.)

D. the blue T-shirt

(WRONG. A suspect can easily change his T-shirt. Also, blue T-shirts are common.)

Answer question 12 based on the following information:

Prior to the start of his patrol, Officer Kevin Johnson learns at the precinct that a female, about 65 years old, had been mugged one hour earlier by a person who the victim described as a "white young man, about twenty years old, with dark hair tied in a shoulder length ponytail, and with severe acne on his face." She also described him as wearing black pants, a yellow T-shirt, and black sneakers.

12. During his patrol, Officer Johnson sees a group of six white males, about 20-25 years old, standing in front of Ernie's Bar. Officer Johnson stops his patrol car about twenty feet away to get a better look at the six males. Which of the following parts of the description provided by the victim is most important for Officer Johnson to consider in his attempt to identify the possible suspect?

A. the yellow T-shirt

(**WRONG.** A suspect can easily change his T-shirt.)

B. the shoulder length pony tail

(**WRONG.** Although the length of the hair may be useful, a suspect can easily change the length of the hair or the hair style.)

C. the black sneakers

(**WRONG.** A suspect can easily change his sneakers. Also, many men wear black sneakers.)

D. the acne on the alleged mugger

(**CORRECT.** This is the best answer because acne cannot easily be changed or hidden.)

Answer questions 13 - 14 based on the following information:

Police Officer Gravitz is assigned to patrol an area which includes four Housing Developments. During the prior four weeks, crime statistics show that four burglaries were reported at the Bellman Housing Development, all between the hours of 10:00 a.m. and 4:00 p.m. At the Diamond Housing Development ten robberies were reported. At the Adrian Housing Development seven mailboxes were broken into. At the Garnacy Housing Development four bicycles were stolen. The robberies all occurred between 9:30 a.m. and 4:30 p.m. The mailboxes were broken into between 9:30 a.m. and 10:30 a.m. The bicycles were all reported stolen in the afternoon and before 5:00 p.m.

-----

13. Officer Gravitz works the 9:00 a.m. to 5:00 p.m. tour. On Monday, his sergeant instructs him to pay careful attention to robberies. To try to reduce the number of robberies, Office Gravitz should patrol the:

A. Garnacy Housing Development

(**WRONG.** At the Garnacy Housing Development four <u>bicycles</u> were stolen.)

B. Bellman Housing Development

(**WRONG** ... four <u>burglaries</u> were reported at the Bellman Housing Development....)

C. Adrian Housing Development

(**WRONG.** At the Adrian Housing Development seven <u>mailboxes</u> were broken into.)

D. Diamond Housing Development

(**CORRECT.** "At the Diamond Housing Development ten <u>robberies</u> were reported." He should patrol this development because it is the most likely housing development to have robberies.)

----

14. On Tuesday Officer Gravitz also works the 9:00 a.m. to 5:00 p.m. tour. On Tuesday, his sergeant tells him that three more mailboxes have been broken into at the same housing development that reported the prior break-ins and instructs him to pay careful attention to mailbox break-ins. To try to reduce the number of break-ins of mailboxes, Office Gravitz should patrol the:

A. Garnacy Housing Development

(**WRONG.** "At the Garnacy Housing Development four <u>bicycles</u> were stolen.")

B. Bellman Housing Development

(**WRONG.** "... four <u>burglaries</u> were reported at the Bellman Housing Development....")

C. Adrian Housing Development

(**CORRECT.** During the prior four weeks, "At the Adrian Housing Development seven <u>mailboxes</u> were broken into.")

D. Diamond Housing Development

(**WRONG.** "At the Diamond Housing Development ten <u>robberies</u> were reported.")

_____

"Success is the sum of all small efforts, repeated day in and day out."

- Robert Collier

INDUCTIVE REASONING

8

These questions test your ability to combine details or separate pieces of information to form general rules or a conclusion so that you may correctly answer a question based on a scenario that is provided.

The information provided may include sections of law, procedures, policies, or situations.

More than one careful reading of the information may be necessary before answering the question.

Question 1

Time Limitations for the Commencement of a Criminal Action

Type of Offense	For the commencement of a criminal action to be timely, an accusatory instrument must be filed within the following time periods after the commission of the offense
Class "A" felony (or rape in the first degree (130.35 PL), or criminal sexual act in the first degree (130.50 PL), or aggravated sexual abuse in the first degree (130.70 PL) or sexual conduct against a child in the first degree	any time
any other felony	within 5 years
misdemeanor	within 2 years
petty offense	within 1 year

1. Based on the above table, which of the following statements is not correct?

A. Prosecution for any felony must be commenced within 5 years of commission of the offense.

B. Where the offense is a misdemeanor, for the commencement of a criminal action to be timely, an accusatory instrument must be filed within 2 years following the commission of the offense.

C. Where the offense charged is aggravated sexual abuse in first degree (130.70 PL), for the commencement of a criminal action to be timely, an accusatory instrument may be filed at any time following the commission of the offense.

D. Where the offense is a petty offense, for the commencement of a criminal action to be timely, an accusatory instrument must be filed within 1 year following the commission of the offense.

Answer 1

A. Prosecution for any felony must be commenced within 5 years of commission of the offense.

The statement is not correct because for certain felonies the prosecution can begin at any time after the offense is committed. These felonies are: "Class "A" felony (or rape in the first degree (130.35 PL), or criminal sexual act in the first degree (130.50 PL), or aggravated sexual abuse in the first degree (130.70 PL) or sexual conduct against a child in the first degree)."

Inductive Reasoning Questions 2 - 3

Answer questions 2 - 3 based on the following summary of "CPL 100.10 Definitions of Local Criminal Court Accusatory Instruments."

CPL 100.10 Definitions of Local Criminal Court accusatory instruments

1. An **Information** is a verified written accusation by a person, charging person(s) with offense(s), none of which is a felony. It may serve as the basis for the commencement of an action and for prosecution.

2. A **Simplified information** is a written accusation by a police officer (or other public servant authorized to issue a simplified information).
    1. A **Simplified parks information** charges parks/recreation offense(s) less than a felony.
    2. A **Simplified environmental conservation information** charges environmental conservation offense(s) less than a felony.
    3. A **Simplified traffic information** charges traffic infractions or misdemeanors.

3. A **Prosecutor's information** is a written accusation filed by the DA, either at the direction of the grand jury or at the direction of the local criminal court, or at the DA's own instance, and charges offense(s) less than a felony.

4. A **Misdemeanor complaint** is a verified written accusation by a person charging offense(s), at least one of which is a misdemeanor, and none is a felony.

5. A **Felony complaint** is a verified written accusation by a person which charges offense(s), one or more of which must be felonies.

-----

2. Based on the preceding (CPL 100.10) definitions, which of the following statements is correct?

A. A Prosecutor's information is the same as a misdemeanor complaint.

B. A felony complaint must be filed by the D.A.

C. A Simplified Parks Information charges a felony.

D. A felony complaint charges at least one felony.

3. Police Officer Gonzalez is reviewing the above definitions sheet of Local Criminal Court accusatory instruments. Based on the definitions, he may correctly conclude that:

A. All accusatory instruments can charge any offense.

B. Simplified informations may be issued by all citizens.

C. Prosecutor's informations and misdemeanor complaints can charge misdemeanors and felonies.

D. None of the above.

Answers 2 - 3

2. Based on the preceding (CPL 100.10) definitions, which of the following statements is correct?

A. A Prosecutor's information is the same as a misdemeanor complaint.

(WRONG. A Prosecutor's Information is a written accusation by the <u>D.A.</u>, whereas a misdemeanor complaint is a written accusation by <u>a person</u>.)

B. A felony complaint must be filed by the D.A.

(WRONG. A felony complaint is a written accusation by <u>a person</u>.)

C. A Simplified Parks Information charges a felony.

(WRONG. A Simplified Parks Information charges <u>less than a felony</u>.)

<u>D. A felony complaint charges at least one felony.</u>

(CORRECT. A felony complaint is a verified written accusation by a person which charges offense(s), <u>one or more of which must be felonies</u>.)

3. Police Officer Gonzalez is reviewing the above definitions sheet of Local Criminal Court accusatory instruments. Based on the definitions, he may correctly conclude that:

A. All accusatory instruments can charge any offense.

(WRONG. Accusatory instruments can charge only <u>specified</u> offenses.)

B. Simplified informations may be issued by all citizens.

(WRONG. Simplified informations can be issued only by a <u>police officer</u> or by other <u>authorized public servants</u>.)

C. Prosecutor's informations and misdemeanor complaints can charge misdemeanors and felonies.

(WRONG. Prosecutor's informations and misdemeanor complaints <u>cannot charge felonies</u>.)

D. None of the above.

(CORRECT ANSWER. All other choices are incorrect.)

Questions 4 - 5

4. While you are on patrol, a male, about 21 years old, reports that he had chained his bicycle to a bicycle parking station and gone into a drugstore to purchase shampoo, only to discover when he came out of the store that his bicycle chain had been cut and his bicycle stolen. You question four witnesses who give you four statements. Which of the following four statements is most likely to be incorrect?

A. The person who cut the chain and rode away with the bicycle was a male, white, about 21 years old and about six feet tall. He was wearing white sneakers, blue dungarees, a yellow T-shirt, and a dark brown backpack. He headed north for one block and then made a left turn.

B. The person who cut the chain was a male, white, about six feet tall. He was wearing black sneakers, blue dungarees, a yellow T-shirt, and a dark brown backpack. He rode the bicycle north for one block and then made a left turn.

C. The person who cut the chain and rode away with the bicycle was a male, white, about six feet tall. He was wearing black sneakers, blue dungarees, a yellow T-shirt, and a dark brown backpack. He pedaled north for one block and then made a left turn.

D. The person who cut the chain and rode away with the bicycle was a male, white, about six feet tall. He was wearing black sneakers, blue dungarees, a yellow T-shirt, and a dark brown backpack. He headed north for one block and then made a left turn.

----

5. Four witnesses to a hit and run accident tell Police Officer Tumi that they memorized the license plate of the car that sped away from the accident. Which of the following is the most like to be correct?

A. 9237SFG

B. 9587SFG

C. 9537SFG

D. 9531SFG

Answers 4 - 5

4. While you are on patrol, a male, about 21 years old, reports that he had chained his bicycle to a bicycle parking station and gone in to a drugstore to purchase shampoo, only to discover when he came out of the store that his bicycle chain had been cut and his bicycle stolen. You question four witnesses who give you four statements. Which of the following four statements is most likely to be incorrect?

A. The person who cut the chain and rode away with the bicycle was a male, white, about 21 years old and about six feet tall. He was wearing white sneakers, blue dungarees, a yellow T-shirt, and a dark brown backpack. He headed north for one block and then made a left turn.

(**MOST LIKELY TO BE INCORRECT.** Although the details of this statement agree with most of the other details in the other three statements below, this statement is the only one which describes the sneakers as being "white" instead of "black.")

B. The person who cut the chain was a male, white, about six feet tall. He was wearing black sneakers, blue dungarees, a yellow T-shirt, and a dark brown backpack. He rode the bicycle north for one block and then made a left turn.

C. The person who cut the chain and rode away with the bicycle was a male, white, about six feet tall. He was wearing black sneakers, blue dungarees, a yellow T-shirt, and a dark brown backpack. He pedaled north for one block and then made a left turn.

D. The person who cut the chain and rode away with the bicycle was a male, white, about six feet tall. He was wearing <u>black</u> sneakers, blue dungarees, a yellow T-shirt, and a dark brown backpack. He headed north for one block and then made a left turn.

----

5. Four witnesses to a hit and run accident tell Police Officer Tumi that they memorized the license plate of the car that sped away from the accident. Which of the following is the most likely to be correct?

A. 9237SFG

Choice "A" is <u>not</u> the most likely to be correct because the second numeral "2" differs from the "5" of the other three choices.

B. 9587SFG

Choice "B" is also <u>not</u> the most likely to be correct because the third numeral "8" differs from the "3" of the other three choices.

C. 9537SFG

(Choice "C" is the most likely to be correct. This is the plate number whose numerals agree with most other plate numbers.)

D. 9531SFG

Choice "D" is also <u>not</u> the most likely to be correct because the fourth numeral "1" differs from the "7" of the other three choices.**)**

Question 6

Answer question 6 based on the following table:

Summonses and Desk Appearance Tickets Issued by Police Officer Rinder

Week	Dates	Parking Summonses	Moving Summonses	Desk Appearance Tickets
1	June 1 – 7	24	11	4
2	June 8 - 14	21	8	7
3	June 15 – 21	26	12	2
4	June 22 – 28	19	9	6
5	June 29 – July 5	28	13	9

6. Police Officer Rinder is adding up the total number of summonses and desk appearance tickets issued by her during the above five-week period. Which of the following four formulas should she use to arrive at the correct total of summonses and desk appearance tickets that she issued?

A. 24+21+26+19+28

B. 28 + 13 + 9

C. 24+11+4+21+8+7+26+12+2+19+9+6+28+13+9

D. 1(24+11+4) + 2(21+8+7) + 3(26+12+2) + 4(19+9+6) + 5(28+13+9)

Answer 6

A. 24+21+26+19+28

(NOT CORRECT. This only includes "Parking Summonses" and does not include "Moving Summonses" and "Desk Appearance Tickets.")

B. 28 + 13 + 9

(NOT CORRECT. This only includes summonses and Desk Appearance Tickets issued during the fifth week, June 29 – July 5).

C. 24+11+4+21+8+7+26+12+2+19+9+6+28+13+9 (Total is 199.)

(CORRECT. This includes all the summonses and Desk Appearance Tickets issued during the entire five weeks.)

D. 1(24+11+4) + 2(21+8+7) + 3(26+12+2) + 4(19+9+6) + 5(28+13+9)

(NOT CORRECT. This mathematical formula would give a result of 617.)

INFORMATION ORDERING

9

These questions evaluate your ability to put in order given rules or actions. The rules or actions can include letters, words, sentences, procedures, pictures, and logical or mathematical operations.

The key to answering this type of question correctly is to make sure that the directions are clear to you.

To obtain maximum clarity, take the time to understand the logical order of the directions. Steps that must be done "before" or "after" or "at the same time" should be noted.

Also, at the time of selecting your answer, refer back to the directions to make sure that you have not mentally mixed up the order or the details of the directions.

Question 1

Answer question 1 based on the following "Bomb Threat Procedure."

Bomb Threat Procedure

Some bomb threats are received by phone. A Police Officer who receives a bomb threat by phone should do the following in the order specified:

> 1. Stay calm. Do not hang up, even if the caller hangs up. Be polite and show interest in what the caller is saying.

> 2. If possible, write a message to a fellow officer or other NYC Police Department employee.

> 3. If your phone displays the caller number, write down the number.

> 4. Even if the caller hangs up, do not hang up your phone. Use a different phone that is not a cell phone to contact the "Bomb Threat Notification Unit."

> 5. As soon as possible, complete the "Bomb Threat Checklist."

-----

1. At a "Bomb Threat Exercise" conducted at the precinct, you are told that you have answered a phone call during which a bomb threat is made. You have written a note and notified a Police Officer working at the desk next to yours. You have also written down the caller's number which displayed on your phone unit. The caller hangs up. The next step you should take is to:

A. Hang up the phone and immediately call the "Bomb Threat Notification Unit."

B. Do not hang up the phone, but use a cell phone to contact the "Bomb Threat Notification Unit."

C. Complete the form "Bomb Threat Checklist."

D. Do not hang up and use a different phone (not a cell phone) to contact the "Bomb Threat Notification Unit."

Answer 1

Answer question 1 based on the following "Bomb Threat Procedure."

Bomb Threat Procedure

Some bomb threats are received by phone. A Police Officer who receives a bomb threat by phone should do the following in the order specified:

> 1. Stay calm. Do not hang up, even if the caller hangs up. Be polite and show interest in what the caller is saying.

> 2. If possible, write a message to a fellow officer or other NYC Police Department employee.

> 3. If your phone displays the caller number, write down the number.

> 4. Even if the caller hangs up, <u>do not hang up your phone. Use a different phone that is not a cell phone</u> to contact the "Bomb Threat Notification Unit."

> 5. As soon as possible, complete the "Bomb Threat Checklist."

-----

1. At a "Bomb Threat Exercise" conducted at the precinct, you are told that you have answered a phone call during which a bomb threat is made. You have written a note and notified a Police Officer working at the desk next to yours. You have also written down the caller's number which displayed on your phone unit. The caller hangs up. The next step you should take is to:

A. Hang up the phone and immediately call the "Bomb Threat Notification Unit."
(WRONG. Number 1 states, "Do <u>not</u> hang up...")

B. Do not hang up the phone, but use a cell phone to contact the "Bomb Threat Notification Unit."
(WRONG. Number 3 states, "Use a different phone that is <u>not</u> a cell phone...")

C. Complete the form "Bomb Threat Checklist."

(**WRONG.** Number 5 states, "complete the form "Bomb Threat Checklist." This is the <u>last</u> step and is done <u>after</u> contacting the "Bomb Threat Notification Unit.")

D. Do not hang up and use a different phone (not a cell phone) to contact the "Bomb Threat Notification Unit."

(**CORRECT.** This is step number four and comes directly after step number three, "...write down the number," which you have already done.)

Question 2

Answer question 2 based on the following "Abandoned Vehicle Procedure."

Police Officer Palenco receives the following new "Abandoned Vehicle Procedure."

Abandoned Vehicle Procedure

1. An abandoned vehicle must be reported to Police Dispatch at 718-555-0105.

2. A police officer will be assigned to attach a notice on the vehicle instructing the owner to remove the vehicle within 48 hours.

3. If the vehicle is not removed within 72 hours, the same officer who reported the abandoned vehicle will complete an AVR (Abandoned Vehicle Information) form and submit it to the precinct (VR Office).

4. The VR office will assign the report an incident report number and e-mail it to the city Department of Environmental Hazards.

5. If the vehicle is not removed within 48 hours, the Department of Environmental Hazards will tow the vehicle to the Waste Metal Recovery Site located in the borough.

-----

2. Officer Palenco is informed by an angry shop owner that a vehicle has been parked in front of his store for the past 3 months without it ever being moved and has accumulated 22 parking tickets. According to the Abandoned Vehicle Procedure, Officer Polanco should:

A. Complete an AVR report and submit it to the precinct (VR Office), as three months have already passed and the shop owner is angry.

B. He should attach a notice on the vehicle instructing the owner to remove the vehicle within 48 hours.

C. Report the abandoned vehicle to Police Dispatch by informing his sergeant, as this will speed up the process.

D. Report the abandoned vehicle to Police Dispatch at 718-555-0105.

Answer 2

Answer question 2 based on the following "Abandoned Vehicle Procedure."

Police Officer Palenco receives the following new "Abandoned Vehicle Procedure."

Abandoned Vehicle Procedure

1. An abandoned vehicle must be reported to Police Dispatch at 718-555-0105.

2. A police officer will be assigned to attach a notice on the vehicle instructing the owner to remove the vehicle within 48 hours.

3. If the vehicle is not removed within 72 hours, the same officer who reported the abandoned vehicle will complete an AVR (Abandoned Vehicle Information) form and submit it to the precinct (VR Office).

4. The VR office will assign the report an incident report number and e-mail it to the city Department of Environmental Hazards.

5. If the vehicle is not removed within 48 hours, the Department of Environmental Hazards will tow the vehicle to the Waste Metal Recovery Site located in the borough.

-----

2. Officer Palenco is informed by an angry shop owner that a vehicle has been parked in front of his store for the past 3 months without it ever being moved and has accumulated 22 parking tickets. According to the Abandoned Vehicle Procedure, Officer Palenco should:

A. Complete an AVR report and submit it to the precinct (VR Office), as three months have already passed and the shop owner is angry.

(WRONG: The first thing he must do is report the abandoned vehicle to Police Dispatch at 718-555-0105.)

B. He should attach a notice on the vehicle instructing the owner to remove the vehicle within 48 hours.

(WRONG. <u>After</u> Police Officer Palenco reports the abandoned vehicle, "A police officer will be assigned to attach a notice on the vehicle instructing the owner to remove the vehicle within 48 hours.")

C. Report the abandoned vehicle to Police Dispatch by informing his sergeant, as this will speed up the process.

(WRONG. The report must be done by telephone and not to his sergeant. There are no steps in the procedure to "speed up the process.")

D. <u>Report the abandoned vehicle to Police Dispatch at 718-555-0105.</u>

(CORRECT. Regardless of how long the vehicle has been there or how angry the shop owner is, the correct first step is to report the abandoned vehicle to Police Dispatch.)

Question 3

Your supervisor gives you five "Complaint Forms" with the following priority numbers:

2867   19643   0344   783   8249

He asks you to organize the forms in ascending priority.

3. According to the above, the third Complaint Form would be Complaint Form number:

A. 8249   C. 783

B. 2867   D. 0344

Answer 3

Examples of <u>ascending order</u> and <u>descending order</u>

Ascending Priority Number Order	Descending Priority Number Order
1	5
2	4
3	3
4	2
5	1

The Complaint Forms in Ascending Priority Number Order are as follows:

1) 0344

2) 783

3) 2867

4) 8249

5) 19643

The third complaint number on the list is 2867, therefore the correct answer is **B) 2867**.

Question 4

Your supervisor gives you five "Requests for Investigation" forms submitted by residents in your precinct. The forms were submitted by the following five persons:

George Felder, Harriet Volker, Ben Halston, Abe Johnson, Diane Molton

He asks you to organize the forms in last name alphabetical order.

4. According to the above, the fourth "Request for Investigation" form is the one submitted by:

A. Halston, Ben

B. Volker, Harriet

C. Molton, Diane

D. Felder, George

Answer 4

The correct listing in last name alphabetical order is:

1) Felder, George

2) Halston, Ben

3) Johnson, Abe

4) Molton, Diane

5) Volker, Harriet

The fourth name on the list is Molton, Diane, therefore the correct answer is **C) Molton, Diane**.

Question 5

5. The ninth letter of the alphabet is:

A) H

B) J

C) I

D. G

Answer 5

The letters of the alphabet (in order) are as follows:

A,   B,   C,   D,   E,   F,   G,   H,   I   J,   K,   L   M.....

1........2.........3.........4.......5.........6.........7.......8........**9**........10.......11.......12.......13....

The correct answer is **C) I.**

Question 6

6. You are assigned to drive the precinct van. Your sergeant asks you to make five stops to pick up police officers. At the first two stops you are to pick up six police officers at each stop. At the last three stops you are to pick up four police officers at each stop. Which of the following mathematical expressions correctly states the total number of police officers that you will pick up at the five stops?

A) 2 + 6 + 3 + 4   B) 2 X 6 X 3 X 4   C) 2 + 3   D) 2(6) + 3(4)

Answer 6

At the first two stops you will pick up six police officers at each stop (6 + 6 = 12 police officers). At the last three stops you will pick up 4 police officers at each stop (4 + 4 + 4 = 12 police officers). The total number of police officers to be picked up is therefore 24 (because 12 + 12 = 24 police officers).

The A, B, C, and D choices would yield the following results:

A) 2 + 6 + 3 + 4 (This gives a total of 15).

B) 2 X 6 X 3 X 4 (This gives a total of 144.)

C) 2 + 3 (This gives a total of 5.)

D) 2(6) + 3(4) = 24

(The mathematical expression 2(6) + 3(4) means (2 X 6) + (3 X 4) = 24. The correct answer therefore is **D) 2(6) + 3(4)**.)

Question 7

Organize the following four sentences in the best logical order:

1. This training includes classroom and "on the street" practice driving.

2. Because of this, they receive proper driving and safety instruction.

3. "On the street" driving is stressed and comprises eighty percent of the training time.

4. Police Officers may be assigned to drive a precinct van.

(A) 1, 3, 4, 2   (B) 2, 3, 4, 1   (C) 3, 2, 1, 4   (D) 4, 2, 1, 3

Answer 7

The correct answer is **(D) 4, 2, 1, 3.**

4. Police Officers may be assigned to drive a precinct van. (This sentence introduces the topic of driving a precinct van.)

2. Because of this, they receive proper driving and safety instruction.

1. This training includes classroom and "on the street" practice driving.

3. "On the street" driving is stressed and comprises eighty percent of the training time.

(After sentence 4, sentences 2, 1, and 3 follow logically in that order.)

Question 8

Your sergeant hands you five "Overtime Request Forms" which you submitted for processing. He reminds you that all overtime requests must be submitted in date order and numbered sequentially. The dates on the overtime forms are as follows:

10-4-2016   9/24/2016   October 1, 2016   September 28, 2016   Sept. 12, 2016

He asks you to number the forms in ascending date order and that you resubmit them.

Assuming that you organize the forms as your supervisor asks and that you number the first request "Request 1," which of the above dated requests would be numbered "Request 3"?

A. 10-4-2016

B. 9/24/2016

C. October 1, 2016

D. September 28, 2016

Answer 8

The correct ascending date order is:

        1) Sept. 12, 2016

        2) 9/24/2016

        3) September 28, 2016

        4) October 1, 2016

        5) 10-4-2016

The third date on the list is September 28, 2016. Therefore, the correct answer is **D). September 28, 2016.**

Question 9

The following are four sentences. Each sentence (listed in random order) is one of the four steps necessary to attach a metal shield to the front of a van. Which one of the following choices (A, B, C, D) lists the order of sentences which best expresses the logical sequence of metal shield installation?

1. Drive the van slowly forward to test whether the shield is securely bolted to the van.

2. Tighten the bolts with heavy duty nuts.

3. Align the front of the van with the shield connectors.

4. Insert connecting bolts in aligned holes of shield and the van's shield connectors.

A. 1, 4, 2, 3

B. 2, 3, 4, 1

C. 4, 1, 3, 2

D. 3, 4, 2, 1

Answer 9

The correct answer is **D. 3, 4, 2, 1.** (In this order, the sentences are logically connected.)

3. Align the front of the van with the shield connectors.

4. Insert connecting bolts in aligned holes of shield and the van's shield connector.

2. Tighten the bolts with heavy duty nuts.

1. Drive the van slowly forward to test whether the shield is securely bolted to the van.

_____

"Successful and unsuccessful people do not vary greatly in their abilities. They vary in their desires to reach their potential."

– John Maxwell

SPATIAL ORIENTATION

10

These questions evaluate your ability to determine your location and the location of an object with respect to you.

For this type of question, try to keep in mind the following North-East-South-West directional diagram.

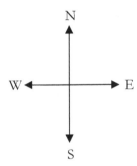

As you read the directional information provided, draw the route (as shown in the answers provided for these types of questions.)

Example: The car travelled east, then south, then west:

Questions 1 – 3

1. You and another officer notice an elderly man laying down on the street and bleeding from his right arm. He tells you that a large dog that was frothing at the mouth just bit him. You notice the dog running down the block northbound to the end of the block where he makes a right turn. While your partner stays with the victim, you follow the dog and observe him continuing to run for two blocks before turning right.

According to the information in the preceding passage, you would be most correct to radio that you last saw the dog running:

A) north   B) south   C) east   D) west

-----

2. While in your patrol car, you notice a car with what seems to be a teenage driver sideswipe a parked car and then drive off southbound without stopping. You follow the car, which after six blocks makes a right turn and then after two more blocks makes a left turn.

According to the information in the preceding passage, you would be most correct to radio that you last saw the car heading:

A) north   B) south   C) east   D) west

-----

3. Your attention is drawn to a shopkeeper shouting "He robbed me!" and pointing to a man running down the block. You shout for the man to stop, but he continues running eastbound. After three blocks, he makes a right turn and runs for two more blocks before making another right turn.

According to the information in the preceding passage, you would be most correct to radio that you last saw the man heading:

A) north   B) south   C) east   D) west

Answers 1 – 3

1. You and another officer notice an elderly man laying down on the street and bleeding from his right arm. He tells you that a large dog that was frothing at the mouth just bit him. You notice the dog running down the block northbound to the end of the block where he makes a right turn. While your partner stays with the victim, you follow the dog and observe him continuing to run for two blocks before turning right.

According to the information in the preceding passage, you would be most correct to radio that you last saw the dog running:

A) north   **B) south**

C) east   D) west

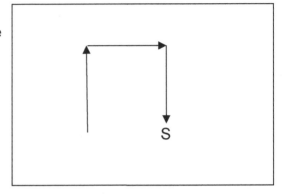

-----

2. While in your patrol car, you notice a car with what seems to be a teenage driver sideswipe a parked car and then drive off southbound without stopping. You follow the car, which after six blocks makes a right turn and then after two more blocks makes a left turn.

According to the information in the preceding passage, you would be most correct to radio that you last saw the car heading:

A) north   **B) south**

C) east   D) west

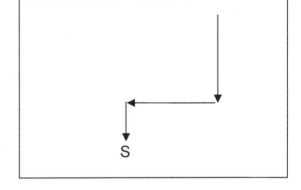

-----

3. Your attention is drawn to a shopkeeper shouting, "He robbed me!" and pointing to a man running down the block. You shout for the man to stop, but he continues running eastbound. After three blocks, he makes a right turn and runs for two more blocks before making another right turn.

According to the information in the preceding passage, you would be most correct to radio that you last saw the man heading:

A) north   B) south

C) east   **D) west**

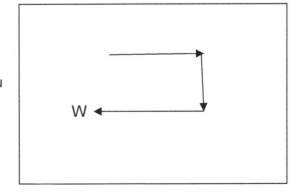

Questions 4 – 6

4. You and another officer witness a masked man snatch a purse from an elderly woman in front of a department store. You shout for the man to stop, but he runs down the block in an eastbound direction. You chase the man for two blocks before he turns right and then runs for another block, at which point he turns left.

According to the information in the preceding passage, you would be most correct to radio that the man was running:

A) north   B) south   C) east   D) west

-----

5. While in your patrol car, you witness two men run out of a bank, both holding a pouch and a revolver. They quickly get into a car and head southbound. You follow. After three six blocks, they make a right turn and then after two more blocks they make another right turn.

According to the information in the preceding passage, you would be most correct to radio that you last saw the car heading:

A) north   B) south   C) east   D) west

-----

6. Your attention is drawn to a pedestrian shouting, "He just ran over me with his bike!" and pointing to a man on a bike pedaling quickly on the sidewalk, away from the pedestrian and in an eastbound direction. After three blocks, he makes a right turn and runs for two more blocks before making another right turn.

According to the information in the preceding passage, you would be most correct to radio that you last saw the man heading:

A) north   B) south   C) east   D) west

Answers 4 - 6

4. You and another officer witness a masked man snatch a purse from an elderly woman in front of a department store. You shout for the man to stop, but he runs down the block in an eastbound direction. You chase the man for two blocks before he turns right and then runs for another block, at which point he turns left.

According to the information in the preceding passage, you would be most correct to radio that the man was running:

A) north   B) south

C) east   D) west

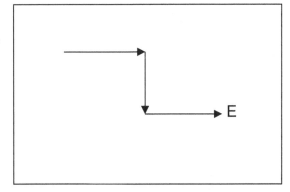

-----

5. While in your patrol car, you witness two men run out of a bank, both holding a pouch and a revolver. They quickly get into a car and head southbound. You follow. After three six blocks, they make a right turn and then after two more blocks they make another right turn.

According to the information in the preceding passage, you would be most correct to radio that you last saw the car heading:

A) north   B) south

C) east   D) west

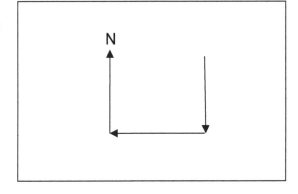

-----

6. Your attention is drawn to a pedestrian shouting, "He just ran over me with his bike!" and pointing to a man on a bike pedaling quickly on the sidewalk, away from the pedestrian and in an eastbound direction. After three blocks, he makes a right turn and runs for two more blocks before making another right turn.

According to the information in the preceding passage, you would be most correct to radio that you last saw the man heading:

A) north   B) south

C) east   **D) west**

VISUALIZATION 11

These questions evaluate your ability to understand how an object would look when it is rotated or unfolded, moved or changed in any manner.

When you examine images that are changed:

1. Look for differences among the images.

2. Cosmetic differences on faces or objects (lipstick, eye shadow, etc., do not make it a different face or object).

When you examine images that are moved or rotated:

1. Try to form a strong mental image of the way it looks originally.

2. Note any distinguishing facts, points, sections, or patterns.

3. Compare carefully the features you have noted in the original image to each of the image choices provided.

Question 1

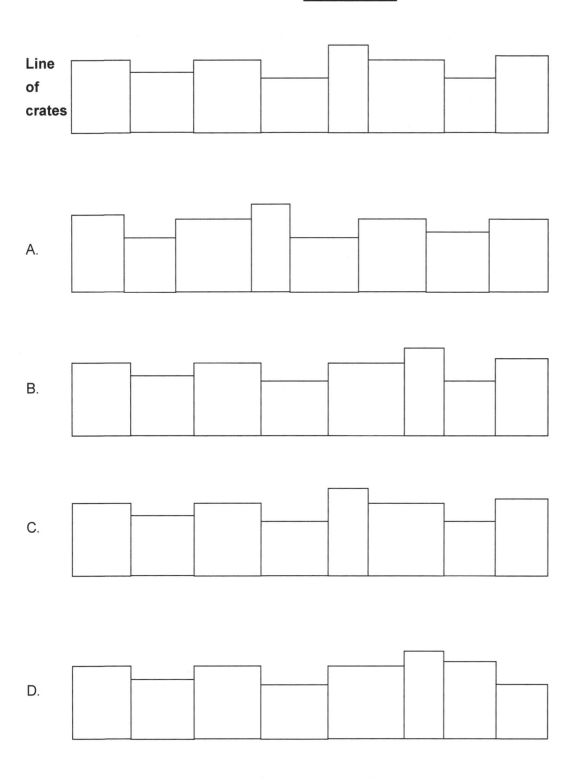

1. Officer Rodriguez is searching for a suspect hiding in a warehouse. He passes a "Line of crates" from the front of the crates. He hears a creek, but keeps walking. A minute later (when he is several rows behind these crates) he decides to return and investigate. How would the "Line of crates" appear as viewed from the back? (A, B, C, or D?)

Questions 2 - 5

Read the following passage, then answer questions 2 - 5 based on the information contained in the passage.

While on patrol, Police Officers Colandro and Feinstein are dispatched to 2834 Boylan Avenue, first floor, "Supreme Arts and Crafts, Inc." at 9:22 p.m. on September 27, 2016. The owner of "Supreme Arts and Crafts, Inc." had just called 911 to report a burglary. They arrive at the store at 9:24 p.m. and are greeted by Mr. Howard Garmen, the owner of the store and Mr. Felix Cuedo, an employee of "Supreme Arts and Crafts, Inc."

Mr. Garmen tells the officers that he and Felix Cuedo had closed the store for the day at 7:00 p.m. They had locked the front and back doors and properly rolled down the security gate and padlocked it. Mr. Garmen discovered the burglary at 9:01 p.m. when at home he happened to glance at the live video of his four security cameras. Although security camera #1 showed the outdoor front entrance and security camera #4 showed the outdoor back door area, it was with security cameras #2 and #3 that he saw the burglars. Security camera #2 covered the outdoor roof skylight and security camera #3 covered the inside area of the store, including the cashier area.

Two burglars, all dressed in black and wearing black face masks, had broken the glass in the skylight and with a rope had descended into the store. The smaller of the two persons descended first and the much taller one followed. The person who descended first carried a black garbage bag and the other person held a flashlight in his right hand.

The two burglars took all the $125.00 cash and coins that had been left in the cash register, a box of collectible statuettes worth $1500.00, three expensive brushes and paints sets worth a total of $900.00, two electric easels worth $179 each, and six original signed watercolor paintings by a local artist worth $129.00 each. Mr. Garmen tells the officers that he will prepare a complete list of missing items as soon as possible.

Mr. Garmen tells Officer Feinstein that he is 58 years old and lives at 2869 Batchelder Avenue in Queens. His cell number is 718-555-2987. Felix Cuedo tells Officer Feinstein that he is 29 years old and lives at 3845 East 289 Street, Brooklyn. His cell number is 718-555-3991.

Police Officers Colandro and Feinstein complete their investigation at 10:05 p.m. Before they completed their crime report, they performed a careful sweep of the store to make sure that the burglars had left.

-----

2. Which of the following security cameras cover the outdoor areas?

A. 1 and 2 only

B. 1, 2, 3, and 4

C. 1, 2, and 4 only

D. 1, 2, and 3 only

----

3. Which of the following statements is correct?

A. The taller man carried a black garbage bag and the smaller man held a flashlight in his right hand.

B. The two burglars were dressed all in grey.

C. The taller person descended first and carried a flashlight in his right hand.

D. The shorter person carried a black garbage bag and the taller person held a flashlight in his right hand.

----

4. Which one of the following statements is correct? Among the items stolen were:

A. three expensive brushes and paints sets worth $900.00 each.

B. two electric easels worth a total of $179.

C. $725.00 cash and coins that had been left in the cash register.

D. six original signed watercolor paintings by a local artist worth a total of $774.00.

----

5. Which of the following statements is correct according to the information provided by Mr. Garmen and Mr. Felix Cuedo?

A. Felix Cuedo tells Officer Feinstein that he is 29 years old and lives at 3845 East 298 Street, Brooklyn. His cell number is 718-555-3991.

B. Mr. Garmen tells Officer Feinstein that he is 58 years old and lives at 2896 Batchelder Avenue in Queens. His cell number is 718-555-2987.

C. Felix Cuedo tells Officer Feinstein that his cell number is 718-555-2987.

D. Mr. Garmen tells Officer Feinstein that he lives at 2869 Batchelder Avenue in Queens.

Answer 1

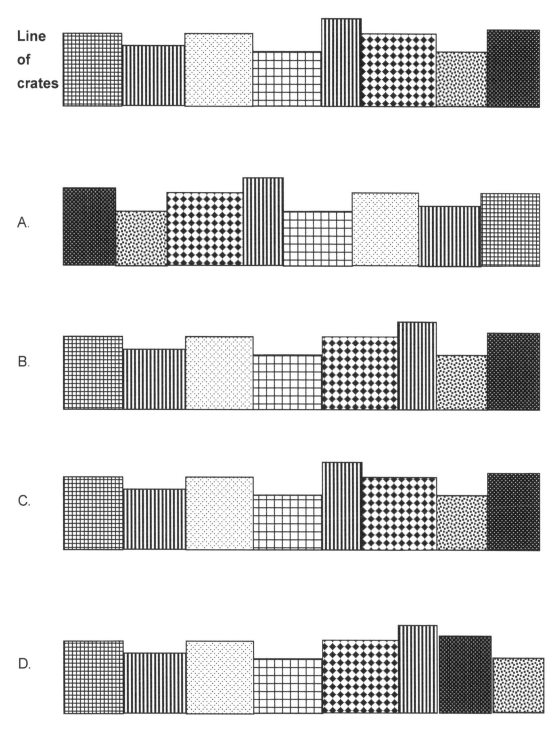

1. The answer is "A."

(To make the answer obvious, we have filled in each corresponding box with the same pattern.)

Answers 2 – 5

2. Which of the following security cameras cover the outdoor areas?

A. 1 and 2 only

B. 1, 2, 3, and 4

C. 1, 2, and 4 only

("...security camera #3 covered the inside area of the store, including the cashier area.")

D. 1, 2, and 3 only

----

3. Which of the following statements is correct?

A. The taller man carried a black garbage bag and the smaller man held a flashlight in his right hand.

(WRONG. The smaller of the two persons descended first and the much taller one followed. The person who descended first carried a black garbage bag and the other person held a flashlight in his right hand.)

B. The two burglars were dressed all in grey.

(WRONG. "The two burglars, all dressed in <u>black</u> and wearing black face masks...)

C. The taller person descended first and carried a flashlight in his right hand.

(WRONG. The <u>smaller</u> of the two persons descended first.)

D. The shorter person carried a black garbage bag and the taller person held a flashlight in the right hand.

(CORRECT. "The smaller of the two persons descended first and the much taller one followed. The person who descended first carried a black garbage bag and the other person held a flashlight in the right hand.")

----

4. Which one of the following statements is correct? Among the items stolen were:

A. three expensive brushes and paints sets worth $900.00 each.

(WRONG. The tree sets <u>totaled</u> $900.00.)

B. two electric easels worth a total of $179.

(**WRONG.** <u>Each</u> easel is worth $179.)

C. $725.00 cash and coins that had been left in the cash register.

(**WRONG.** The correct amount of cash and coins is $125.)

D. six original signed watercolor paintings by a local artist worth a total of $774.00.

(**CORRECT.** "$129.00 each X 6 = $774.00)

----

5. Which of the following statements is correct according to the information provided by Mr. Garmen and Mr. Felix Cuedo?

A. Felix Cuedo tells Officer Feinstein that he is 29 years old and lives at 3845 East 298 Street, Brooklyn. His cell number is 555-3991.

(**WRONG.** Felix Cuedo lives at East <u>289</u> Street.)

B. Mr. Garmen tells Officer Feinstein that he is 58 years old and lives at 2896 Batchelder Avenue in Queens. His cell number is 718-555-2987.

(**WRONG.** The correct street address is <u>2869</u> Batchelder Avenue.)

C. Felix Cuedo tells Officer Feinstein that his cell number is 718-555-2987.

(**WRONG.** The correct cell number is <u>718-555-3991</u>.)

D. Mr. Garmen tells Officer Feinstein that he lives at 2869 Batchelder Avenue in Queens.

(**CORRECT.** "Mr. Garmen tells Officer Feinstein that he is 58 years old and lives at 2869 Batchelder Avenue in Queens.")

"Focused, hard work is the key to success."

– John Carmack

Question 6

During her patrol, Police Officer Dawn Heller is called to the scene of an accident. The driver/owner of vehicle #3 stated that he was driving on Vine St. and making a right turn to Hart Avenue when car #1 hit his car from behind, causing him to hit vehicle number 2.

Assume that all 3 vehicles were in their proper lanes of traffic.

Which of the following 4 diagrams best matches the statement of the driver of vehicle #3?

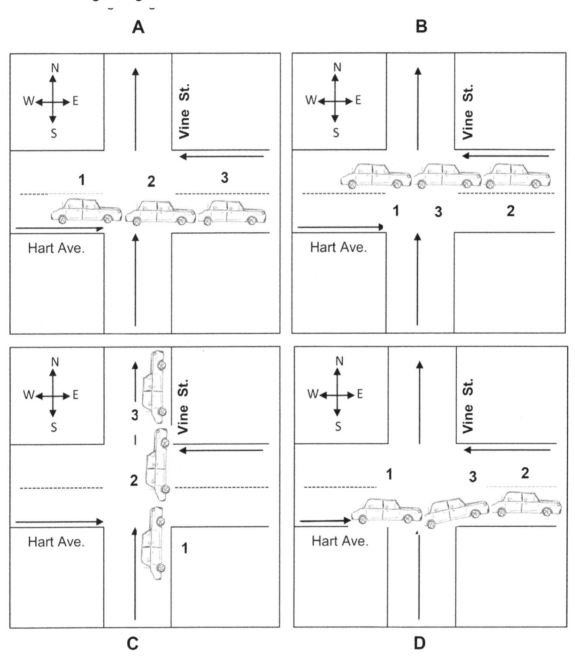

6. The diagram which best matches the statement of driver of vehicle #3 is:

A. diagram "A"

B. diagram "B"

C. diagram "C"

D. diagram "D"

Answer 6

6. The diagram which best matches the statement of driver of vehicle #3 is:

A. diagram "A"   C. diagram "C"

B. diagram "B"   **D. diagram "D" (Answer)**

Why?

According to the question, "The driver/owner of vehicle #3 stated that he was driving on Vine St. and making a right turn when car #1 hit his car from behind, causing him to hit vehicle number 2."

"Car 1 hits Car 3 which hits Car 2"

1 > 3 > 2

The only choice which displays the collision in this sequence <u>and in the proper lane</u> is choice **"D."**

Questions 7 - 9

Answer question 7 based on the following information.

Officer Lagnier collects the following information at the scene of an auto accident:

Date of Accident: August 16, 2016

Time of accident: 5:02 p.m.

Place of accident: intersection of Ferndale Avenue and Willows Avenue, Bronx

Driver: Alfred Kearns

Vehicle: 2007 Toyota Sienna

Damage: Vehicle struck a bicycle partially parked on the sidewalk, but protruding into the street.

-----

7. Officer Lagnier is preparing a report of the accident and has four drafts of the report. He wishes to use the draft that expresses the information most clearly, accurately and completely. Which draft should he choose?

A. At 5:02 p.m., on August 16, 2016, at the intersection of Ferndale Avenue and Willows Avenue, Bronx, a vehicle driven by Alfred Kearns struck a bicycle partially parked on the sidewalk, but protruding into the street.

B. On August 16, 2016, at 5:02 p.m., at the intersection of Ferndale Avenue and Willows Avenue, Bronx, a 2007 Toyota Sienna driven by Alfred Karns struck a bicycle partially parked on the sidewalk, but protruding into the street.

C. On August 16, 2016, at 5:02 p.m., at the intersection of Ferndale Avenue and Willows Avenue, Bronx, a 2007 Toyota Sienna driven by Alfred Kearns struck a bicycle partially parked on the sidewalk, but protruding into the street.

D. At the intersection of Ferndale Avenue and Willows Avenue, Bronx, on August 16, 2016, at 2:05 p.m., a 2007 Toyota Sienna driven by Alfred Kearns struck a bicycle partially parked on the sidewalk, but protruding into the street.

Answer question 8 based on the following information.

Officer Pintkin responds to a car theft. She questions the owner of the vehicle who reported the car stolen and obtains the following information:

Suspect: Unidentified

Date of crime: August 15, 2016

Time of crime: between 6:20 p.m. and 11:30 p.m.

Crime: theft of car

Vehicle stolen: 2012 Nissan

Victim: owner of car, Lance Bedford

Place of crime: driveway in front of 167 28th Street, Staten Island

-----

8. Officer Pintkin is preparing a report of the theft and has prepared four drafts of the report. She wishes to use the draft that expresses the information most clearly, accurately and completely. Which of the following drafts should she choose?

A. A car theft of a 2012 Nissan happened at the driveway in front of 167 28th Street, Staten Island where Lance Bedford's car was parked for the night. The alleged thief is unidentified, as the theft happened in the afternoon.

B. On August 15, 2016, between 6:20 p.m. and 11:30 p.m., at the driveway in front of 167 28th Street, Staten Island, a 2012 Nissan owned by Lance Bedford was stolen by an unidentified suspect.

C. A car was stolen on August 15, 2016, between 6:20 p.m. and 11:30 p.m., at the driveway in front of 167 28th Street, Staten Island, owned by Lance Bedford. The suspect is unidentified.

D. On August 15, 2016, at the driveway in front of 167 28th Street, Staten Island, between 6:30 p.m. and 11:30 p.m., a 2012 Nissan owned by Lance Bedford was stolen by an unidentified suspect.

Answer question 9 based on the following procedure.

When a criminal case is pending in the courts, the Police Officer who made the arrest is prohibited from discussing the case with any newspaper, magazine, TV reporters, and all other media. Exceptions to this are when:

1. a New York court of competent jurisdiction formally orders the Police Officer to discuss one or more particulars of the case.

2. a NYPD authorized Department orders such discussion.

3. the Police Officer is subpoenaed to testify before an authorized NYC, NYS, or federal board.

The officer must in all cases refer all requests for information to the officer's supervisor.

-----

9. Police Officer Janet Peters arrests a person suspected of kidnapping a child who is still missing. The suspect has been indicted and is in jail, waiting for trial. A newspaper reporter, Brian Collins, contacts Officer Janet Peters and asks for information that might help the reporter to investigate the kidnapping and perhaps locate the missing child. Officer Janet Peters should:

A. give assistance to Brian Collins by providing information that might help to locate the missing child.

B. give assistance only if the reporter can guarantee that the child will be found.

C. provide only information relating to locating the child, and not any other information.

D. not provide any information and report the request to her supervisors.

Answers 7 - 9

Answer question 7 based on the following information.

Officer Lagnier collects the following information at the scene of an auto accident:

Date of Accident: August 16, 2016

Time of accident: 5:02 p.m.

Place of accident: intersection of Ferndale Avenue and Willows Avenue, Bronx

Driver: Alfred Kearns

Vehicle: 2007 Toyota Sienna

Damage: Vehicle struck a bicycle partially parked on the sidewalk, but protruding into the street.

7. Officer Lagnier is preparing a report of the accident and has four drafts of the report. He wishes to use the draft that expresses the information most clearly, accurately and completely. Which draft should he choose?

A. At 5:02 p.m., on August 16, 2016, at the intersection of Ferndale Avenue and Willows Avenue, Bronx, a vehicle driven by Alfred Kearns struck a bicycle partially parked on the sidewalk, but protruding into the street.

(**WRONG.** The information is not complete. The type of vehicle, "2007 Toyota Sienna", is not stated.)

B. On August 16, 2016, at 5:02 p.m., at the intersection of Ferndale Avenue and Willows Avenue, Bronx, a 2007 Toyota Sienna driven by Alfred <u>Karns</u> struck a bicycle partially parked on the sidewalk, but protruding into the street.

(**WRONG.** The name of the driver, "Kearns," is misspelled "Karns.")

C. On August 16, 2016, at 5:02 p.m., at the intersection of Ferndale Avenue and Willows Avenue, Bronx, a 2007 Toyota Sienna driven by Alfred Kearns struck a bicycle partially parked on the sidewalk, but protruding into the street.

(**CORRECT.** The information is accurate and complete.)

D. At the intersection of Ferndale Avenue and Willows Avenue, Bronx, on August 16, 2016, at <u>2:05 p.m.,</u> a 2007 Toyota Sienna driven by Alfred Kearns struck a bicycle partially parked on the sidewalk, but protruding into the street.

(**WRONG.** The time of the accident is not correct. The accident occurred at <u>5:02</u> p.m. and not <u>2:05</u> p.m.)

Answer question 8 based on the following information.

Officer Pintkin responds to a car theft. She questions the owner of the vehicle who reported the car stolen and obtains the following information:

Suspect: Unidentified

Date of crime: August 15, 2016

Time of crime: between 6:20 p.m. and 11:30 p.m.

Crime: theft of car

Vehicle stolen: 2012 Nissan

Victim: owner of car, Lance Bedford

Place of crime: driveway in front of 167 28th Street, Staten Island

8. Officer Pintkin is preparing a report of the theft and has prepared four drafts of the report. She wishes to use the draft that expresses the information most clearly, accurately and completely. Which of the following drafts should she choose?

A. A car theft of a 2012 Nissan happened at the driveway in front of 167 28th Street, Staten Island where Lance Bedford's car was parked for the night. The alleged thief is unidentified, as the theft happened in the <u>afternoon</u>.

(**WRONG.** The date of the crime is missing and the time of the crime is missing. Also, the statement that "The alleged thief is unidentified, as the theft happened in the afternoon" is not correct because it occurred in the evening.)

B. On August 15, 2016, between 6:20 p.m. and 11:30 p.m., at the driveway in front of 167 28th Street, Staten Island, a 2012 Nissan owned by Lance Bedford was stolen by an unidentified suspect.

(**CORRECT.** The information is accurate and complete.)

C. A car was stolen on August 15, 2016, between 6:20 p.m. and 11:30 p.m., at the driveway in front of 167 28th Street, Staten Island, owned by Lance Bedford. The suspect is unidentified.

(**WRONG. The t**ype of car, "2012 Nissan", is omitted and the statement is clumsy.)

D. On August 15, 2016, at the driveway in front of 167 28th Street, Staten Island, between 6:30 a.m. and <u>11:30 a.m.,</u> a 2012 Nissan owned by Lance Bedford was stolen by an unidentified suspect.

(**WRONG.** The time of the crime is wrong. The summary states "a.m." and it should be "<u>p.m.</u>")

Answer question 9 based on the following procedure.

When a criminal case is pending in the courts, the Police Officer who made the arrest is prohibited from discussing the case with any newspaper, magazine, TV reporters, and all other media. Exceptions to this are when:

1. a New York court of competent jurisdiction formally orders the Police Officer to discuss one or more particulars of the case.

2. a NYPD authorized Department orders such discussion.

3. the Police Officer is subpoenaed to testify before an authorized NYC, NYS, or federal board.

The officer must in all cases refer all requests for information to the officer's supervisor.

-----

9. Police Officer Janet Peters arrests a person suspected of kidnapping a child who is still missing. The suspect has been indicted and is in jail, waiting for trial. A newspaper reporter, Brian Collins, contacts Officer Janet Peters and asks for information that might help the reporter to investigate the kidnapping and perhaps locate the missing child. Officer Janet Peters should:

A. give assistance to Brian Collins by providing information that might help to locate the missing child.

(WRONG. This does not qualify as one of the three exception to the prohibition from discussing the case.)

B. give assistance only if the reporter can guarantee that the child will be found.

(WRONG. This does not qualify as one of the three exception to the prohibition from discussing the case.)

C. provide only information relating to locating the child, and not any other information.

(WRONG. This does not qualify as one of the three exception to the prohibition from discussing the case.)

D. not provide any information and report the request to her supervisors.

(CORRECT. All the other choices do not qualify as exceptions. Officer Peters cannot supply information and must "refer all requests for information to the officer's supervisor," as stated in the last sentence.)

FACIAL RECOGNITION QUESTIONS

On the test, you may see a type of question which tests your sensitivity to differences in facial features. The face of a suspect may be shown, along with a number of other faces of other persons that may look like the suspect, and also the original face (disguised by makeup, some loss of weight, different hair style, facial hair, different hat or clothing, etc.) You are asked to choose the face that looks most like the original face.

The most important thing to keep in mind when answering these types of questions is to not consider makeup, a different haircut, or the wearing of a different hat, etc. when comparing the faces. Only compare permanent features, such as the size of the chin, the shape of the eyes and nose, the thickness of the lips, etc. These are features that are not easily changed (except by cosmetic surgery) and are therefore excellent for comparison.

POLICE OFFICER EXAM NEW YORK CITY

Example: Consider the following comparisons of facial features:

SUSPECT	A	B	C	D

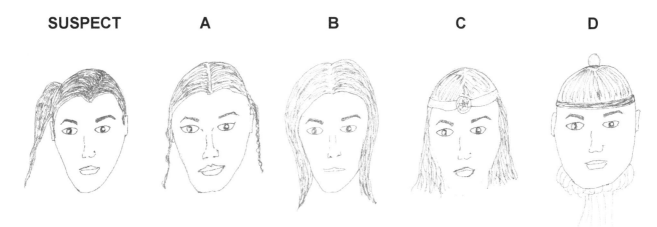

Question: Which of the four images (A, B, C, D) best matches the image of the suspect?

To answer this question, let's list the differences between the "Suspect" and the four choices and decide which differences are permanent features which we should consider in choosing our answer.

1. The noticeable differences between "Suspect" and "A" are:

   a. different hair style (We should <u>not</u> consider this because hairstyles may be changed.)

   b. The eyes of "A' slant differently. (Consider this difference.)

   c. The noses of the "Suspect" and "A" have a different shape. (This is a significant and permanent difference.)

   d. The face of "A" is wider than that of the "Suspect." (This is a significant and permanent difference.)

   e. the upper lip of "A" has a "V" middle section, which the "Suspect" does not have. (This is a significant permanent difference.)

   Conclusion: "Suspect" and "A" are <u>NOT</u> the same person.

2. The noticeable differences between "Suspect" and "B" are:

   a. different hair style (We should <u>not</u> consider this because hairstyles may be easily changed.)

   b. The noses of the "Suspect" and "A" have a different shape. (This is a significant and permanent difference.)

   c. "B" has thinner lips than the "Suspect." (This is a significant, permanent difference.)

   d. "B" has a squarer chin than the "Suspect." (This is a significant, permanent difference.)
   Conclusion: "Suspect" and "B" are <u>NOT</u> the same person.

3. **("C" IS THE CORRECT CHOICE.)** Other than the temporary hairstyle and the possibility that "C" is wearing lipstick, there are no permanent features that differ between the "Suspect" and "C".

4. The "Suspect" and "D" have a very big difference in the shape of the face, with the face of "D" being much broader than that of the "Suspect."

During the exam, try to follow a similar analysis. These questions are relatively easy. A careful examination of the images will give you the correct answer.

Consider the facial features of the persons below and then select the image (A, B, C, D) that best matches the image of the suspect.

SUSPECT   A   B   C   D

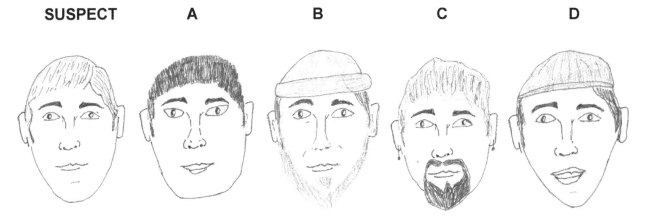

1. The eyes of "A" have an upward slant, which the "Suspect" does not have. Also, the face of "A" is broader and the nose is different. Therefore "A" is not the correct choice.

2. "B" is closer to the "Suspect" than "A." We don't consider the difference in hairstyle because a hairstyle can be quickly changed. However, "B" has a different type of nose, a facial feature that cannot be changed without plastic surgery. Therefore, "B" is not the correct choice.

3. "C" is wearing earrings, has a different hairstyle (and a goatee) and a dot (a mole?) on his cheek. These are all things that are matters of style and not permanent features. Other than these "cosmetic" differences, the "Suspect" image and the "C" image are the same. **Therefore, "C" is the correct choice.**

4. The permanent features that make "D" different from the "Suspect" are the thicker lips, thinner face, and slightly different nose. Therefore, "D" is not the correct choice.

Remember

The most important thing to keep in mind when answering these questions is to not consider temporary elements such as makeup, a different haircut, or the wearing of a different hat, etc. when comparing the faces. Only compare **permanent** head and facial features, such as the shape of the head, the size of the chin, the shape of the eyes and nose, the thickness of the lips, etc. These are features that are not easily changed without cosmetic surgery and are therefore excellent for identification purposes.

PRACTICE TEST #1
QUESTIONS

Memory Question

Study the photo below for the next ten minutes. Try to remember as many details about the people and objects as you can. During the ten minutes, you are not permitted to take any notes or write anything.

At the end of the ten minutes you will be asked to answer questions 1 – 10 (without looking back at the picture.)

(After ten minutes)

Instructions for questions 1 – 10:

Without looking back at the picture, answer questions 1 – 10 on the following page.

POLICE OFFICER EXAM NEW YORK CITY

1. The number of protestors not wearing any type of mask is:

A. 0   B. 1   C. 2   D. 3

2. How many signboards are displayed in the picture?

A. 6   B. 7   C. 8   D. 9

3. How many people are wearing a white mask?

A. 2   B. 3   C. 4   D. 5

4. The capital letter that appears alone on one of the signs is:

A. "B"   B. "Z"   C. "R"   D. none of the above

5. The two protestors that are holding signs with "USA" and the crossed-out "51" on them:

A. are wearing black shirts.

B. are both wearing white jackets.

C. are of the same height.

D. are wearing black face masks.

6. The dark signboard that is ripped at the corner:

A. has the word "Peace" on it.

B. has the word "NO" on it.

C. has the letters "USA" on it.

D. none of the above

7. How many signs have the letters "USA" on the sign?

A. 1   B. 2   C. 3   D. 4

8. The "smiley face":

A. is on a white background.

B. is being held above the heads of the crowd.

C. is on two signs.

D. does not have a nose.

9. How many signs have a "star" drawn on them?

A. 1   B. 2   C. 3   D. 4

10. How many signs do not have anything written, printed or displayed on them?

A. 0   B. 1   C. 2   D. 3

Questions 11 - 15

Answer questions 11 - 15 based on the information contained in the following paragraphs.

Police Officers Frank Torres and Diane Washington were on patrol on August 13, 2016 when at 9:45 p.m. they witnessed a minor traffic accident (at East 16th Street and Kings Highway in Brooklyn). Officer Torres called the Police Dispatcher at 9:50 p.m. and reported that the two drivers, and two passengers (one in each vehicle) did not sustain any personal injuries. One of the vehicles, the one driven by a male named Felix Upton, did have minor damage to the windshield, and the other vehicle, driven by a male named Mark Levington, had extensive damage to the driver's side front door.

Officer Washington examined the driver's licenses, vehicle registration certificates and vehicle insurance identification cards. The auto driven by Felix Upton, age 46, was a black 2012 Ford Edge, N.Y. license plate 4357ZB, owned by the driver, residing at 1942 West 58th Street, New York, N.Y. Mr. Upton's N.Y. driver's license identification number is D274 43 662 and the expiration date is December 31, 2016.

The driver of the other auto was Mark Levington, age 52, residing at 2686 Manor Street, Brooklyn, N.Y. Mr. Levington's auto was a blue 2011 Ford Escape, NY license plate 607PHB. Mr. Levington's driver's license identification number is A214 295 337 and the expiration is December 31, 2016.

Officers Torres and Washington completed a Vehicle Accident Report at 10:15 p.m. The report number was 48392747332.

-----

11. What is the time of the accident?
A. 9:50 p.m.
B. 10:15 p.m.
C. 9:45 p.m.
D. before 9:30 a.m.

----

12. How many persons were injured as a result of the traffic accident?
A. 1
B. 0
C. 2
D. none of the above

----

13. Which car sustained extensive damage to the driver's side front door?
A. NY plate #607PHB, black 2012 Ford Edge
B. NY plate #4357ZN, black 2012 Ford Edge
C. NY plate #4357ZN, blue 2011 Ford Escape
D. NY plate #607PHB, blue 2011 Ford Escape

14. Which of the following statements is not correct?
A. The auto driven by Felix Upton, age 46, was a black 2012 Ford Edge.
B. The vehicle Accident Report number was 4839274732.
C. Mark Levington, age 52, resides at 2686 Manor Street, Brooklyn, N.Y.
D. Mr. Upton's N.Y. driver's license identification number is D274 43 662.

----

15. Which of the following is correct?
A. The person residing at 1942 West 58th Street, New York, N.Y. has a N.Y. driver's license identification number D274 43 665 with an expiration date of December 31, 2016.
B. Mark Levington, age 25, resides at 2686 Manor Street, Brooklyn, N.Y.
C. The auto driven by Felix Upton, is a black 2012 Ford Edge, N.Y. license plate 4357ZB.
D. The accident occurred at East 16th Street and Kings Highway in the Bronx.

Questions 16 - 20

Answer questions 16 - 20 based on the information contained in the following paragraphs.

Police Officers George Elton and Jasmine Colbert were on patrol in their squad car on September 17, 2016 when at 9:35 p.m. a man approached them. The man pointed to his parked car, a silver Toyota, and stated that the red Ford Taurus parked behind it had just done some damage to the back of his car while the Taurus was parking. Police Officer George Elton called the police dispatcher at 9:40 p.m. and reported the traffic accident, which occurred in front of 924 6th Avenue, Staten Island. Police Officer Jasmine Colbert questioned the driver of the Taurus. Both Police Officers reported to the dispatcher that the driver of the silver Toyota and the driver of the damaged red Ford Taurus did not sustain any injuries. Also, there were no passengers in the two cars. One of the vehicles, the silver Toyota, was driven and owned by a male, Fred Elkinson. It had moderate damage to the back bumper and rear tail lights. The other vehicle, owned by a female, Barbara Baker, sustained no damage.

Officer Elton examined the driver's licenses, vehicle registration certificates and vehicle insurance identification cards. The auto driven by Fred Elkinson, age 51, was a 2008 silver Toyota, N.Y. license plate 36823EL, owned by the driver, residing at 62 West Garry Road, Brooklyn, N.Y. Mr. Elkinson's N.Y. driver's license identification number is R3241 35532 32578 and the expiration date is October 31, 2016.

The owner of the Taurus was Barbara Baker, age 46, residing at 234 West 9th Street, Queens, N.Y. Ms. Baker's auto was a 2009 red Ford Taurus, NY license plate KB3463H. Ms. Baker's driver's license identification number is D413 742 533 and the expiration is November 30, 2016.
Officers Elton and Colbert completed a Vehicle Accident Report at 9:50 p.m.
The report number was 224376654522.

16. Select the best answer: The time closest to the time of the accident is:
A. 9:35 a.m.   C. 9:40 p.m.
B. 6:50 p.m.   D. 9:35 p.m.

----

17. Which car sustained damage to the rear bumper and rear tail lights?
A. NY plate #36823EL, red Ford Taurus
B. NY plate #3463HKB, silver 2008 Toyota
C. NY plate #36823EL, silver 2008 Toyota
D. NY plate #3463HKB, red Ford Taurus

----

18. At what time was the Vehicle Accident Report completed?
A. 9:35 p.m.   B. 9:40 p.m.   C. 9:50 p.m.   D. 9:55 p.m.

----

19. Which of the following statements is correct?
A. The license plate number of the car owned by Barbara Baker is KD3463H.
B. The report number is 224376654522.
C. Police Officer Jasmine Colbert called the police dispatcher at 9:40 p.m.
D. The vehicle driven and owned by Fred Elkinson had moderate damage to the front bumper and rear tail lights.

----

20. Which of the following statements is correct?
A. Police Officer Jasmine Colbert questioned the driver of the Toyota.
B. Barbara Baker is 64 years old.
C. Officers Elton and Colbert completed a Vehicle Accident Report at 9:05 p.m.
D. Mr. Fred Elkinson's N.Y. driver's license identification number is R3241 35532 32578.

Questions 21 - 26

Answer questions 21 - 26 based on the information contained in the following paragraphs.

Police Officers David Alberts and Carol Sumpter were on patrol in their squad car on August 23, 2016 when at 8:25 p.m. a female approached them. The female stated that she had just been involved in a car accident with the black Honda that was now stopped next to her car, a red Ford. Police Officer David Alberts called the police dispatcher at 8:33 p.m. and reported the traffic accident (which occurred in front of 1976 East 17th Street, Jamaica). Police Officer Carol Sumpter questioned the driver of the black Honda. Both Police Officers reported to the dispatcher that both drivers did not sustain any injuries. Also, there were no passengers in the two cars. One of the vehicles, the red Ford, was driven and owned by a female, Nancy Wright. It had damage to the rear bumper. The other vehicle, driven by a female, Tania Salters, had damage to the front bumper.

Officer Alberts examined the driver's licenses, vehicle registration certificates and vehicle insurance cards. The auto driven by Nancy Wright, age 38, was a red 2006 Ford, N.Y. license plate 35434DE, owned by the driver, residing at 304 West Almeria Road, Brooklyn, N.Y. Ms. Wright's N.Y. driver's license identification number is W3547 28592 12332 and the expiration date is September 30, 2016.

The driver and owner of the other auto was Tania Salters, age 26, residing at 183 Madison Street, Bronx, N.Y. Ms. Salters' auto was a 2007 black Honda, NY license plate 4492GDX. Ms. Salters' driver's license identification number is H215 594 732 and the expiration is November 30, 2016.

Officers Alberts and Sumpter completed a Vehicle Accident Report at 8:40 p.m. The report number was 224376754321.

-----

21. Select the best answer. The closest time of the accident is approximately:
A. after 8:35 p.m.
B. after 8:30 p.m.
C. before 8:25 p.m.
D. after 8:40 p.m.

----

22. Which car sustained damage to the front bumper?
A. NY plate #4492GDX, red 2007 Honda
B. NY plate #35434DE, red 2006 Ford
C. NY plate #35434DE, black 2006 Ford
D. NY plate #4492GDX, black 2007 Honda

----

23. What is the total number of persons involved in the accident?
A. 1   C. 3
B. 2   D. none of the above

----

24. The owner of the parked vehicle with damage to the rear bumper resides at:
A. 304 West Almeria Road, Jamaica
B. 183 Madison Street, Bronx, N.Y.
C. 304 West Almeria Road, Brooklyn
D. 183 Madison Street, Jamaica, N.Y.

----

25. Which of the following is correct?
A. The driver and owner of the red Honda is Tania Salters.
B. Ms. Wright's N.Y. driver's license identification number is W3547 28592 12323.
C. Officers Alberts and Sumpter completed a Vehicle Accident Report at 8:04 p.m.
D. Nancy Wright lives at 304 West Almeria Road, Brooklyn.

----

26. Which of the following is not correct?
A. The vehicle driven by Tania Salters had damage to the front bumper.
B. The vehicle driven and owned by Nancy Wright was a red 2009 Ford.
C. Tania Salters is 26 years old.
D. Ms. Salters' auto was a 2007 black Honda, NY license plate 4492GDX.

Questions 27 - 34

27. An officer is reviewing a report she is preparing. It contains the following two rough drafts. Which of the two sentences are grammatically correct?

    1. The man who assaulted him, the cashier said, was about twenty years old and was wearing blue pants and a black, turtleneck sweater.

    2. The cashier stated that the male who assaulted him was about twenty years old and was wearing blue pants and a black, turtleneck sweater.

A. Only sentence 1 is grammatically correct.
B. Only sentence 2 is grammatically correct.
C. Both sentences 1 and 2 are grammatically correct.
D. Neither sentence 1 nor sentence 2 is grammatically correct.

----

28. An officer is asked by his partner to review a speech that the officer is preparing to give to new recruits. It contains the following two versions of one part of the speech. Which are grammatically correct?

    1. And other reasons why police should know the neighborhood is they can learn about drug dealers where they sell where they store their supply and other facts.

    2. Police should know drug dealers the neighborhood for the reason where they sell and hide their supply and other facts.

A. Only version 1 is grammatically correct.
B. Only version 2 is grammatically correct.
C. Both version 1 and 2 are grammatically correct.
D. Neither version 1 nor version 2 is grammatically correct.

----

29. An officer is preparing a report and has not decided which of two versions of a specific section he wishes to use. Which of the two versions are grammatically correct?

    1. The alleged burglar and his alleged accomplice has decided not to speak with the officer. Both stated that they will not cooperate in any manner.

    2. Both the alleged burglar and his alleged accomplice stated that they will not cooperate in any way and that they will not speak with the officer.

A. Only version 1 is grammatically correct.
B. Only version 2 is grammatically correct.
C. Both versions 1 and 2 are grammatically correct.
D. Neither version 1 nor version 2 is grammatically correct.

----

30. Police Officer Bruce Manow is preparing a speech that he will give to an elementary school class which his sergeant has asked him to visit. Which of the following two versions are grammatically correct?

    1. The police officer job is not easy to get. Police officer candidates must do well on a written test and then pass a number of other qualifying tests.

    2. The police officer job is not easy to get must do well on a written test and then pass a number of other qualifying tests.

A. 1 only is correct.

B. 2 only is correct.

C. Neither 1 nor 2 is correct.

D. Both 1 and 2 are correct.

31. Police Officer Susan Houston is preparing an instruction sheet on how to respond to oral inquiries. Which of the following two sentences are correct?

1. When responding to oral inquiries from the public, the police officer should keep in mind that the manner in which the response is given is as important as the accuracy of the response.

2. When a police officer responds to oral inquiries from the public, the police officer should keep in mind that the manner in which the response is given is as important as the accuracy of the response.

A. 1 only is correct.

B. 2 only is correct.

C. Neither 1 nor 2 is correct.

D. Both 1 and 2 are correct.

----

32. Police Officer James Valerios is checking the correctness of sentences in one of his reports. Which of the following two choices are correct?

1. Police Officers wear uniforms and are required to act professionally and be impartial. Because Police Officers are highly visible, the impression which Police Officers create is important in establishing in the public a sense of trust and fairness.

2. Police Officers wear uniforms and are required to act professionally and be impartial, because Police Officers are highly visible, the impression which Police Officers create is important in establishing in the public a sense of trust and fairness.

A. 1 only is correct.   C. Neither 1 nor 2 is correct.

B. 2 only is correct.   D. Both 1 and 2 are correct.

----

33. Officer Follins is asked to select the best summary (A, B, C, or D) of the following information: (The best summary is the one that expresses the information in the most clear, accurate and complete manner).

Place of accident: in front of 2625 North 77th Street, Jamaica

Time of accident: 10:15 P.M.

Date of accident: October 12, 2016

Vehicle involved: 2007 Armada

Driver: Helen Kierston

Damage: cracked rear headlights and cracked rear bumper

Details: a metal garbage container rolled into the street and struck the 2007 Armada

-----

A. On October 12, 2016, at 10:15 a.m., in front of 2625 North 77th Street., Jamaica, a metal garbage container rolled into the street and struck the 2007 Armada, driven by Helen Kierston.

B. On October 12, 2016, in front of 2625 North 77th Street., Jamaica, a metal garbage container rolled into the street and struck the 2007 Armada, driven by Helen Kierston.

C. On October 12, 2016, at 10:15 p.m., in front of 2625 North 7th Street., Jamaica, a metal garbage container rolled into the street and struck the 2007 Armada, driven by Helen Kierston.

D. On October 12, 2016, at 10:15 p.m., in front of 2625 North 77th Street., Jamaica, a metal garbage container rolled into the street and struck the 2007 Armada, driven by Helen Kierston, causing cracked rear headlights and cracked rear bumper.

----

34. Police Officer Quinones obtains the following information at the scene of a traffic accident:

Date of accident: November 5, 2016

Time of accident: 3:15 P.M.

Place of accident: intersection of 7th Avenue and 67th Street, New York

Vehicles involved: 2008 Nissan and 2006 Buick

Drivers: Benjamin Fogel (2008 Nissan) and Annette Traynor (2006 Buick)

Damage: dent on front passenger door of 2006 Buick

Police Officer Quinones drafts four versions to express the above information. Which of the following four versions is most clear, accurate and complete?

A. On November 2, 2016, at 3:15 P.M., at the intersection of 7th Avenue and

67ᵗʰ Street, New York, a 2008 Nissan and a 2006 Buick were involved in a traffic accident. The 2006 Buick, owned by Annette Traynor, sustained a dent on the passenger's front door. The 2008 Nissan, driven by Benjamin Fogel, did not sustain any damage.

B. On November 5, 2016, at 3:15 P.M., at the intersection of 7ᵗʰ Avenue and 67ᵗʰ Avenue, New York, a 2008 Nissan and a 2006 Buick were involved in a traffic accident. The 2006 Buick, owned by Annette Traynor, sustained a dent on the passenger's front door. The 2008 Nissan, driven by Benjamin Fogel, did not sustain any damage.

C. On November 5, 2016, at 3:12 P.M., at the intersection of 7ᵗʰ Avenue and 67ᵗʰ Street, New York, a 2008 Nissan and a 2006 Buick were involved in a traffic accident. The 2006 Buick, driven by Annette Traynor, sustained a dent on the passenger's front door. The 2008 Nissan, driven by Benjamin Fogel, did not sustain any damage.

D. On November 5, 2016 , at 3:15 P.M., at the intersection of 7ᵗʰ Avenue and 67ᵗʰ Street, New York, a 2008 Nissan and a 2006 Buick were involved in a traffic accident. The 2006 Buick, driven by Annette Traynor, sustained a dent on the passenger's front door. The 2008 Nissan, driven by Benjamin Fogel, did not sustain any damage.

Questions 35 - 40

35. Police Officer Haas is informed by a female whose pocketbook was yanked from her hands while she was waiting for the bus that the perpetrator was a male with a red baseball cap, about five feet eleven inches tall and wearing a white T-shirt and dark pants.

Officer Haas looks down the street in an attempt to spot the perpetrator. According to the information provided by the victim, Police Officer Haas should: (Choose the best answer.)

A. question all males and females on the street.

B. question all males and females wearing a red baseball cap.

C. question all persons with the height of five feet ten inches to five feet twelve inches.

D. question all males on the street who are wearing a red baseball cap and are about five feet eleven inches tall.

---

36. Police Officer Gregorius notices that repulsive smelling fumes are emanating from a fire in a city garbage container at the corner of a crowded street. Police Officer Gregorius should:

A. immediately run into a nearby store and see if they have a fire extinguisher.

B. take off his shirt and throw it on the fire.

C. warn everyone to stay clear and contact the proper authorities.

D. wait for the fire to burn itself out before checking it out.

37. While on patrol, Police Officer Ben McDonnel discovers that a manhole cover in the middle of a busy street has been removed and pungent smoke is coming out of it.

Based on the preceding information, what is the first step that Police Officer McDonnel should take?

A. Call for backup since he is on patrol alone.

B. Quickly get all the persons and traffic away from the manhole and then notify the proper authorities.

C. Look for the manhole cover as it may be nearby.

D. Call the highway department and complain.

----

38. Your sergeant asks that you interview a Mr. Jeffrey Fredrich regarding a complaint received by his neighbor, Gail Sealy, that he is always leaving his dog unleashed and free to roam in Ms. Sealy's back yard. You have knowledge that there is a Mr. Jeffrey Fredrich, Sr. and a Mr. Jeffrey Fredrich, Jr. because they are the owners of a coffee shop where you are a customer. What is the first step you should take in this situation?

A. At the Fredrich home, interview both Jeffrey Fredrich, Sr. and Jeffrey Fredrich, Jr. as they have the same name.

B. Ask the sergeant for clarification of the name of the person to be interviewed.

C. Disregard the sergeant's instructions because you know both Mr. Fredrich. Sr. and Mr. Fredrich, Jr. and they are both fine people.

D. Do not ask questions of the sergeant, as he might get upset.

----

39. Police Officer Lorna Kelman is on patrol when a shop owner runs out of his store with his hands on his head, trying to stem a serious bleeding wound. The man yells out that he was robbed a minute ago, and that the robbers sped away in a car.

Based on the preceding information, what should Police Officer Kelman do first?

A. Take the man back into the liquor store and question him regarding the robbery.

B. Interview all nearby persons to determine whether any of them witnessed the robbery.

C. Apply first aid to the shop owner to stop the bleeding and call for medical assistance and officer backup.

D. Officer Kelman should get in her patrol car and attempt to catch up to the robbers.

----

40. Prior to the start of your patrol, your sergeant gives the name and address of an elderly female who reported that she had been mugged and instructs you to interview her. From prior experience, you know that this female is prone to hallucinations. What is the first step you should take?

A. Quickly carry out the instructions of the sergeant.

B. Don't interview the female, as this would be a waste of time.

C. Prepare a report that includes that the woman is prone to hallucinations and that because of that you prepared the report without interviewing her.

D. Check with her relatives to see if she has been hallucinating recently.

Questions 41 - 43

PL 70.05 MAXIMUM SENTENCE OF IMPRISONMENT FOR JUVENILE OFFENDER

TYPE OF CONVICTION	MAXIMUM TERM OF IMPRISONMENT
Type "A" felony (murder second degree)	life imprisonment
Type "A" felony (arson first degree or kidnapping first degree)	at least 12, but not more than 15 years
Type "B" felony	10 years
Type "C" felony	7 years
Type "D" felony	4 years

41. According to the preceding table, which of the following choices is a correct maximum term of imprisonment for conviction of the stated offense?

A. Murder in the second degree committed by a Juvenile Offender (maximum 15 years)

B. "C" felony committed by a Juvenile Offender (maximum 10 years)

C. "B" felony committed by a Juvenile Offender (at least 12 nor more than 15 years)

D. "C" felony committed by Juvenile Offender (7 years)

CPL 120.10 Warrant of arrest definition, function, form, and content

1. A warrant of arrest is issued by a local criminal court after the filing of an accusatory instrument for the purpose of arraignment. It directs a police officer or designated peace officers to arrest a defendant and bring him to court for arraignment.

2. It is signed by the issuing judge and must state the following:

  (a) name of issuing court,

  (b) date of issuance of the warrant,

  (c) name of offense(s) charged in the accusatory instrument,

  (d) name of defendant to be arrested (or alias or description),

  (e) police or peace officer(s) to whom warrant is addressed,

  (f) direction that officer arrest defendant and bring him to court.

3. A warrant of arrest may be addressed to an individual police officer or classification of officers.

Multiple copies of a warrant may be issued.

-----

42. According to CPL 120.10, which of the following statements is correct?

A. A warrant of arrest must contain the date of the issuance of the warrant.

B. A warrant of arrest must have the signature of the D.A.

C. A warrant of arrest directs that the officer bring the defendant to the local penitentiary.

D. For privacy reasons, a warrant of arrest cannot contain the name of the defendant.

CPL 170.55 Adjournment in contemplation of dismissal (ACD)

After arraignment and before entry of plea of guilty or commencement of trial, the court MAY upon motion of the people or defendant, or upon its own motion and consent of both the people and the defendant, order an ACD (ADJOURNMENT IN CONTEMPLATION OF DISMISSAL).

The case is adjourned without a date. People may make an application to restore the case within 6 months. If that occurs, the court may restore it and proceed to trial. If the case is not restored, the accusatory instrument is deemed to have been dismissed in furtherance of justice at the end of the six-month period.

In case of a family offense, the ACD is for 1 year. The people may make an application to restore the case within 1 year.

The court can impose conditions (performance of public service, counseling, etc.) as part of an ACD.

An ACD is NOT a conviction or admission of guilt.

-----

43. According to CPL 170.55, which of the following statements is not correct?

A. An ACD is not an admission of guilt.

B. An ACD in a family offense proceeding is for one year.

C. When an ACD is ordered, the case is adjourned without a date.

D. The people must in all cases consent to the ordering of an ACD by the judge.

Question 44

Which of the following circles (A, B, C, D) matches the image of the "Dissected Circle?"

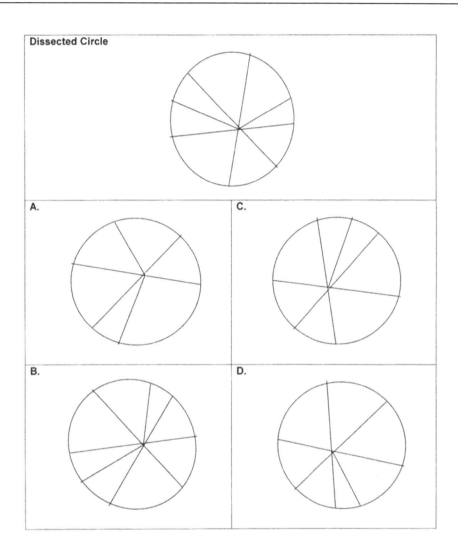

44. The drawing which best matches the image of the "Dissected Circle" is:

    A. Drawing A   B. Drawing B

    C. Drawing C   D. Drawing D

Questions 45 - 47

Answer questions 45 - 47 based on the following extracts of two Criminal Procedure Law sections, CPL 120.70 and CPL 120.80.

CPL 120.70 A warrant of arrest issued by a district court, NYC criminal court or a superior court judge sitting as a local criminal court can be executed anywhere in the state.

A warrant of arrest issued by a city, town, or village court can be executed in the county of issuance or adjoining county (or anywhere in NYS upon the written endorsement of a local criminal court of the county in which arrest is to be made).

CPL 120.80 A warrant of arrest is executed any day of the week, any hour of the day or night.

The arresting police officer is not required to have the warrant in his possession at the time of making the arrest.

-----

45. Police Officer Marino, a NYPD Officer assigned to a precinct in Queens County, has in his possession a warrant of arrest issued by a district court for a person named Jack Wringer. Which of the following choices is correct?

A. Police Officer Marino cannot execute the warrant of arrest because it was issued by a district court and not a New York City court.

B. Jack Wringer cannot be arrested on that warrant if he is outside the county served by the district court.

C. Police Officer Marino may execute the warrant outside the state of New York.

D. Police Officer Marino may execute the warrant because it was issued by a district court.

----

46. Police Officer Jane Goodwin, a NYPD Officer assigned to a precinct in Brooklyn, has in her possession a warrant of arrest issued by a town court in Nassau County. Which of the following statements is correct?

A. Officer Goodwin can execute the warrant in Brooklyn.

B. Officer Goodwin can execute the warrant only on weekdays in Brooklyn.

C. Officer Goodwin can execute the warrant in Brooklyn only if it has the written endorsement of a local criminal court of the county in which the arrest is to be made, in this case Kings County (Brooklyn).

D. Officer Goodwin can execute the warrant in New Jersey.

47. According to CPL 120.70, which of the following is not correct?

A. A warrant of arrest issued by a superior court judge sitting as a local criminal court can be executed anywhere in the state.

B. A warrant of arrest issued by the NYC criminal court can be executed anywhere in the state.

C. A warrant of arrest issued by the board of a school district can be executed anywhere in the state.

D. Some warrants of arrest may be executed anywhere in the state.

"Because a thing is difficult for you to do, do not think that it is impossible for any man; but whatever is possible for any man to do and right for his nature, think that you can achieve it too."

- Marcus Aurelius

Questions 48 - 51 are based on the following map.

In answering the questions, follow the flow of traffic, as indicated by the arrows. Names of streets, buildings, public areas, and points 1-9 are indicated on the map.

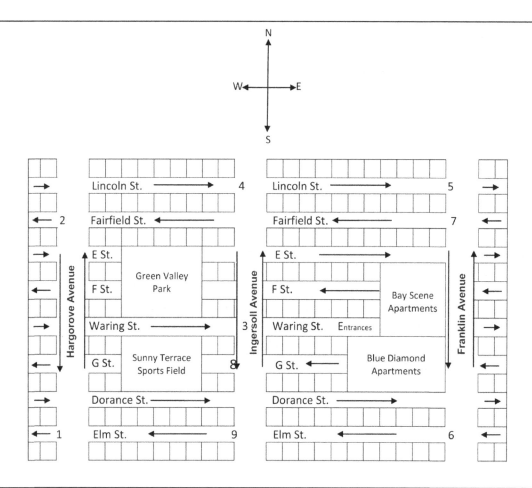

48. Imagine that you are at Hargrove Avenue and Lincoln Street and then drive east to Franklin Avenue, then drive south to Elm St., then travel west to Ingersoll Avenue, you will be closest to which one of the following points?

A. 2   B. 4   C. 5   D. 9

49. If you start your drive at point number 7, then drive west to Ingersoll Avenue, then drive south to Dorance St., then east to Franklin Avenue, then drive south to Elm St., you will be closest to which one of the following points?

A. 1   B. 5   C. 6   D. 9

50. You are driving south in your patrol car and are at the intersection of Lincoln St. and Franklin Avenue. You are informed that an auto accident has just occurred at the intersection of Waring Street and Ingersoll Avenue. Assuming you must obey all traffic signs, which one of the following four choices describes the most direct route?

A. Drive south on Franklin Avenue to Fairfield St, then drive east on Fairfield St. to Ingersoll Avenue, then south to the intersection of Dorance Street and Ingersoll Avenue.

B. Drive south on Franklin Avenue to Fairfield St, then drive west on Fairfield St. to Ingersoll Avenue, then north to the intersection of Dorance Street and Ingersoll Avenue.

C. Drive north on Franklin Avenue to Fairfield St, then drive east on Fairfield St. to Ingersoll Avenue, then north to the intersection of Dorance Street and Ingersoll Avenue.

D. Drive south on Franklin Avenue to Fairfield St, then drive west on Fairfield St. to Ingersoll Avenue, then south to the intersection of Waring Street and Ingersoll Avenue.

----

51. You are driving north in your patrol car and are at Hargrove Avenue and E St. You are informed that a fight between two men is happening at the corner of Lincoln St. and Ingersoll Avenue. Which one of the following four choices describes the most direct route?

A. Drive south to Lincoln St. then west on Lincoln St. to the corner of Lincoln St. and Ingersoll Avenue.

B. Drive north to Lincoln St. then west on Lincoln St. to the corner of Lincoln St. and Ingersoll Avenue.

C. Drive south to Dorance St. then east on Dorance St. to Ingersoll Avenue, then north to Lincoln Street and Ingersoll Avenue.

D. Drive north to Lincoln St. then east on Lincoln St. to the corner of Lincoln St. and Ingersoll Avenue.

----

52. During the month of August 2016 there were 14 purse snatchings reported in Police Officer Devon's precinct. In five of the purse snatchings, the victims reported that the perpetrator was a white male, about 5 feet ten inches, shoulder length dark hair, "with a small, black star tattoo on the right side of his neck." All five victims reported that the man was carrying a large brown backpack. The five also reported that he had been wearing black dungarees and a black T-shirt.

During his patrol, Officer Devon stops four white males for questioning. He had recorded in his memo book the description given by the five witnesses. Which piece of information should Officer Devon consider the most important in identifying the suspected purse snatcher?

A. the black dungarees and black T-shirt

B. the shoulder length dark hair

C. the small, black star tattoo on his neck

D. the color of his skin

53. Prior to the start of his patrol, Officer Charles Briggs learns at the precinct that a female, about 75 years old, had been mugged one hour earlier by a person who the victim described as a "Hispanic, about twenty years old, with red hair tied in a shoulder length ponytail, and with a very crooked nose." She also described him as wearing black pants, a black T-shirt, and black sneakers.

During his patrol, Officer Briggs sees a group of four white or Hispanic males, about 20-25 years old, standing in front of Junior's Delicatessen. Officer Briggs stops his patrol car about twenty feet away to get a better look at the four males. Which of the following parts of the description provided by the victim is most important for Officer Briggs to consider in his attempt to identify the possible suspect?

A. the black T-shirt

B. the red hair tied in a shoulder length pony tail

C. the black sneakers

D. the crooked nose.

----

54. Police Officer Hanson is assigned to patrol an area which includes four public parks. During the prior four weeks, crime statistics show that four muggings were reported at the Jackson Park, all between the hours of 10:00 a.m. and 4:00 p.m. At the Washington Park six purse snatchings were reported. At the Bellmore Park eight strollers were stolen. At the Green Valley Park four bicycles were stolen. The muggings all occurred between 9:30 a.m. and 4:30 p.m. The purse snatchings occurred between 9:30 a.m. and 10:30 a.m. The strollers were stolen in the afternoon and before 3:00 p.m.

Officer Hanson works the 9:00 a.m. to 5:00 p.m. tour. On Monday, his sergeant instructs him to pay careful attention to stroller robberies. To try to reduce the number of stroller robberies, Office Hanson should patrol:

A. Washington Park

B. Green Valley Park

C. Bellmore Park

D. Green Valley Park and Washington Park

----

55. On Tuesday Officer Hanson works the 9:00 a.m. to 5:00 p.m. tour. His sergeant tells him that six bicycles have been stolen at the same park where four bicycles were stolen during the prior four weeks. To try to reduce the number of bicycles being stolen, Officer Hanson should patrol:

A. Washington Park

B. Green Valley Park

C. Bellmore Park

D. Columbus Park

Question 56 - 57

Answer questions 56 - 57 based on the following "Procedure for an Arrest on a Felony Offense."

Procedure for an Arrest on a Felony Offense

1. A person arrested for a felony offense must be handcuffed by the arresting officer.

2. The accused must be held in a police station or jail pending his or her ability to post bail in the amount set by the Judge at the first court appearance.

3. If the accused cannot post bail, the accused must be held in a secure facility.

4. If the accused posts bail, he or she must be released and ordered to appear at the next court date.

5. If the accused does not appear on the next scheduled court date, he or she forfeits any bail the Judge may have ordered and the Judge must order the issuance of an arrest warrant.

56. A person arrested on a felony charge appears before the Judge in court. The Judge sets a bail of $250,000.00. The person posts the entire bail and is released and ordered by the Judge to return on a specified date. On the return date, he does not appear. Based on the above "Procedure for an Arrest on a Felony Offense," which of the following statements is correct?

A. The person must be notified to appear on the next court date or a warrant of arrest will be issued.

B. The bail must be held on deposit by the court and returned to the person when he comes to court on the next court date.

C. If a warrant of arrest is ordered by the Judge, the bail is not forfeited.

D. The bail must be forfeited and a warrant of arrest must be ordered by the Judge.

57. According to the "Procedure for an Arrest on a Felony Offense," which of the following statements is correct?

A. If the accused refuses to post bail, he or she must be released and ordered to appear at the next court date.

B. The accused must be held in a police station or jail pending his or her ability to post bail in the amount set by the Police Captain.

C. A person arrested for a felony must not be handcuffed.

D. The Judge must order the issuance of an arrest warrant if the accused does not appear on the next scheduled court date.

"The secret of success is constancy of purpose."

- Bible

Questions 58 - 59

Answer questions 58 - 59 based on the following "Lost Property Procedure."

Lost Property Procedure

1. Any lost property in the possession of a Police Officer must be delivered by the officer to the "Lost Property Office" in the precinct by the end of the Officer's tour of the day.

2. The Lost Property Officer must inventory the property and safeguard it according to the requirements in the "Property Safeguarding Manual."

3. Property not claimed within 30 days shall be delivered by the Lost Property Officer to the "Central Lost Property Office" at One Police Plaza.

4. If the article is not claimed within one year following the delivery to the "Central Lost Property Office" at One Police Plaza, the article must be sold at auction pursuant to "Lost Property Auction Rules."

5. Funds collected at the auction, net of expenses, must be forwarded by the Central Lost Property Officer to the New York City Finance Administrator.

58. Officer Rolands receives a copy of the above "Lost Property Procedure" the same day in which a pedestrian hands him a diamond ring which he has found on the sidewalk. Officer Rolands used to work in a jewelry store and believes the ring to be costume jewelry. There is one hour remaining before Officer Roland's daily tour ends. Which of the following statements is correct procedure?

A. Officer Rolands should return the ring to the pedestrian and tell him it is costume jewelry.

B. Officer Rolands should take the ring to a jewelry store and have it examined before the end of his tour.

C. Officer Rolands should take the ring to the precinct's "Lost Property Office" before the end of his tour.

D. Officer Rolands should hold on to the ring for at least the following day and have it examined before wasting time delivering it to the "Lost Property Office."

----

59. After the passage of one year from the date property is delivered to the "Central Lost Property Office," the property:

A. must be returned to the precinct Lost Property Office.

B. must be forwarded to the office of the New York City Finance Administrator.

C. must be sold at auction pursuant to "Lost Property Auction Rules, 2014."

D. may be returned to the officer who found the property.

Questions 60 – 68

60. You and another officer notice an elderly woman on the sidewalk. She tells you that a "tall man" just knocked her down and stole her pocketbook. You notice a "tall man" running down the block southbound to the end of the block where he makes a right turn. While your partner stays with the victim, you follow the man and observe him continuing to run for two blocks before making another right turn.

According to the information in the preceding passage, you would be most correct to radio that you last saw the man running:

A) north   B) south   C) east   D) west

----

61. While in your patrol car, you notice a car sideswipe a parked car and then continue northbound without stopping. You follow the car, which after four blocks makes a right turn and then after two more blocks makes a left turn.

According to the information in the preceding passage, you would be most correct to radio that you last saw the car heading:

A) north   B) south   C) east   D) west

----

62. A jewelry store employee runs out of a jewelry store, points down the block and shouts, "That guy just robbed me!" You shout for the man to stop, but he continues running westbound. After three blocks, he makes a left turn and runs for two more blocks before making another left turn.

According to the information in the preceding passage, you would be most correct to radio that you last saw the suspect heading:

A) north   B) south   C) east   D) west

----

63. You and another officer witness a purse being snatched from an elderly woman in front of the entrance to Ulmer Park. You shout for the man to stop, but he runs down the block in a westbound direction. You chase the man for three blocks before he turns left and then runs for another block, at which point he turns right.

According to the information in the preceding passage, you would be most correct to radio that the man was running:

A) north   B) south   C) east   D) west

----

64. While in your patrol car, you witness two men run out of a bar, each holding a pouch and a revolver. They quickly get into a car and head northbound. You follow. After three blocks, they make a right turn and then after two more blocks they make another right turn.

According to the information in the preceding passage, you would be most correct to radio that you last saw the car heading:

A) north   B) south   C) east   D) west

----

65. Your attention is drawn to a pedestrian shouting, "He took my bike!" and pointing to a man on a bike pedaling quickly on the sidewalk, away from the pedestrian and in a westbound direction. After three blocks, he makes a right turn and then after two more blocks he makes a left turn.

According to the information in the preceding passage, you would be most correct to radio that you last saw the man heading:

A) north   B) south   C) east   D) west

----

66. You and another officer notice a man in a wheelchair moaning on the sidewalk. He tells you that a "crazy looking man" just punched him on the head and then ran away. You notice a man running down the block northbound to the end of the block where he makes a left turn. While your partner stays with the victim, you follow the man and observe him continuing to run for three blocks before turning left.

According to the information in the preceding passage, you would be most correct to radio that you last saw the man running:

A) north   B) south   C) east   D) west

----

67. While in your patrol car, you notice a red car sideswipe a parked car and then drive off southbound without stopping. You follow the car, which after sixteen blocks makes a right turn and then after two more blocks makes another right turn.

According to the information in the preceding passage, you would be most correct to radio that you last saw the car heading:

A) east   B) south   C) north   D) west

----

68. A shoe store employee runs out of a shoe store, points down the block and shouts, "That guy just robbed the store!" You shout for the running man to stop, but he continues running northbound. After four blocks, he makes a left turn and runs for two more blocks before making a right turn.

According to the information in the preceding passage, you would be most correct to radio that you last saw the suspect heading:

A) north   B) south   C) east   D) west

"Let me tell you what has led me to my goal. My strength lies solely in my tenacity."

- Louis Pasteur

Question 69

Line of crates

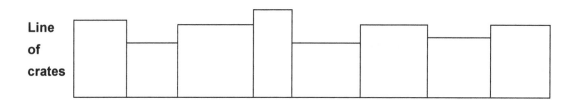

A.

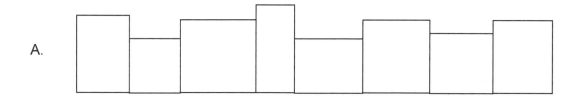

B.

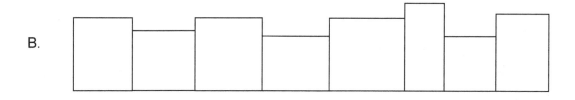

C.

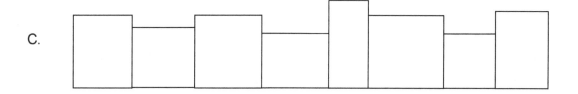

D.

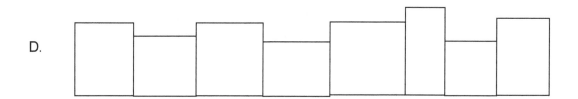

69. The above "Line of Crates" when viewed from the back would appear as which of the following choices?

A. Choice A
B. Choice B

C. Choice C
D. Choice D

Questions 70 - 75

Answer questions 70 - 75 based on the information contained in the following passage.

While on patrol, Police Officers Collins and Fogel are dispatched to 1673 Brittany Avenue, first floor "Archer Discount Store" at 9:45 p.m. on October 29, 2016. The owner of "Archer Discount Store" had just called 911 to report a burglary. They arrive at the store at 9:49 p.m. and are greeted by Mr. James Fontaine, the owner of the store and Mr. John Brighton, an employee of "Archer Discount Store."

Mr. Fontaine tells the officers that he and John Brighton had closed the store for the day at 8:00 p.m. They had locked the front and back doors and properly rolled down the security gate and padlocked it. Mr. Fontaine discovered the burglary at 9:30 p.m. when at home he happened to glance at the live video of his four security cameras. Although security camera #1 showed the outdoor front entrance and security camera #4 showed the outdoor back door area, it was with security cameras #2 and #3 that he saw the burglars. Security camera # 2 covered the outdoor roof skylight and security camera # 3 covered the inside area of the store, including the cashier area.

Two burglars, all dressed in dark blue and wearing black face masks, had broken the glass in the skylight and with a rope had lowered themselves into the store. The smaller of the two persons descended first and the much taller one followed. The person who descended first carried a black garbage bag and the other person held a flashlight in his right hand.

The two burglars took the $225.00 cash and coins that had been left in the cash register, an entire box of seven identical collectible statuettes worth a total of $1200.00, three expensive, identical watches worth a total of $900.00, two electric toasters worth $49.00 each, and six original signed watercolor paintings by a local artist worth $99.00 each. Mr. Fontaine tells the officers that he will prepare a complete list of missing items as soon as possible.

Mr. Fontaine tells Officer Fogel that he is 57 years old and lives at 3465 Baton Rouge Avenue in the Bronx. His cell number is 718-555-1283. John Brighton tells Officer Fogel that he is 27 years old and lives at 2835 West 125 Street, Brooklyn. His cell number is 781-555-2944.

Police Officers Collins and Fogel complete their investigation at 10:25 p.m. Before they completed their crime report, they performed a careful sweep of the store to make certain that the burglars had left.

-----

70. What was the most expensive individual item (one piece) stolen?

A. statuette

B. watch

C. watercolor painting

D. electric toaster

----

71. Which of the following statements is correct?

A. Mr. John Brighton, the owner of the store, is 57 years old.

B. Each of the burglars took $225.00 in cash and coins (total of $450.00).

C. Mr. John Brighton lives at 3465 Baton Rouge Avenue in the Bronx.

D. The total value of the watercolor paintings is $594.00.

72. Which one of the following statements is correct? Among the items stolen were:

A. six identical collectible statuettes worth a total of $1200.00.

B. two electric toasters worth a total of $49.00.

C. $450.00 cash and coins that had been left in the cash register.

D. three expensive, identical watches worth $300.00 each.

----

73. Which of the following statements is correct according to the information provided by Mr. Fontaine and Mr. Brighton?

A. Mr. Fontaine tells Officer Fogel that he is 57 years old and lives at 3645 Baton Rouge Avenue in the Bronx. His cell number is 718-555-1283

B. John Brighton tells Officer Fogel that he is 27 years old and lives at 2853 West 125 Street, Brooklyn. His cell number is 781-555-2944.

C. John Brighton tells Officer Fogel that he is 27 years old and lives at 2835 West 125 Street, Bronx. His cell number is 781-555-2944.

D. Mr. Fontaine tells Officer Fogel that he is 57 years old and lives at 3465 Baton Rouge Avenue in the Bronx. His cell number is 718-555-1283.

----

74. Choose the best answer: The value of each of the statuettes that were stolen is closest to:

A. $171

B. $140

C. $150

D. $183

----

75. The total value of all items missing is:

A. $2,453

B. $3,617

C. $2,968

D. $3,017

Question 76

During his patrol, Police Officer Dawn Heller is called to the scene of an accident. The driver/owner of vehicle #3 stated that he was driving on Vine St. when car #1 hit his rear bumper, causing him to hit vehicle number 2.

Assume that all 3 vehicles were in their proper lanes of traffic.

Which of the following 4 diagrams best matches the statement of the driver of vehicle #3?

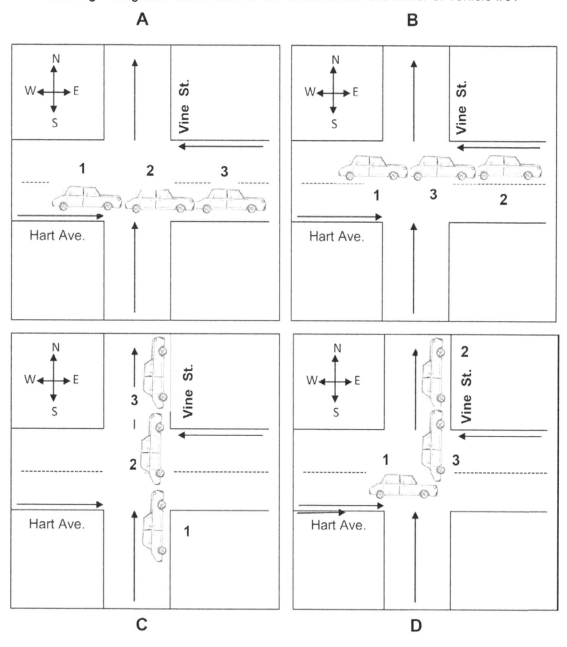

76. The diagram which best matches the statement of the driver of vehicle #3 is:

A. diagram "A"

B. diagram "B"

C. diagram "C"

D. diagram "D"

Questions 77 - 78

Answer questions 77 – 78 based on the following accident details.

Officer Nordstrum collects the following information at the scene of an auto accident:

Date of Accident: September 9, 2016

Time of accident: 4:15 p.m.

Place of accident: Intersection of Lavin Avenue and Reiker Avenue, Bronx

Driver: Barry Jones

Vehicle: 2008 Toyota Sienna

Damage: Vehicle struck a commercial metal garbage container protruding into the street.

-----

77. Officer Nordstrum is preparing a report of the accident and has four drafts of the report. He wishes to use the draft that expresses the information most clearly, accurately and completely. Which draft should he choose?

A. At 4:15 p.m., on September 9, 2016, at the intersection of Lavin Avenue and Reiker Avenue, Bronx, a vehicle driven by Barry Jones struck a commercial metal garbage container protruding into the street.

B. On September 9, 2016, at 4:15 p.m., at the intersection of Lavin Avenue and Reiker Avenue, Bronx, a 2008 Toyota Sienna driven by Barry Lones struck a commercial metal garbage container protruding into the street.

C. On September 9, 2016, at 4:25 p.m., at the intersection of Lavin Avenue and Reiker Avenue, Bronx, a 2008 Toyota Sienna driven by Barry Jones struck a commercial metal garbage container protruding into the street.

D. On September 9, 2016, at 4:15 p.m., at the intersection of Lavin Avenue and Reiker Avenue, Bronx, a 2008 Toyota Sienna driven by Barry Jones struck a commercial metal garbage container protruding into the street.

----

78. Officer Nordstrum is comparing the information he recorded in his memo pad (at the scene of the accident) to the information in his report. Which of the above choices (A, B, C, or D) has a detail that does not agree with the information in the officer's memo pad?

A. Date of Accident: September 9, 2016; Time of accident: 4:15 p.m.

B. Place of accident: Intersection of Lavin Avenue and Reiker Avenue, Bronx

C. Driver: Barry Jones: Vehicle: 2008 Toyota Sienna

D. Damage: Vehicle struck a commercial plastic garbage container protruding into the street

Answer questions 79 - 80 based on the following information gathered at a crime scene.

Officer Samuels responds to a car theft. She questions the owner of the vehicle who reported the car stolen and obtains the following information:

Suspect: Unidentified

Date of crime: August 25, 2016

Time of crime: between 7:20 p.m. and 11:40 p.m.

Crime: theft of car

Vehicle stolen: 2012 Volvo

Victim: owner of car, Frank Dolin

Place of crime: driveway in front of 247 18th Street, Staten Island

-----

79. Officer Samuels is preparing a report of the accident and has prepared four drafts of the report. She wishes to use the draft that expresses the information most clearly, accurately and completely. Which of the following drafts should she choose?

A. A car theft of a 2012 Volvo happened at the driveway in front of 247 18th Street, Staten Island, where Frank Dolin's car was parked for the night. The alleged thief is unidentified, as the theft happened in the evening hours.

B. On August 25, 2016, between 7:20 p.m. and 11:40 p.m., at the driveway in front of 247 18th Street, a 2012 Volvo owned by Frank Dolin was stolen by an unidentified suspect.

C. A car was stolen on August 25, 2016, between 7:20 p.m. and 11:40 p.m., at the driveway in front of 247 18th Street, owned by Frank Dolin. The suspect is unidentified.

D. On August 25, 2016, 247 18th Street, Staten Island, between 7:20 a.m. and 11:40 a.m., a 2012 Volvo owned by Frank Dolin was stolen by an unidentified suspect.

----

80. Officer Samuels is comparing the information he recorded in his memo pad (at the scene of the accident) to the information in his report. Which of the above choices (A, B, C, or D) has one detail that does not agree with the information in the officer's memo pad?

A. Date of crime: August 25, 2016; Time of crime: between 7:20 p.m. and 11:40 p.m.

B. Crime: theft of car; Vehicle stolen: 2012 Volvo

C. Victim: owner of car, Frank Dolin

D. Place of crime: driveway in front of 247 18th Avenue, Staten Island

----

Answer question 81 based on the following "Media Inquiry Procedure."

Media Inquiry Procedure

When a criminal case is pending in the courts, the Police Officer who made the arrest is prohibited from discussing the case with any newspaper, magazine, TV reporters and all other media. Exceptions to this are cases where:

1. a New York court of competent jurisdiction formally orders the Police Officer to discuss one or more particulars of the case.

2. a NYPD authorized Department orders such discussion.

3. the Police Officer is subpoenaed to testify by an authorized NYC, NYS or federal board.

In all cases, media inquiries made to the officer should be referred to HQ Media Services at One Police Plaza.

-----

81. Police Officer Jane Hollis arrests a drug suspect and confiscates two pounds of heroin. The suspect has been indicted and is in jail, waiting for trial. A newspaper reporter, Abigail Briggs, contacts Officer Jane Hollis and asks a quick question, the answer to which might help the reporter to investigate drug trafficking in the city. Officer Jane Hollis should:

A. Answer the question since it is a quick question.

B. Tell the reporter to contact her sergeant.

C. Answer the question only if the reporter is trustworthy.

D. Tell the reporter to contact HQ Media Services at One Police Plaza.

Questions 82 - 83

Answer questions 82 - 83 based on the following highlights of "CPL 500.10: Definitions."

CPL 500.10: Definitions

SECURED BAIL BOND is a bond secured by:

1) personal property greater than or equal to the undertaking, or

2) real property at least 2 times the value of the undertaking (assessed value divided by equalization rate, or special assessing unit as defined in article 18 of real property tax law).

PARTIALLY SECURED BAIL BOND is a bond secured by a deposit of money not in excess of 10 per cent of the total amount of the undertaking.

UNSECURED BAIL BOND is a bail bond (other than an insurance company bail bond) that is not secured by any deposit or lien.

-----

82. Which of the following is an example of an unsecured bail bond?

A. a bail bond secured by a deposit of money not in excess of 10 per cent of the total amount of the undertaking

B. a bail bond secured by personal property greater than or equal to undertaking

C. a bail bond (other than an insurance company bail bond) that is not secured by any deposit or lien

D. a bond secured by real property at least 2 times the value of the undertaking

83. A bail bond secured by a deposit of money not in excess of 10 per cent of the total amount of the undertaking is a:

A. secured bail bond.

B. unsecured bail bond.

C. questionable secured bail bond.

D. partially secured bail bond.

----

84. Four witnesses to a hit and run accident tell Police Officer Valenti that they memorized the license plate number of the car that sped away from the accident. Which of the following license plate numbers is the most likely to be correct?

A. 8337AFR

B. 8587AFR

C. 8537AFR

D. 8531AFR

Answer question 85 based on the following table:

Summonses and Desk Appearance Tickets Issued by Police Officer Archer

Week	Dates	Parking Summonses	Moving Summonses	Desk Appearance Tickets
1	Nov. 1 – 7	14	15	4
2	Nov 8 -14	11	3	6
3	Nov 15 – 21	16	10	1
4	Nov 22 – 28	9	12	5
5	Nov 29 – Dec 5	14	10	7

85. Police Officer Archer is adding up the total number of all summonses and Desk Appearance Tickets issued by her during the above five-week period. Which of the following four formulas should she use to arrive at the correct number of summonses and Desk Appearance Tickets that she issued?

A. 14+10+7

B. 4+6+1+5+7

C. 14+11+16+9+14+15+3+10+12+10+4+6+1+5+7

D. 1(14+11+16+9+14) + 2(15+3+10+12+10) + 3(4+6+1+5+7)

<u>END OF PRACTICE TEST #1</u>

"The race is not to the swift nor the battle to the strong."

- Bible

PRACTICE TEST #1
ANSWERS

Memory Answers

Study the photo below for the next ten minutes. Try to remember as many details about the people and objects as you can. During the ten minutes, you are not permitted to take any notes or write anything.

At the end of the ten minutes you will be asked to answer questions 1 – 10 (<u>without</u> looking back at the picture.)

(After ten minutes)

Instructions for questions 1 – 10:

<u>Without</u> looking back at the picture, answer questions 1 – 10 on the following page.

1. The number of protestors not wearing any type of mask is:

A. 0   B. 1   C. 2   D. 3

2. How many signboards are displayed in the picture?

A. 6   B. 7   **C. 8**   D. 9

3. How many people are wearing a white mask?

A. 2   **B. 3**   C. 4   D. 5

4. The capital letter that appears alone on one of the signs is:

A. "B"   B. "Z"   C. "R"   **D. none of the above**

5. The two protestors that are holding signs with "USA" and the crossed-out number "51" on them:

A. both are wearing black shirts.   C. are of the same height.

B. are both wearing white jackets.   D. are wearing black face masks.

6. The dark signboard that is ripped at the corner:

A. has the word "Peace" on it.

B. has the word "NO" on it.

C. has the letters "USA" on it.

D. none of the above (It is blank.)

7. How many signs have the letters "USA" on the sign?

A. 1   **B. 2**   C. 3   D. 4

8. The "smiley face":

A. is on a white background.

B. is being held above the heads of the crowd.

C. is on two signs.

D. does not have a nose.

9. How many signs have a "star" drawn on them?

A. 1   B. 2   C. 3   D. 4

10. How many signs do not have anything written, printed or displayed on them?

A. 0   **B. 1**   C 2   D. 3

POLICE OFFICER EXAM NEW YORK CITY

Answers 11 - 15

Answer questions 11 - 15 based on the information contained in the following paragraphs.

Police Officers Frank Torres and Diane Washington were on patrol on August 13, 2016 when at **9:45 p.m.** they witnessed a minor traffic accident (at East 16th Street and Kings Highway in Brooklyn). Officer Torres called the Police Dispatcher at 9:50 p.m. and reported that **the two drivers, and two passengers (one in each vehicle) did not sustain any personal injuries**. One of the vehicles, the one driven by a male named Felix Upton, did have minor damage to the windshield, and the other vehicle, driven by a male named Mark Levington, had extensive damage to the driver's side front door.

Officer Washington examined the driver's licenses, vehicle registration certificates and vehicle insurance identification cards. The auto driven by **Felix Upton, age 46, was a black 2012 Ford Edge, N.Y. license plate 4357ZB**, owned by the driver, residing at 1942 West 58th Street, New York, N.Y. Mr. Upton's N.Y. driver's license identification number is D274 43 662 and the expiration date is December 31, 2016.

The driver of the other auto was Mark Levington, age 52, residing at 2686 Manor Street, Brooklyn, N.Y. Mr. Levington's auto was a **blue 2011 Ford Escape, NY license plate 607PHB**. Mr. Levington's driver's license identification number is A214 295 337 and the expiration is December 31, 2016.

Officers Torres and Washington completed a Vehicle Accident Report at 10:15 p.m. The report number was **48392747332**.

-----

11. What is the time of the accident?
A. 9:50 p.m.
B. 10:15 p.m.
C. 9:45 p.m.
D. before 9:30 a.m.
(The passage states, "...at 9:45 p.m. they witnessed a minor traffic accident....")

----

12. How many persons were injured as a result of the traffic accident?
A. 1
B. 0
C. 2
D. none of the above
(The passage states, "...the two drivers, and two passengers (one in each vehicle) did not sustain any personal injuries....")

----

13. Which car sustained extensive damage to the driver's side front door?
A. NY plate #607PHB, black 2012 Ford Edge
B. NY plate #4357ZN, black 2012 Ford Edge
C. NY plate #4357ZN, blue 2011 Ford Escape
D. NY plate #607PHB, blue 2011 Ford Escape
(The passage states, "…vehicle driven by a male named Mark Levington, had extensive damage to the driver's door…Mr. Levington's auto was a blue 2011 Ford Escape, NY license plate 607PHB.")

----

14. Which of the following statements is not correct?

A. The auto driven by Felix Upton, age 46, was a black 2012 Ford Edge.

B. The vehicle Accident Report number was 4839274732.
(The correct Accident Report number is 48392747332.)

C. Mark Levington, age 52, resides at 2686 Manor Street, Brooklyn, N.Y.

D. Mr. Upton's N.Y. driver's license identification number is D274 43 662.

----

15. Which of the following is correct?

A. The person residing at 1942 West 58th Street, New York, N.Y. has a N.Y. driver's license identification number D274 43 665 with an expiration date of December 31, 2016.
(WRONG. The correct driver's license identification number D274 43 662.)

B. Mark Levington, age **25**, resides at 2686 Manor Street, Brooklyn, N.Y.
(WRONG. "The driver of the other auto was Mark Levington, age 52….)

C. The auto driven by Felix Upton, is a black 2012 Ford Edge, N.Y. license plate 4357ZB.
(CORRECT. "The auto driven by Felix Upton, age 46, was a black 2012 Ford Edge, N.Y. license plate 4357ZB.)

D. The accident occurred at East 16th Street and Kings Highway in the Bronx.
(WRONG. "…they witnessed a minor traffic accident at East 16th Street and Kings Highway in Brooklyn.)

Answers 16 - 20

Answer questions 16 - 20 based on the information contained in the following paragraphs.

Police Officers George Elton and Jasmine Colbert were on patrol in their squad car on September 17, 2016 when at **9:35 p.m.** a man approached them. The man pointed to his parked car, a silver Toyota, and stated that the red Ford Taurus parked behind it had just done some damage to the back of his car while the Taurus was parking. Police Officer George Elton called the police dispatcher at 9:40 p.m. and reported the traffic accident, which occurred in front of 924 6th Avenue, Staten Island. Police Officer Jasmine Colbert questioned the driver of the Taurus. Both Police Officers reported to the dispatcher that the driver of the silver Toyota and the driver of the damaged red Ford Taurus did not sustain any injuries. Also, there were no passengers in the two cars. One of the vehicles, **the silver Toyota, was driven and owned by a male, Fred Elkinson. It had moderate damage to the back bumper and rear tail lights**. The other vehicle, owned by a female, Barbara Baker, sustained no damage.

Officer Elton examined the driver's licenses, vehicle registration certificates and vehicle insurance identification cards. The auto driven by Fred Elkinson, age 51, was a 2008 silver Toyota, N.Y. license plate 36823EL, owned by the driver, residing at 62 West Garry Road, Brooklyn, N.Y. **Mr. Elkinson's N.Y. driver's license identification number is R3241 35532 32578** and the expiration date is October 31, 2016.

The owner of the Taurus was Barbara Baker, age 46, residing at 234 West 9th Street, Queens, N.Y. Ms. Baker's auto was a 2009 red Ford Taurus, NY license plate KB3463H. Ms. Baker's driver's license identification number is D413 742 533 and the expiration is November 30, 2016.

Officers Elton and Colbert completed a Vehicle Accident Report at **9:50 p.m**. The report number was **224376654522.**

-----

16. Select the best answer: The time closest to the time of the accident is:
A. 9:35 a.m.   C. 9:40 p.m.
B. 6:50 p.m.   **D. 9:35 p.m.**
(**"D" is CORRECT.** "...when at 9:35 p.m. a man approached them. The man pointed to his parked car, a silver Toyota, and stated that the red Ford Taurus parked behind it had just done some damage to the back of his car while the Taurus was parking.")

----

17. Which car sustained damage to the rear bumper and rear tail lights?

A.   NY plate #36823EL, red Ford Taurus

B.   NY plate #3463HKB, silver 2008 Toyota

C.   NY plate #36823EL, silver 2008 Toyota
("C" is CORRECT. One of the vehicles, the silver Toyota, was driven and owned by a male, Fred Elkinson. "The auto driven by Fred Elkinson, age 51, was a 2008 silver Toyota, N.Y. license plate 36823EL…It had moderate damage to the back bumper and rear tail lights.")

D.   NY plate #3463HKB, red Ford Taurus

----

18. At what time was the Vehicle Accident Report completed?

A. 9:35 p.m.

B. 9:40 p.m.

C. 9:50 p.m.
("C" is CORRECT. "Officers Elton and Colbert completed a Vehicle Accident Report at 9:50 p.m.")

D. 9:55 p.m.

----

19. Which of the following statements is correct?

A. The license plate number of the car owned by Barbara Baker is KD3463H.
(WRONG. Correct plate number is KB3463H)

B. The report number is 224376654522.
(CORRECT)

C. Police Officer Jasmine Colbert called the police dispatcher at 9:40 p.m.
(WRONG. Officer Elton called the dispatcher.)

D. The vehicle driven and owned by Fred Elkinson had moderate damage to the front bumper and rear tail lights.
(WRONG. Damage was to the back bumper and rear tail lights.)

----

20. Which of the following statements is correct?

A. Police Officer Jasmine Colbert questioned the driver of the Toyota.
(WRONG. Police Officer Jasmine Colbert questioned the driver of the Taurus)

B. Barbara Baker is 64 years old.
(WRONG. Correct age is 46 years old.)

C. Officers Elton and Colbert completed a Vehicle Accident Report at <u>9:05 p.m.</u>
(**WRONG.** Correct time is <u>9:50 p.m.</u>)

D. Mr. Fred Elkinson's N.Y. driver's license identification number is R3241 35532 32578.
(**CORRECT**)

Answers 21 - 26

Answer questions 21 - 26 based on the information contained in the following paragraphs.

Police Officers David Alberts and Carol Sumpter were on patrol in their squad car on August 23, 2016 when at **8:25 p.m.** a female approached them. The female stated that she had just been involved in a car accident with the black Honda that was now stopped next to her car, a red Ford. Police Officer David Alberts called the police dispatcher at 8:33 p.m. and reported the traffic accident (which occurred in front of 1976 East 17th Street, Jamaica). Police Officer Carol Sumpter questioned the driver of the black Honda. Both Police Officers reported to the dispatcher that both drivers did not sustain any injuries. **Also, there were no passengers in the two cars.** One of the vehicles, **the red Ford, was driven and owned by a female, Nancy Wright. It had damage to the rear bumper**. The other vehicle, driven by a female, Tania **Salters, had damage to the front bumper.**

Officer Alberts examined the driver's licenses, vehicle registration certificates and vehicle insurance cards. **The auto driven by Nancy Wright, age 38, was a red 2006 Ford, N.Y. license plate 35434DE, owned by the driver, residing at 304 West Almeria Road**, Brooklyn, N.Y. Ms. Wright's N.Y. driver's license identification number is W3547 28592 12332 and the expiration date is September 30, 2016.

The driver and owner of the other auto was Tania Salters, age 26, residing at 183 Madison Street, Bronx, N.Y. Ms. Salters' auto was a 2007 black Honda, NY license plate 4492GDX. Ms. Salters' driver's license identification number is H215 594 732 and the expiration is November 30, 2016.

Officers Alberts and Sumpter completed a Vehicle Accident Report at 8:40 p.m. The report number was 224376754321.

-----

21. Select the best answer. The closest time of the accident is approximately:

A. after 8:35 p.m.

B. after 8:30 p.m.

C. before 8:25 p.m.
(**"C" is CORRECT.** The officers learned of the accident at 8:25 p.m. Choices A, B, and D are all times after 8:25 p.m. and are therefore incorrect.)

D. after 8:40 p.m.

----

22. Which car sustained damage to the front bumper?

A.   NY plate #4492GDX, red 2007 Honda

B.   NY plate #35434DE, red 2006 Ford

C.   NY plate #35434DE, black 2006 Ford

D.   NY plate #4492GDX, black 2007 Honda
(Choice "D" has the correct details for the car driven by Tania Salters, the car which sustained the damage to the front bumper.)

----

23. What is the total number of persons involved in the accident?

A. 1

B. 2
("B" is CORRECT. "There were no passengers in the two cars." Therefore, the drivers were the only persons involved.)

C. 3

D. none of the above

----

24. The owner of the parked vehicle with damage to the rear bumper resides at:

A. 304 West Almeria Road, Jamaica

B. 183 Madison Street, Bronx, N.Y.

C. 304 West Almeria Road, Brooklyn
(Choice "C" has the correct details for the car owned by Nancy Wright, the car which sustained the damage to the rear bumper.)

D. 183 Madison Street, Jamaica, N.Y.

----

25. Which of the following is correct?

A. The driver and owner of the red Honda is Tania Salters.
(WRONG. Color of car is a <u>black</u> Honda.)

B. Ms. Wright's N.Y. driver's license identification number is W3547 28592 12323**.**
(WRONG. Correct number is W3547 28592 123<u>32.</u>)

C. Officers Alberts and Sumpter completed a Vehicle Accident Report at 8:04 p.m.
(WRONG. Correct time is <u>8:40</u> p.m.)

D. Nancy Wright lives at 304 West Almeria Road, Brooklyn.
("D" is CORRECT. "The auto driven by Nancy Wright, age 38, was a red 2006 Ford, N.Y. license plate 35434DE, owned by the driver, <u>residing at 304 West Almeria Road, Brooklyn</u>....")

----

26. Which of the following is not correct?

A. The vehicle driven by Tania Salters had damage to the front bumper.

B. The vehicle driven and owned by Nancy Wright was a red 2009 Ford.
(This statement is not correct. The correct year of the Ford is <u>2006.</u>)

C. Tania Salters is 26 years old.

D. Ms. Salters' auto was a 2007 black Honda, NY license plate 4492GDX.

Answers 27 - 34

27. An officer is reviewing a report she is preparing. It contains the following two rough drafts. Which of the two sentences are grammatically correct?

    1. The man who assaulted him, the cashier said, was about twenty years old and was wearing blue pants and a black, turtleneck sweater.

    2. The cashier stated that the male who assaulted him was about twenty years old and was wearing blue pants and a black, turtleneck sweater.

A. Only sentence 1 is grammatically correct.

B. Only sentence 2 is grammatically correct.

C. Both sentences 1 and 2 are grammatically correct.

D. Neither sentence 1 nor sentence 2 is grammatically correct.

28. An officer is asked by his partner to review a speech that the officer is preparing to give to new recruits. It contains the following two versions of one part of the speech. Which are grammatically correct?

    1. And other reasons why police should know the neighborhood is they can learn about drug dealers where they sell where they store their supply and other facts.

    2. Police should know drug dealers the neighborhood for the reason where they sell and store their supply and other facts.

A. Only version 1 is grammatically correct.

B. Only version 2 is grammatically correct.

C. Both versions 1 and 2 are grammatically correct.

D. Neither version 1 nor version 2 is grammatically correct.

(Version 1 starts with "And" – which is commonly frowned upon. It also needs commas, as in the following version:

Other reasons why police should know the neighborhood is that they can learn about drug dealers, where they sell, and where they store their supply.

Version 2 is a run-on sentence. Two or more sentences are joined without proper connecting words.)

----

29. An officer is preparing a report and has not decided which of two versions of a specific section he wishes to use. Which of the two versions are grammatically correct?

    1. The alleged burglar and his alleged accomplice has decided not to speak with the officer. Both stated that they will not cooperate in any manner.

    2. Both the alleged burglar and his alleged accomplice stated that they will not cooperate in any way and that they will not speak with the officer.

A. Only version 1 is grammatically correct.

B. Only version 2 is grammatically correct.
(In version 1 the subject of the sentence "alleged burglar and his alleged accomplice" (plural) disagrees with the verb "has (singular)." A correct version would be:

The alleged burglar and his alleged accomplice <u>have</u> decided not to speak with the officer. Both stated that they will not cooperate in any manner.

C. Both versions 1 and 2 are grammatically correct.

D. Neither version 1 nor version 2 is grammatically correct.

----

30. Police Officer Bruce Manow is preparing a speech that he will give to an elementary school class which his sergeant has asked him to visit. Which of the following two versions are grammatically correct?

    1. The police officer job is not easy to get. Police officer candidates must do well on a written test and then pass a number of other qualifying tests.

    2. The police officer job is not easy to get must do well on a written test and then pass a number of other qualifying tests.

A. 1 only is correct.

(Version 2 is a run-on sentence. It needs to be expressed in two sentences.)

B. 2 only is correct.

C. Neither 1 nor 2 is correct.

D. Both 1 and 2 are correct.

----

31. Police Officer Susan Houston is preparing an instruction sheet on how to respond to oral inquiries. Which of the following two sentences are correct?

    1. When responding to oral inquiries from the public, the police officer should keep in mind that the manner in which the response is given is as important as the accuracy of the response.

    2. When a police officer responds to oral inquiries from the public, the police officer should keep in mind that the manner in which the response is given is as important as the accuracy of the response.

A. 1 only is correct.

B. 2 only is correct.

C. Neither 1 nor 2 is correct.

D. Both 1 and 2 are correct.

----

32. Police Officer James Valerios is checking the correctness of sentences in one of his reports. Which of the following two choices are correct?

1. Police Officers wear uniforms and are required to act professionally and be impartial. Because Police Officers are highly visible, the impression which Police Officers create is important in establishing in the public a sense of trust and fairness.

2. Police Officers wear uniforms and are required to act professionally and be impartial, because Police Officers are highly visible, the impression which Police Officers create is important in establishing in the public a sense of trust and fairness.

A. 1 only is correct.

(Sentence 2 is a run-on sentence. Two or more sentences are joined without proper connecting words.)

B. 2 only is correct.

C. Neither 1 nor 2 is correct.

D. Both 1 and 2 are correct.

----

33. Officer Follins is asked to select the best summary (A, B, C, or D) of the following information: (The best summary is the one that expresses the information in the most clear, accurate and complete manner).

Place of accident: in front of 2625 North 77th Street, Jamaica
Time of accident: 10:15 P.M.
Date of accident: October 12, 2016
Vehicle involved: 2007 Armada
Driver: Helen Kierston
Damage: cracked rear headlights and cracked rear bumper
Details: a metal garbage container rolled into the street and struck the 2007 Armada

-----

A. On October 12, 2016, at 10:15 a.m., in front of 2625 North 77th Street., Jamaica, a metal garbage container rolled into the street and struck the 2007 Armada, driven by Helen Kierston. **(WRONG.** Correct time is 10:15 P.M.)

B. On October 12, 2016, in front of 2625 North 77th Street., Jamaica, a metal garbage container rolled into the street and struck the 2007 Armada, driven by Helen Kierston. **(WRONG.** The time of the accident, "10:15 P.M.", is omitted.)

C. On October 12, 2016, at 10:15 p.m., in front of 2625 North 7<u>th</u> Street., Jamaica, a metal garbage container rolled into the street and struck the 2007 Armada, driven by Helen Kierston. **(WRONG.** Correct address is 2625 North 77<u>th</u> Street., Jamaica.)

D. On October 12, 2016, at 10:15 p.m., in front of 2625 North 77<u>th</u> Street., Jamaica, a metal garbage container rolled into the street and struck the 2007 Armada, driven by Helen Kierston, causing cracked rear headlights and cracked rear bumper.
(CORRECT. Choice "D" includes all the information and has no factual errors.)

----

34. Police Officer Quinones obtains the following information at the scene of a traffic accident:

Date of accident: November 5, 2016
Time of accident: 3:15 P.M.
Place of accident: intersection of 7<u>th</u> Avenue and 67<u>th</u> Street, New York
Vehicles involved: 2008 Nissan and 2006 Buick
Drivers: Benjamin Fogel (2008 Nissan) and Annette Traynor (2006 Buick)
Damage: dent on front passenger door of 2006 Buick

Police Officer Quinones drafts four versions to express the above information. Which of the following four versions is most clear, accurate and complete?

A. On November <u>2</u>, 2016, at 3:15 P.M., at the intersection of 7<u>th</u> Avenue and 67<u>th</u> Street, New York, a 2008 Nissan and a 2006 Buick were involved in a traffic accident. The 2006 Buick, owned by Annette Traynor, sustained a dent on the passenger's front door. The 2008 Nissan, driven by Benjamin Fogel, did not sustain any damage.
(WRONG. Correct date is November <u>5</u>, 2016.)

B. On November 5, 2016, at 3:15 P.M., at the intersection of 7<u>th</u> Avenue and 67<u>th</u> <u>Avenue</u>, New York, a 2008 Nissan and a 2006 Buick were involved in a traffic accident. The 2006 Buick, owned by Annette Traynor, sustained a dent on the passenger's front door. The 2008 Nissan, driven by Benjamin Fogel, did not sustain any damage.
(WRONG. 67th <u>Avenue</u> should be 67<u>th</u> <u>Street</u>. Also, vehicle is <u>driven</u> and not <u>owned</u> by Annette Traynor.)

C. On November 5, 2016, at <u>3:12 P.M.</u>, at the intersection of 7<u>th</u> Avenue and 67<u>th</u> Street, New York, a 2008 Nissan and a 2006 Buick were involved in a traffic accident. The 2006 Buick, <u>driven</u> by Annette Traynor, sustained a dent on the passenger's front door. The 2008 Nissan, driven by Benjamin Fogel, did not sustain any damage.
(WRONG. Time should be <u>3:15</u> P.M.)

D. On November 5, 2016, at 3:15 P.M., at the intersection of 7th Avenue and 67th Street, New York, a 2008 Nissan and a 2006 Buick were involved in a traffic accident. The 2006 Buick, driven by Annette Traynor, sustained a dent on the passenger's front door. The 2008 Nissan, driven by Benjamin Fogel, did not sustain any damage.

(**CORRECT.** Choice "D" includes all the information and has no factual errors.)

Answers 35 - 40

35. Police Officer Haas is informed by a female whose pocketbook was yanked from her hands while she was waiting for the bus that the perpetrator was a male with a red baseball cap, about five feet eleven inches tall and wearing a white T-shirt and dark pants.

Officer Haas looks down the street in an attempt to spot the perpetrator. According to the information provided by the victim, Police Officer Haas should: (Choose the best answer.)

A. question all males and females on the street.

B. question all males and females wearing a red baseball cap.

C. question all persons with the height of five feet ten inches to five feet twelve inches.

D. question all males on the street who are wearing a red baseball cap and are about five feet eleven inches tall.

(**"D" is correct** because questioning all persons who fit just one of the description items is not logical. The combination of a red baseball cap, appropriate height, and the person being a male zeroes in on possible suspects without wasting time or involving other people.)

---

36. Police Officer Gregorius notices that repulsive smelling fumes are emanating from a fire in a city garbage container at the corner of a crowded street. Police Officer Gregorius should:

A. immediately run into a nearby store and see if they have a fire extinguisher.

B. take off his shirt and throw it on the fire.

C. warn everyone to stay clear and contact the proper authorities.

(**"C" is correct** because the "repulsive smelling fumes" might be an indication of dangerous chemicals. This is a possible emergency situation. To protect the public, he should warn them to stay clear. Also, the proper authorities should be contacted so they can investigate the nature of the fumes and extinguish the fire.)

D. wait for the fire to burn itself out before checking it out.

----

37. While on patrol, Police Officer Ben McDonnel discovers that a manhole cover in the middle of a busy street has been removed and pungent smoke is coming out of it.

Based on the preceding information, what is the first step that Police Officer McDonnel should take?

A. Call for backup since he is on patrol alone.

B. Quickly get all the persons and traffic away from the manhole and then notify the proper authorities.

(**"B" is correct** because the "repulsive smelling fumes" might be an indication of hazardous chemicals. This is a possible emergency situation. To protect the public, he should warn them to stay clear. Also, the proper authorities should be contacted so they can investigate the toxicity of the fumes and extinguish the fire.)

C. Look for the manhole cover as it may be nearby.

D. Call the highway department and complain.

----

38. Your sergeant asks that you interview a Mr. Jeffrey Fredrich regarding a complaint received by his neighbor, Gail Sealy, that he is always leaving his dog unleashed and free to roam in Ms. Sealy's back yard. You have knowledge that there is a Mr. Jeffrey Fredrich, Sr. and a Mr. Jeffrey Fredrich, Jr. because they are the owners of a coffee shop where you are a customer. What is the first step you should take in this situation?

A. At the Fredrich home, interview both Jeffrey Fredrich, Sr. and Jeffrey Fredrich, Jr. as they have the same name.

B. Ask the sergeant for clarification of the name of the person to be interviewed.

("B" is correct because Police Officers should always get clarification when they have questions about instructions given to them by their supervisors. This helps the officer to properly carry out the instructions and helps to diminish unnecessary negative consequences that may result from misunderstood instructions.)

C. Disregard the sergeant's instructions because you know both Mr. Fredrich, Sr. and Mr. Fredrich, Jr. and they are both fine people.

D. Do not ask questions of the sergeant, as he might get upset.

----

39. Police Officer Lorna Kelman is on patrol when a shop owner runs out of his store with his hands on his head, trying to stem a serious bleeding wound. The man yells out that he was robbed a minute ago, and that the robbers sped away in a car.

Based on the preceding information, what should Police Officer Kelman do first?

A. Take the man back into the liquor store and question him regarding the robbery.

B. Interview all nearby persons to determine whether any of them witnessed the robbery.

C. Apply first aid to the shop owner to stop the bleeding and call for medical assistance and officer backup.

("C" is correct because immediate medical attention is required to stem the bleeding wound before the officer takes other action.)

D. Officer Kelman should get in her patrol car and attempt to catch up to the robbers.

----

40. Prior to the start of your patrol, your sergeant gives the name and address of an elderly female who reported that she had been mugged and instructs you to interview her. From prior experience, you know that this female is prone to hallucinations. What is the first step you should take?

A. Quickly carry out the instructions of the sergeant.

("A" is correct because proper instructions should be carried out. If the officer has questions or suggestions, the officer should bring them to the attention of the sergeant and not modify or disregard them.)

B. Don't interview the female, as this would be a waste of time.

(**WRONG.** Proper instructions should be carried out.)

C. Prepare a report that includes that the woman is prone to hallucinations and that because of that you prepared the report without interviewing her.

(**WRONG.** By doing this, the instructions are not being carried out.)

D. Check with her relatives to see if she has been hallucinating recently.

(**WRONG.** The instructions should be carried out. Any proper investigation may be done after.)

Deductive Reasoning Answers 41 - 43

PL 70.05 MAXIMUM SENTENCE OF IMPRISONMENT FOR JUVENILE OFFENDER

TYPE OF CONVICTION	MAXIMUM TERM OF IMPRISONMENT
Type "A" felony (murder second degree)	life imprisonment
Type "A" felony (arson first degree or kidnapping first degree)	at least 12, but not more than 15 years
Type "B" felony	10 years
Type "C" felony	7 years
Type "D" felony	4 years

41. According to the preceding table, which of the following choices is a correct maximum term of imprisonment for conviction of the stated offense?

A. Murder in the second degree committed by a Juvenile Offender (maximum 15 years)

(**WRONG.** Maximum is <u>life imprisonment</u>.)

B. "C" felony committed by a Juvenile Offender (maximum 10 years)

(**WRONG.** Maximum is <u>7 years</u>.)

C. "B" felony committed by a Juvenile Offender (at least 12 nor more than 15 years)

(**WRONG.** Maximum is <u>10 years</u>.)

D. "C" felony committed by Juvenile Offender (7 years)

(**CORRECT.** A "C" felony maximum term is <u>7 years</u>.)

CPL 120.10 Warrant of arrest definition, function, form, and content

1. A warrant of arrest is issued by a local criminal court after the filing of an accusatory instrument for the purpose of arraignment. It directs a police officer or designated peace officers to arrest a defendant and bring him to court for arraignment.

2. It is signed by the issuing judge and must state the following:

  (a) name of issuing court,

  (b) date of issuance of the warrant,

  (c) name of offense(s) charged in the accusatory instrument,

  (d) name of defendant to be arrested (or alias or description),

  (e) police or peace officer(s) to whom warrant is addressed,

  (f) direction that officer arrest defendant and bring him to court.

3. A warrant of arrest may be addressed to an individual police officer or classification of officers.

Multiple copies of a warrant may be issued.

-----

42. According to CPL 120.10, which of the following statements is correct?

A. A warrant of arrest must contain the date of the issuance of the warrant.
(CORRECT. "A warrant of arrest: 2. It is signed by the issuing judge and must state the following:

  (a) name of issuing court,

  (b) date of issuance of the warrant....)"

B. A warrant of arrest must have the signature of the D.A.
(WRONG. "It is signed by the issuing judge.")

C. A warrant of arrest directs that the officer bring the defendant to the local penitentiary.
(WRONG. A warrant of arrest directs the officer to bring the defendant to court.)

D. For privacy reasons, a warrant of arrest cannot contain the name of the defendant.
(WRONG. A warrant of arrest can contain the name of the defendant, or alias or description.)

CPL 170.55 Adjournment in contemplation of dismissal (ACD)

After arraignment and before entry of plea of guilty or commencement of trial, the court MAY upon motion of the people or defendant, or upon its own motion and consent of both the people and the defendant, order an ACD (ADJOURNMENT IN CONTEMPLATION OF DISMISSAL).

The case is adjourned without a date. People may make an application to restore the case within 6 months. If that occurs, the court may restore it and proceed to trial. If the case is not restored, the accusatory instrument is deemed to have been dismissed in furtherance of justice at the end of the six-month period.

In case of a family offense, the ACD is for 1 year. The people may make an application to restore the case within 1 year.

The court can impose conditions (performance of public service, counseling, etc.) as part of an ACD.

An ACD is NOT a conviction or admission of guilt.

-----

43. According to CPL 170.55, which of the following statements is not correct?

A. An ACD is not an admission of guilt.

B. An ACD in a family offense proceeding is for one year.

C. When an ACD is ordered, the case is adjourned without a date.

D. The people must in all cases consent to the ordering of an ACD by the judge.

(This statement is not correct because "After arraignment and before entry of plea of guilty or commencement of trial, court may upon motion of people or defendant, or upon its own motion and consent of both the people and the defendant, order an ACD.)

"The starting point of all achievement is desire."

– Napoleon Hill

Answer 44

Which of the following circles (A, B, C, D) matches the image of the "Dissected Circle?"

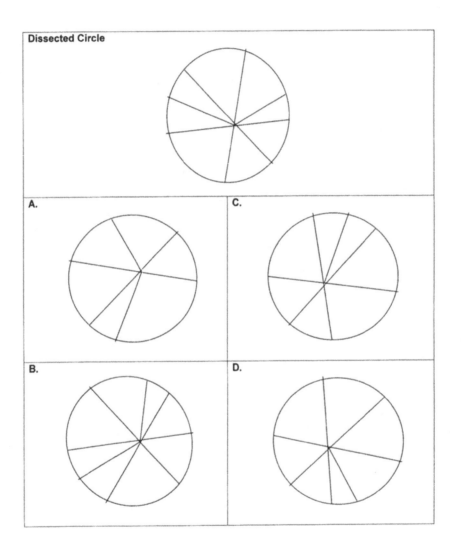

Dissected Circle

A.

C.

B.

D.

44. The drawing which best matches the image of the "Dissected Circle" is:

A. Drawing A (only 6 slices)   **B. Drawing B (identical 8 slices)**

C. Drawing C (only 7 slices)   D. Drawing D (only 7 slices)

Answers 45 - 47

Answer questions 45 - 47 based on the following extracts of two Criminal Procedure Law sections, CPL 120.70 and CPL 120.80.

CPL 120.70 A warrant of arrest issued by a district court, NYC criminal court or a superior court judge sitting as a local criminal court can be executed anywhere in the state.

A warrant of arrest issued by a city, town, or village court can be executed in the county of issuance or adjoining county (or anywhere in NYS upon the written endorsement of a local criminal court of the county in which arrest is to be made).

CPL 120.80 A warrant of arrest is executed any day of the week, any hour of the day or night.

The arresting police officer is not required to have the warrant in his possession at the time of making the arrest.

-----

45. Police Officer Marino, a NYPD Officer assigned to a precinct in Queens County, has in his possession a warrant of arrest issued by a district court for a person named Jack Wringer. Which of the following choices is correct?

A. Police Officer Marino cannot execute the warrant of arrest because it was issued by a district court and not a New York City court.

(WRONG. A warrant of arrest issued by a district court can be executed anywhere in the state.)

B. Jack Wringer cannot be arrested on that warrant if he is outside the county served by the district court.

(WRONG. A warrant of arrest issued by a district court can be executed anywhere in the state.)

C. Police Officer Marino may execute the warrant outside the state of New York.

(WRONG. A warrant of arrest issued by a district court, NYC criminal court or a superior court judge sitting as a local criminal court can be executed anywhere in the state.)

D. Police Officer Marino may execute the warrant because it was issued by a district court.

(CORRECT. A warrant of arrest issued by a district court, NYC criminal court or a superior court judge sitting as a local criminal court can be executed anywhere in the state.)

46. Police Officer Jane Goodwin, a NYPD Officer assigned to a precinct in Brooklyn, has in her possession a warrant of arrest issued by a town court in Nassau County. Which of the following statements is correct?

A. Officer Goodwin can execute the warrant in Brooklyn.

B. Officer Goodwin can execute the warrant only on weekdays in Brooklyn.

C. Officer Goodwin can execute the warrant in Brooklyn only if it has the written endorsement of a local criminal court of the county in which the arrest is to be made, in this case, Kings County (Brooklyn).

(CORRECT. A warrant of arrest issued by a city, town, or village court can be executed in the county of issuance or adjoining county, <u>or anywhere in NYS upon the written endorsement of a local criminal court of the county in which arrest is to be made</u>).

D. Officer Goodwin can execute the warrant in New Jersey.

----

47. According to CPL 120.70, which of the following is not correct?

A. A warrant of arrest issued by a superior court judge sitting as a local criminal court can be executed anywhere in the state.

B. A warrant of arrest issued by the NYC criminal court can be executed anywhere in the state.

C. A warrant of arrest issued by the board of a school district can be executed anywhere in the state.

(CPL 120.70 does not address warrants of arrest issued by the board of a <u>school</u> district. Therefore, this statement is not correct.)

D. Some warrants of arrest may be executed anywhere in the state.

Answer 48

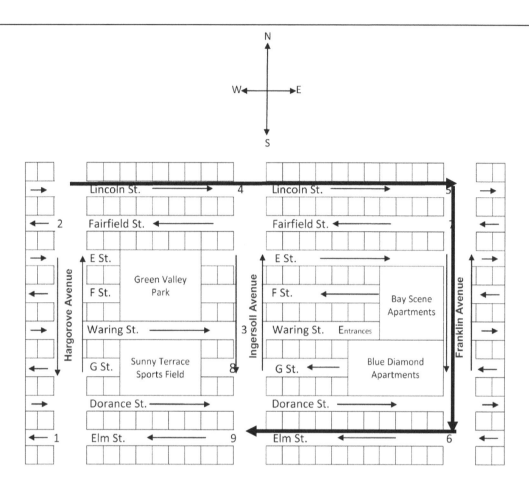

48. Imagine that you are at Hargrove Avenue and Lincoln Street and then drive east to Franklin Avenue, then drive south to Elm St., then travel west to Ingersoll Avenue, you will be closest to which one of the following points?

A. 2   B. 4   C. 5   **D. 9**

(For correct route, see dark arrows, above.)

Answer 49

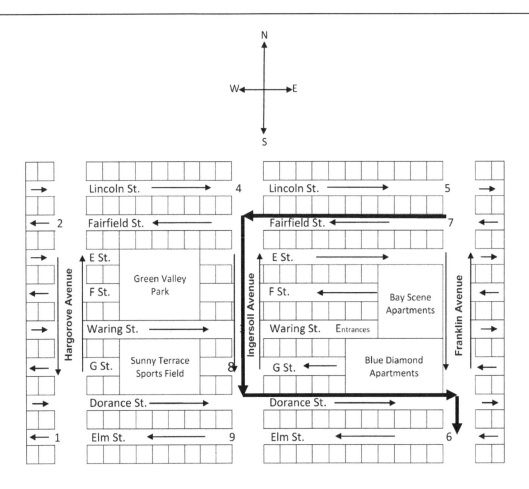

49. If you start your drive at point number 7, then drive west to Ingersoll Avenue, then drive south to Dorance St., then east to Franklin Avenue, then drive south to Elm St., you will be closest to which one of the following points?

A. 1   B. 5   **C. 6**   D. 9

Answer 50

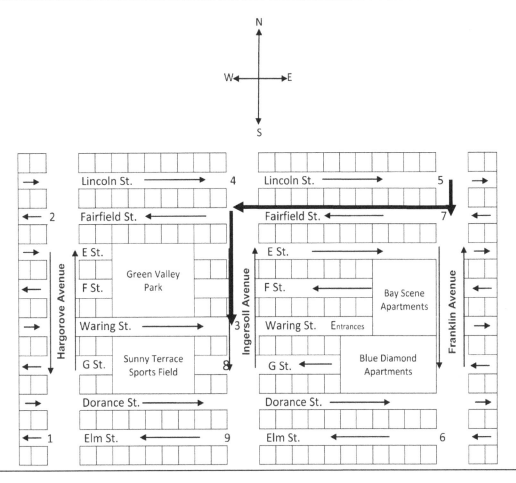

50. You are drining south in your patrol car and are at the intersection of Lincoln St. and Franklin Avenue. You are informed that an auto accident has just occurred at the intersection of Waring Street and Ingersoll Avenue. Assuming you must obey all traffic signs, which one of the following four choices describes the most direct route?

A. Drive south on Franklin Avenue to Fairfield St, then drive east on Fairfield St. to Ingersoll Avenue, then south to the intersection of Dorance Street and Ingersoll Avenue.

B. Drive south on Franklin Avenue to Fairfield St, then drive west on Fairfield St. to Ingersoll Avenue, then north to the intersection of Dorance Street and Ingersoll Avenue.

C. Drive north on Franklin Avenue to Fairfield St, then drive east on Fairfield St. to Ingersoll Avenue, then north to the intersection of Dorance Street and Ingersoll Avenue.

D. Drive south on Franklin Avenue to Fairfield St, then drive west on Fairfield St. to Ingersoll Avenue, then south to the intersection of Waring Street and Ingersoll Avenue.

Answer 51

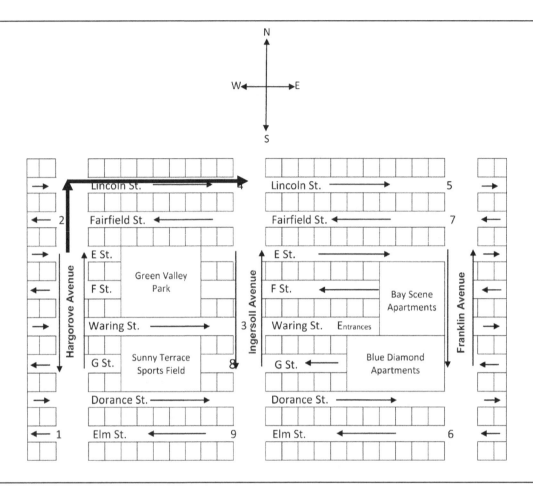

51. You are driving north in your patrol car and are at Hargrove Avenue and E St. You are informed that a fight between two men is happening at the corner of Lincoln St. and Ingersoll Avenue. Which one of the following four choices describes the most direct route?

A. Drive south to Lincoln St. then west on Lincoln St. to the corner of Lincoln St. and Ingersoll Avenue.

B. Drive north to Lincoln St. then west on Lincoln St. to the corner of Lincoln St. and Ingersoll Avenue.

C. Drive south to Dorance St. then east on Dorance St. to Ingersoll Avenue, then north to Lincoln Street and Ingersoll Avenue.

D. Drive north to Lincoln St. then east on Lincoln St. to the corner of Lincoln St. and Ingersoll Avenue.

52. During the month of August 2016 there were 14 purse snatchings reported in Police Officer Devon's precinct. In five of the purse snatchings, the victims reported that the perpetrator was a white male, about 5 feet ten inches, shoulder length dark hair, "with a small, black star tattoo on the right side of his neck." All five victims reported that the man was carrying a large brown backpack. The five also reported that he had been wearing black dungarees and a black T-shirt.

During his patrol, Officer Devon stops four white males for questioning. He had recorded in his memo book the description given by the five witnesses. Which piece of information should Officer Devon consider the most important in identifying the suspected purse snatcher?

A. the black dungarees and black T-shirt

B. the shoulder length dark hair

C. the small, black star tattoo on his neck

(CORRECT. Unlike the items listed in choices "A," "B," and "D," this is the piece of the description that cannot be easily changed or disguised and that is also not too broad, like skin color.)

D. the color of his skin

----

53. Prior to the start of his patrol, Officer Charles Briggs learns at the precinct that a female, about 75 years old, had been mugged one hour earlier by a person who the victim described as a "Hispanic, about twenty years old, with red hair tied in a shoulder length ponytail, and with a very crooked nose." She also described him as wearing black pants, a black T-shirt, and black sneakers.

During his patrol, Officer Briggs sees a group of four white or Hispanic males, about 20-25 years old, standing in front of Junior's Delicatessen. Officer Briggs stops his patrol car about twenty feet away to get a better look at the four males. Which of the following parts of the description provided by the victim is most important for Officer Briggs to consider in his attempt to identify the possible suspect?

A. the black T-shirt

B. the red hair tied in a shoulder length pony tail

C. the black sneakers

D. the crooked nose.

(CORRECT. Unlike the items listed in choices "A," "B," and "C," this is the one piece of the description that cannot be easily changed or disguised.)

54. Police Officer Hanson is assigned to patrol an area which includes four public parks. During the prior four weeks, crime statistics show that four muggings were reported at the Jackson Park, all between the hours of 10:00 a.m. and 4:00 p.m. At the Washington Park six purse snatchings were reported. **At the Bellmore Park eight <u>strollers</u> were stolen. At the Green Valley Park four <u>bicycles</u> were stolen.** The muggings all occurred between 9:30 a.m. and 4:30 p.m. The purse snatchings occurred between 9:30 a.m. and 10:30 a.m. The strollers were stolen in the afternoon and before 3:00 p.m.

Officer Hanson works the 9:00 a.m. to 5:00 p.m. tour. On Monday, his sergeant instructs him to pay careful attention to stroller robberies. To try to reduce the number of stroller robberies, Office Hanson should patrol:

A. Washington Park

B. Green Valley Park

C. Bellmore Park
("At the Bellmore Park eight <u>strollers</u> were stolen" during the prior four weeks.)

D. Green Valley Park and Washington Park

----

55. On Tuesday Officer Hanson works the 9:00 a.m. to 5:00 p.m. tour. His sergeant tells him that six bicycles have been stolen at the same park where four bicycles were stolen during the prior four weeks. To try to reduce the number of bicycles being stolen, Officer Hanson should patrol:

A. Washington Park

B. Green Valley Park
("At the Green Valley Park four <u>bicycles</u> were stolen" during the prior four weeks.)

C. Bellmore Park

D. Columbus Park

Answers 56 - 57

Answer questions 56 - 57 based on the following "Procedure for an Arrest on a Felony Offense."

Procedure for an Arrest on a Felony Offense

1. A person arrested for a felony offense must be handcuffed by the arresting officer.

2. The accused must be held in a police station or jail pending his or her ability to post bail in the amount set by the Judge at the first court appearance.

3. If the accused cannot post bail, the accused must be held in a secure facility.

4. If the accused posts bail, he or she must be released and ordered to appear at the next court date.

5. If the accused does not appear on the next scheduled court date, he or she forfeits any bail the Judge may have ordered and the Judge must order the issuance of an arrest warrant.

56. A person arrested on a felony charge appears before the Judge in court. The Judge sets a bail of $250,000.00. The person posts the entire bail and is released and ordered by the Judge to return on a specified date. On the return date, he does not appear. Based on the above "Procedure for an Arrest on a Felony Offense," which of the following statements is correct?

A. The person must be notified to appear on the next court date or a warrant of arrest will be issued.
(**NOT CORRECT** because bail must be forfeited and the judge must order a warrant of arrest.)

B. The bail must be held on deposit by the court and returned to the person when he comes to court on the next court date.
(**NOT CORRECT** because bail must be forfeited now and the judge must order a warrant of arrest.)

C. If a warrant of arrest is ordered by the Judge, the bail is not forfeited.
(**NOT CORRECT**. Bail is forfeited.)

D. The bail must be forfeited and a warrant of arrest must be ordered by the Judge.

(CORRECT. "If the accused does not appear on the next scheduled court date, he or she forfeits any bail the Judge may have ordered and the Judge must order the issuance of an arrest warrant.")

----

57. According to the "Procedure for an Arrest on a Felony Offense," which of the following statements is correct?

A. If the accused refuses to post bail, he or she must be released and ordered to appear at the next court date.

(NOT CORRECT. Person must <u>not</u> be released if he does not post bail.)

B. The accused must be held in a police station or jail pending his or her ability to post bail in the amount set by the <u>Police Captain</u>.

(NOT CORRECT. Bail is set by the <u>judge</u>.)

C. A person arrested for a felony must not be handcuffed.

(NOT CORRECT. The person <u>must</u> be handcuffed.)

D. The Judge must order the issuance of an arrest warrant if the accused does not appear on the next scheduled court date.

(CORRECT. "If the accused does not appear on the next scheduled court date, he or she forfeits any bail the Judge may have ordered and the Judge must order the issuance of an arrest warrant.")

Answers 58 - 59

Answer questions 58 - 59 based on the following "Lost Property Procedure."

Lost Property Procedure

1. Any lost property in the possession of a Police Officer must be delivered by the officer to the "Lost Property Office" in the precinct by the end of the Officer's tour of the day.

2. The Lost Property Officer must inventory the property and safeguard it according to the requirements in the "Property Safeguarding Manual."

3. Property not claimed within 30 days shall be delivered by the Lost Property Officer to the "Central Lost Property Office" at One Police Plaza.

4. If the article is not claimed within one year following the delivery to the "Central Lost Property Office" at One Police Plaza, the article must be sold at auction pursuant to "Lost Property Auction Rules."

5. Funds collected at the auction, net of expenses, must be forwarded by the Central Lost Property Officer to the New York City Finance Administrator.

58. Officer Rolands receives a copy of the above "Lost Property Procedure" the same day in which a pedestrian hands him a diamond ring which he has found on the sidewalk. Officer Rolands used to work in a jewelry store and believes the ring to be costume jewelry. There is one hour remaining before Officer Roland's daily tour ends. Which of the following statements is correct procedure?

A. Officer Rolands should return the ring to the pedestrian and tell him it is costume jewelry.
(**NOT CORRECT**. This is contrary to the Lost Property Procedure.)

B. Officer Rolands should take the ring to a jewelry store and have it examined before the end of his tour.
(**NOT CORRECT**. This is not one of the stated procedures.)

C. Officer Rolands should take the ring to the precinct's "Lost Property Office" before the end of his tour.

(**CORRECT.** Any lost property in the possession of a Police Officer must be delivered by the officer to the "Lost Property Office" in the precinct by the end of the Officer's tour of the day.)

D. Officer Rolands should hold on to the ring for at least the following day and have it examined before wasting time delivering it to the "Lost Property Office."

(**NOT CORRECT.** The ring must be delivered to the Lost Property Office before the end of the tour.)

----

59. After the passage of one year from the date property is delivered to the "Central Lost Property Office," the property:

A. must be returned to the precinct Lost Property Office.

B. must be forwarded to the office of the New York City Finance Administrator.

C. must be sold at auction pursuant to "Lost Property Auction Rules, 2014."

(**"C" is CORRECT.** "4. If the article is not claimed within one year following the delivery to the "Central Lost Property Office" at One Police Plaza, the article must be sold at auction pursuant to "Lost Property Auction Rules, 2014." Choices A, B, and D are contrary to the procedure.)

D. may be returned to the officer who found the property.

_____

Answers 60 – 68

60. You and another officer notice an elderly woman on the sidewalk. She tells you that a "tall man" just knocked her down and stole her pocketbook. You notice a "tall man" running down the block southbound to the end of the block where he makes a right turn. While your partner stays with the victim, you follow the man and observe him continuing to run for two blocks before making another right turn.

According to the information in the preceding passage, you would be most correct to radio that you last saw the man running:

A) north

B) south

C) east

D) west

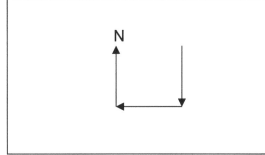

----

61. While in your patrol car, you notice a car sideswipe a parked car and then continue northbound without stopping. You follow the car, which after four blocks makes a right turn and then after two more blocks makes a left turn.

According to the information in the preceding passage, you would be most correct to radio that you last saw the car heading:

A) north

B) south

C) east

D) west

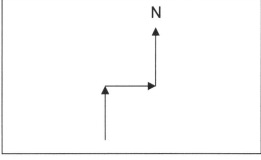

----

62. A jewelry store employee runs out of a jewelry store, points down the block and shouts, "That guy just robbed me!" You shout for the man to stop, but he continues running westbound. After three blocks, he makes a left turn and runs for two more blocks before making another left turn.

According to the information in the preceding passage, you would be most correct to radio that you last saw the suspect heading:

A) north

B) south

C) east

D) west

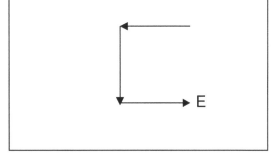

63. You and another officer witness a purse being snatched from an elderly woman in front of the entrance to Ulmer Park. You shout for the man to stop, but he runs down the block in a westbound direction. You chase the man for three blocks before he turns left and then runs for another block, at which point he turns right.

According to the information in the preceding passage, you would be most correct to radio that the man was running:

A) north

B) south

C) east

D) west

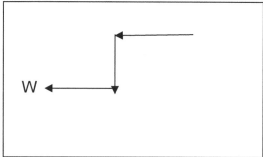

----

64. While in your patrol car, you witness two men run out of a bar, each holding a pouch and a revolver. They quickly get into a car and head northbound. You follow. After three blocks, they make a right turn and then after two more blocks they make another right turn.

According to the information in the preceding passage, you would be most correct to radio that you last saw the car heading:

A) north

B) south

C) east

D) west

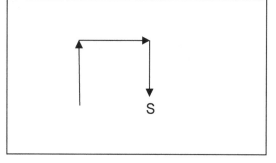

----

65. Your attention is drawn to a pedestrian shouting, "He took my bike!" and pointing to a man on a bike pedaling quickly on the sidewalk, away from the pedestrian and in a westbound direction. After three blocks, he makes a right turn and then after two more blocks he makes a left turn.

According to the information in the preceding passage, you would be most correct to radio that you last saw the man heading:

A) north

B) south

C) east

D) west

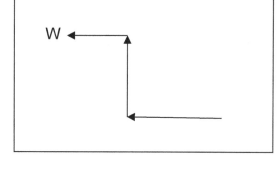

----

66. You and another officer notice a man in a wheelchair moaning on the sidewalk. He tells you that a "crazy looking man" just punched him on the head and then ran away. You notice a man running down the block northbound to the end of the block where he makes a left turn. While your partner stays with the victim, you follow the man and observe him continuing to run for three blocks before turning left.

According to the information in the preceding passage, you would be most correct to radio that you last saw the man running:

A) north

B) south

C) east

D) west

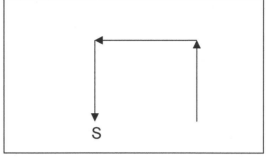

----

67. While in your patrol car, you notice a red car sideswipe a parked car and then drive off southbound without stopping. You follow the car, which after sixteen blocks makes a right turn and then after two more blocks makes another right turn.

According to the information in the preceding passage, you would be most correct to radio that you last saw the car heading:

A) east

B) south

C) north

D) west

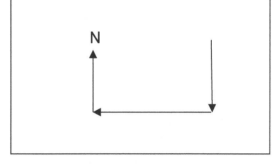

----

68. A shoe store employee runs out of a shoe store, points down the block and shouts, "That guy just robbed the store!" You shout for the running man to stop, but he continues running northbound. After four blocks, he makes a left turn and runs for two more blocks before making a right turn.

According to the information in the preceding passage, you would be most correct to radio that you last saw the suspect heading:

A) north

B) south

C) east

D) west

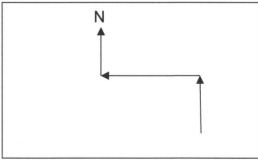

Answer 69

Line
of
crates

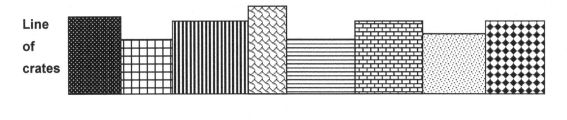

A.

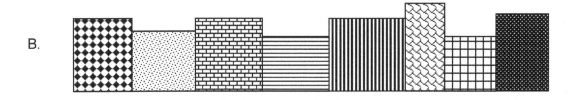

B.

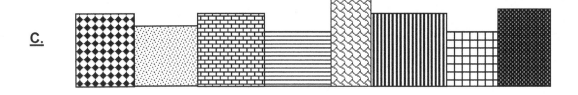

C.

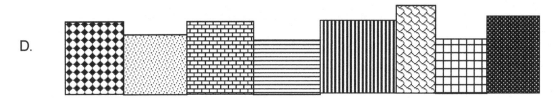

D.

69. The above "Line of Crates" when viewed from the back would appear as which of the following choices?

A. Choice A

C. Choice C

B. Choice B

D. Choice D

The answer is "C." (To make the answer clear, we have filled-in each corresponding box with the same pattern.)

Answers 70 - 75

Answer questions 70 - 75 based on the information contained in the following passage.

While on patrol, Police Officers Collins and Fogel are dispatched to 1673 Brittany Avenue, first floor "Archer Discount Store" at 9:45 p.m. on October 29, 2016. The owner of "Archer Discount Store" had just called 911 to report a burglary. They arrive at the store at 9:49 p.m. and are greeted by Mr. James Fontaine, the owner of the store and Mr. John Brighton, an employee of "Archer Discount Store."

Mr. Fontaine tells the officers that he and John Brighton had closed the store for the day at 8:00 p.m. They had locked the front and back doors and properly rolled down the security gate and padlocked it. Mr. Fontaine discovered the burglary at 9:30 p.m. when at home he happened to glance at the live video of his four security cameras. Although security camera #1 showed the outdoor front entrance and security camera #4 showed the outdoor back door area, it was with security cameras #2 and #3 that he saw the burglars. Security camera # 2 covered the outdoor roof skylight and security camera # 3 covered the inside area of the store, including the cashier area.

Two burglars, all dressed in dark blue and wearing black face masks, had broken the glass in the skylight and with a rope had lowered themselves into the store. The smaller of the two persons descended first and the much taller one followed. The person who descended first carried a black garbage bag and the other person held a flashlight in his right hand.

The two burglars took the $225.00 cash and coins that had been left in the cash register, an entire box of seven identical collectible statuettes worth a total of $1200.00, three expensive, identical watches worth a total of $900.00, two electric toasters worth $49.00 each, and six original signed watercolor paintings by a local artist worth $99.00 each. Mr. Fontaine tells the officers that he will prepare a complete list of missing items as soon as possible.

Mr. Fontaine tells Officer Fogel that he is 57 years old and lives at 3465 Baton Rouge Avenue in the Bronx. His cell number is 718-555-1283. John Brighton tells Officer Fogel that he is 27 years old and lives at 2835 West 125 Street, Brooklyn. His cell number is 781-555-2944.

Police Officers Collins and Fogel complete their investigation at 10:25 p.m. Before they completed their crime report, they performed a careful sweep of the store to make certain that the burglars had left.

-----

70. What was the most expensive individual item (one piece) stolen?

A. statuette

(Each statuette is worth approximately $171 ($1200.00 divided by 7.)

B. watch

(THIS IS THE ANSWER. Each watch is worth $300.00 because 3 watches are worth $900.)

C. watercolor painting

(Each painting is worth $99.)

D. electric toaster

(Each toaster is worth $49.)

71. Which of the following statements is correct?

A. Mr. John Brighton, the owner of the store, is 57 years old.

(**WRONG**. Mr. <u>Fontaine</u> is 57 years old. Mr. <u>Brighton</u> is 27 years old.)

B. Each of the burglars took $225.00 in cash (total of $450.00).

(**WRONG**. <u>Total</u> cash and coins was <u>$225</u>.)

C. Mr. John Brighton lives at 3465 Baton Rouge Avenue in the Bronx.

(**WRONG**. Mr. <u>Fontaine</u> lives at this address.)

D. The total value of the watercolor paintings is $594.00.

(**CORRECT**. 6 watercolor paintings at $99 each = $594.)

----

72. Which one of the following statements is correct? Among the items stolen were:

A. six identical collectible statuettes worth a total of $1200.00

(**WRONG**. There were <u>seven</u> statuettes.)

B. two electric toasters worth a total of $49.00.

(**WRONG**. <u>Each</u> toaster is worth $49.)

C. $450.00 cash and coins that had been left in the cash register

(**WRONG**. Total cash and coins is <u>$225</u>.)

D. three expensive, identical watches worth $300.00 each.

(**CORRECT**. Paragraph 3: "three expensive watches worth a total of $900.00" – or <u>$300 each</u>.)

----

73. Which of the following statements is correct according to the information provided by Mr. Fontaine and Mr. Brighton?

A. Mr. Fontaine tells Officer Fogel that he is 57 years old and lives at <u>3645</u> Baton Rouge Avenue in the Bronx. His cell number is 718-555-1283

(**WRONG**. The correct street number is <u>3465</u>.)

B. John Brighton tells Officer Fogel that he is 27 years old and lives at <u>2853</u> West 125 Street, Brooklyn. His cell number is 781-555-2944.

(**WRONG.** The correct building number is <u>2835</u>.")

C. John Brighton tells Officer Fogel that he is 27 years old and lives at 2835 West 125 Street, <u>Bronx</u>. His cell number is 781-555-2944.

(**WRONG.** John Brighton lives in <u>Brooklyn</u>.)

D. Mr. Fontaine tells Officer Fogel that he is 57 years old and lives at 3465 Baton Rouge Avenue in the Bronx. His cell number is 718-555-1283.

(**CORRECT.** All the information is correct.)

----

74. Choose the best answer: The value of each of the statuettes that were stolen is closest to:

A. $171

(**CORRECT.** This is the best "approximate" value. "…an entire box of seven identical collectible statuettes worth a total of $1200.00,": $1,200 divided by 7 = <u>$171.42</u>.)

B. $140

C. $150

D. $183

----

75. The total value of all items missing is:

A. $2,453

B. $3,617

C. $2,968

D. $3,017

Cash $	225
7 statuettes	1,200
3 watches for a total of	900
2 toaster, $49 each;	98
6 paintings, $99	594
Total	$ 3017

Answer 76

During his patrol, Police Officer Dawn Heller is called to the scene of an accident. The driver/owner of vehicle #3 stated that he was driving on Vine St. when car #1 hit his rear bumper, causing him to hit vehicle number 2.

Assume that all 3 vehicles were in their proper lanes of traffic.

Which of the following 4 diagrams best matches the statement of the driver of vehicle #3?

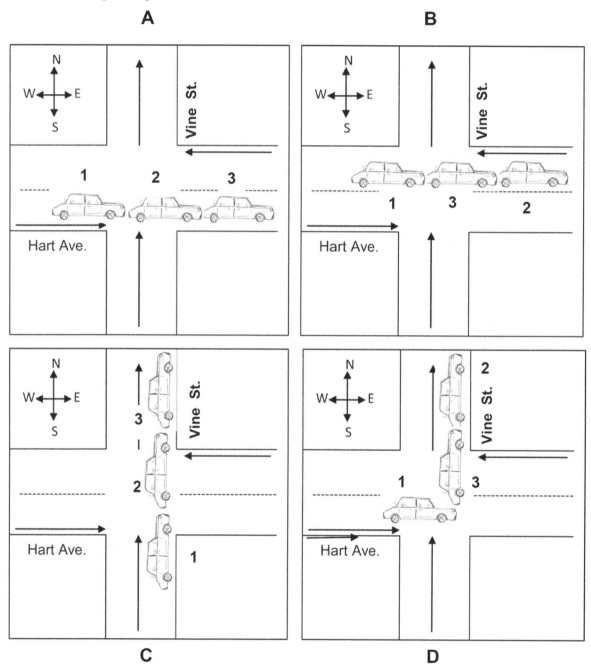

76. The diagram which best matches the statement of the driver of vehicle #3 is:

A. diagram "A"   C. diagram "C"

B. diagram "B"   **D. diagram "D"**

(In proper lanes, "Car 1 hits car 3 which then hits car 2" is only displayed in <u>Diagram "D."</u>)

Answers 77 - 78

Answer questions 77 – 78 based on the following accident details.

Officer Nordstrum collects the following information at the scene of an auto accident:

Date of Accident: September 9, 2016

Time of accident: 4:15 p.m.

Place of accident: Intersection of Lavin Avenue and Reiker Avenue, Bronx

Driver: Barry Jones

Vehicle: 2008 Toyota Sienna

Damage: Vehicle struck a commercial metal garbage container protruding into the street.

-----

77. Officer Nordstrum is preparing a report of the accident and has four drafts of the report. He wishes to use the draft that expresses the information most clearly, accurately and completely. Which draft should he choose?

A. At 4:15 p.m., on September 9, 2016, at the intersection of Lavin Avenue and Reiker Avenue, Bronx, a vehicle driven by Barry Jones struck a commercial metal garbage container protruding into the street.

(WRONG. Type of vehicle, <u>a 2008 Toyota Sienna</u>, is not stated.)

B. On September 9, 2016, at 4:15 p.m., at the intersection of Lavin Avenue and Reiker Avenue, Bronx, a 2008 Toyota Sienna driven by Barry <u>Lones</u> struck a commercial metal garbage container protruding into the street.

(WRONG. Jones is misspelled <u>Lones</u>.)

C. On September 9, 2016, at <u>4:25 p.m.</u>, at the intersection of Lavin Avenue and Reiker Avenue, Bronx, a 2008 Toyota Slenna driven by Barry Jones struck a commercial metal garbage container protruding into the street.

(WRONG. Time is not correct. Time should be <u>4:15 p.m.</u>)

D. On September 9, 2016, at 4:15 p.m., at the intersection of Lavin Avenue and Reiker Avenue, Bronx, a 2008 Toyota Sienna driven by Barry Jones struck a commercial metal garbage container protruding into the street.

(BEST DRAFT. All the information is stated and is accurate.)

----

78. Officer Nordstrum is comparing the information he recorded in his memo pad (at the scene of the accident) to the information in his report. Which of the above choices (A, B, C, or D) has a detail that does not agree with the information in the officer's memo pad?

A. Date of Accident: September 9, 2016; Time of accident: 4:15 p.m.

B. Place of accident: Intersection of Lavin Avenue and Reiker Avenue, Bronx

C. Driver: Barry Jones: Vehicle: 2008 Toyota Sienna

D. Damage: Vehicle struck a commercial plastic garbage container protruding into the street
(ONE DETAIL IS WRONG. The garbage container is <u>metal</u> and not <u>plastic</u>.)

Answer questions 79 - 80 based on the following information gathered at a crime scene.

_____

Officer Samuels responds to a car theft. She questions the owner of the vehicle who reported the car stolen and obtains the following information:

Suspect: Unidentified

Date of crime: August 25, 2016

Time of crime: between 7:20 p.m. and 11:40 p.m.

Crime: theft of car

Vehicle stolen: 2012 Volvo

Victim: owner of car, Frank Dolin

Place of crime: driveway in front of 247 18th Street, Staten Island

-----

79. Officer Samuels is preparing a report of the accident and has prepared four drafts of the report. She wishes to use the draft that expresses the information most clearly, accurately and completely. Which of the following drafts should she choose?

A. A car theft of a 2012 Volvo happened at the driveway in front of 247 18th Street, Staten Island where Frank Dolin's car was parked for the night. The alleged thief is unidentified, as the theft happened in the evening hours.
(WRONG. Date is missing. Time is missing. Language is sloppy.)

B. On August 25, 2016, between 7:20 p.m. and 11:40 p.m., at the driveway in front of 247 18th Street, Staten Island, a 2012 Volvo owned by Frank Dolin was stolen by an unidentified suspect.
(CORRECT. This is the best draft. It has all the information and is accurate.)

C. A car was stolen on August 25, 2016, between 7:20 p.m. and 11:40 p.m., at the driveway in front of 247 18th Street, Staten Island, owned by Frank Dolin. The suspect is unidentified. **(WRONG.** Type of car is not stated. Language is sloppy.)

D. On August 25, 2016, 247 18th Street, Staten Island, between <u>7:20 a.m.</u> and <u>11:40 a.m.</u>, a 2012 Volvo owned by Frank Dolin was stolen by an unidentified suspect.

(WRONG. Time is not correct. It should be "between 7:20 <u>p.m.</u> and 11:40 <u>p.m.)</u>

----

80. Officer Samuels is comparing the information he recorded in his memo pad (at the scene of the accident) to the information in his report. Which of the above choices (A, B, C, or D) has one detail that does not agree with the information in the officer's memo pad?

A. Date of crime: August 25, 2016; Time of crime: between 7:20 p.m. and 11:40 p.m.

B. Crime: theft of car; Vehicle stolen: 2012 Volvo

C. Victim: owner of car, Frank Dolin

D. Place of crime: driveway in front of 247 18th Avenue, Staten Island
(The address should be <u>"Street"</u> and not <u>"Avenue."</u>)

Answer question 81 based on the following "Media Inquiry Procedure."

Media Inquiry Procedure

When a criminal case is pending in the courts, the Police Officer who made the arrest is prohibited from discussing the case with any newspaper, magazine, TV reporters and all other media. Exceptions to this are cases where:

1. a New York court of competent jurisdiction formally orders the Police Officer to discuss one or more particulars of the case.

2. a NYPD authorized Department orders such discussion

3. the Police Officer is subpoenaed to testify by an authorized NYC, NYS, or federal board.

In all cases, media inquiries made to the officer should be referred to HQ Media Services at One Police Plaza.

-----

81. Police Officer Jane Hollis arrests a drug suspect and confiscates two pounds of heroin. The suspect has been indicted and is in jail, waiting for trial. A newspaper reporter, Abigail Briggs, contacts Officer Jane Hollis and asks a quick question, the answer to which might help the reporter to investigate drug trafficking in the city. Officer Jane Hollis should:

A. Answer the question since it is a quick question.

B. Tell the reporter to contact her sergeant.

C. Answer the question only if the reporter is trustworthy.

D. tell the reporter to contact HQ Media Services at One Police Plaza.

(CORRECT. Choices A, B, and C are contrary to the Media Inquiry Procedure.)

Answers 82 - 83

Answer questions 82 - 83 based on the following highlights of "CPL 500.10: Definitions."

CPL 500.10: Definitions

SECURED BAIL BOND is a bond secured by:

1) personal property greater than or equal to the undertaking, or

2) real property at least 2 times the value of the undertaking (assessed value divided by equalization rate, or special assessing unit as defined in article 18 of real property tax law)

PARTIALLY SECURED BAIL BOND is a bond secured by a deposit of money not in excess of 10 per cent of the total amount of the undertaking.

UNSECURED BAIL BOND is a bail bond (other than an insurance company bail bond) that is not secured by any deposit or lien.

----

82. Which of the following is an example of an unsecured bail bond?

A. a bail bond secured by a deposit of money not in excess of 10 per cent of the total amount of the undertaking

(WRONG. This is the definition of a <u>partially</u> secured bail bond.)

B. a bail bond secured by personal property greater than or equal to undertaking

(WRONG. This is the definition of a <u>secured</u> bail bond.)

C. a bail bond (other than an insurance company bail bond) that is not secured by any deposit or lien

(**CORRECT.** This is the definition of an <u>"Unsecured bail bond."</u>)

D. a bond secured by real property at least 2 times the value of the undertaking

(**WRONG.** This is the definition of a <u>secured</u> bail bond.)

----

83. A bail bond secured by a deposit of money not in excess of 10 per cent of the total amount of the undertaking is a:

A. secured bail bond.

B. unsecured bail bond.

C. questionable secured bail bond.

D. partially secured bail bond.

"PARTIALLY SECURED BAIL BOND is a bond secured by a deposit of money not in excess of 10 per cent of the total amount of the undertaking."

----

84. Four witnesses to a hit and run accident tell Police Officer Valenti that they memorized the license plate number of the car that sped away from the accident. Which of the following license plate numbers is the most likely to be correct?

A. 8337AFR

B. 8587AFR

C. 8537AFR

D. 8531AFR

Explanation:

The first digit "8" is the same in all choices.

Choice "A" differs from all other choices in that the second digit is "3" instead of "5." We can eliminate "A".

Choice "B" differs from the remaining choices by having an "8" as the third digit instead of "3." This leaves choices "C" and" D."

Choice "D" differs from the other choices in that the fourth digit is "1" instead of "7."

The correct choice is therefore **"C."**

Answer question 85 based on the following table.

Summonses and Desk Appearance Tickets Issued by Police Officer Archer

Week	Dates	Parking Summonses	Moving Summonses	Desk Appearance Tickets
1	Nov. 1 – 7	14	15	4
2	Nov 8 -14	11	3	6
3	Nov 15 – 21	16	10	1
4	Nov 22 – 28	9	12	5
5	Nov 29 – Dec 5	14	10	7

85. Police Officer Archer is adding up the total number of all summonses and Desk Appearance Tickets issued by her during the above five-week period. Which of the following four formulas should she use to arrive at the correct number of summonses and Desk Appearance Tickets that she issued?

A. 14+10+7

(WRONG. This totals only summonses and Desk Appearance Tickets issued Nov 29 – Dec 5.)

B. 4+6+1+5+7

(WRONG. This only totals the Desk Appearance Tickets issued.)

C. 14+11+16+9+14+15+3+10+12+10+4+6+1+5+7

(CORRECT. This gives us the total (137) of all summonses and Desk Appearance Tickets issued.)

D. 1(14+11+16+9+14) + 2(15+3+10+12+10) +3 (4+6+1+5+7)

(WRONG. This mathematical formula multiplies each parenthetical group of summonses issued by the number preceding the parenthesis and gives an incorrect total of 233 for the summonses and Desk Appearance Tickets issued.)

END OF PRACTICE TEST #1

PRACTICE TEST #2
QUESTIONS

Memory Question

Study the photo below for the next ten minutes. Try to remember as many details about the people and objects as you can. During the ten minutes, you are not permitted to take any notes or write anything.

At the end of the ten minutes you will be asked to answer questions 1 – 10 (without looking back at the picture.)

(After ten minutes)

Instructions for questions 1 – 10:

Without looking back at the picture, answer questions 1 – 10 on the following page.

POLICE OFFICER EXAM NEW YORK CITY

1. The number of people in the picture is:

A. 4   B. 5   C. 6   D. 7

2. Choose the best answer.

The person holding the cookie tray in the center of the picture is:

A. male white   B. female white   C. male black   D. female black

3. The man holding the wine bottle:

A. is wearing a T-shirt

B. has blonde hair

C. is wearing white pants

D. is wearing short pants

4. The woman on the extreme right is:

A. cutting meat

B. pouring a drink

C. mixing a salad

D. none of the above

5. The number of bottles in the picture is:

A. four

B. two

C. three

D. one

6. In the picture there are:

A. two women and three men

B. three women and three men

C. two men and three women

D. none of the above

7. Choose the best answer.

The person on the far right is wearing a _____ shirt.

A. white

B. black

C. plaid

D. none of the above

8. On the back wall there is a:

A. a painting of the New York skyline.

B. a painting of the Eifel Tower.

C. a painting of a beach scene.

D. none of the above

9. The person holding the glass is:

A. a male with dark hair

B. a male with blonde hair

C. a female with blonde hair and taller than the person holding the wine bottle.

D. none of the above

10. The person holding the cookie tray is wearing a glove that can be described as:

A. white

B. black

C. checkered

D. none of the above.

> "All our dreams can come true if we have the courage to pursue them."
>
> – Walt Disney

Questions 11 - 15

Answer questions 11 - 15 based on the information contained in the following paragraphs.

Police Officers Jack Ellis and Rhonda Cordan were on patrol on November 3, 2016 when at 7:15 p.m. they witnessed a minor traffic accident (in front of 2455 Elmer Street, in Staten Island). Officer Ellis called the Police Dispatcher at 7:25 p.m. and reported that the two drivers and four passengers (two in each vehicle) did not sustain any personal injuries. One of the vehicles, the one driven by a male named Fred Ulmer, did have minor damage to the driver's side door, and the other vehicle, driven by a male named Oswald Trunger, had minor damage to the front bumper.

Officer Cordan examined the driver's licenses, vehicle registration certificates and vehicle insurance identification cards. The auto driven by Fred Ulmer, age 49, was a white 2010 Acura, N.Y. license plate 2845AB, owned by the driver, residing at 282 Carle Road, New York, N.Y. Mr. Ulmer's N.Y. driver's license identification number is E172 73 561 and the expiration date is December 31, 2016

The driver of the other auto was Oswald Trunger, age 50, residing at 3857 Elm Street, Brooklyn, N.Y. Mr. Trunger's auto was a silver 2012 Ford Escape, NY license plate 325DKL. Mr. Trunger's driver's license identification number is R261 392 142 and the expiration is November 30, 2016.

Officers Ellis and Cordan completed a Vehicle Accident Report at 7:35 p.m. The report number was 28332757362.

-----

11. What is the time of the accident?
A. 7:25 p.m.   C. 7:25 a.m.
B. 7:15 p.m.   D. before 7:10 p.m.

----

12. How many persons were injured as a result of the traffic accident?
A. 1   C. 2
B. 0   D. 4

----

13. Which car sustained damage to the front bumper?
A. NY plate #2845AB, white 2010 Acura
B. NY plate #2845AB, white 2012 Acura

C.   NY plate #325DKL, silver 2012 Ford Escape
D.   NY plate #325DKL, white 2012 Ford Escape

----

14. Which of the following statements is not correct?
A. The auto driven by Oswald Trunger, age 50, was a silver 2012 Ford Escape.
B. The vehicle Accident Report number was 2832757362.
C. Fred Ulmer, age 49, resides at 282 Carle Road, New York, N.Y.
D. Mr. Trunger's license plate number is 325DKL.

----

15. Which of the following is not correct?
A. The person residing at 282 Carle Road, New York, N.Y., has a N.Y. driver's license
   identification number of E172 73 561, expiration date of December 31, 2016.
B. Mr. Trunger, age 50, resides at 3857 Elm Street, Brooklyn, N.Y.
C. The auto driven by Fred Ulmer was a black 2010 Acura.
D. The accident occurred in front of 2455 Elmer Street, in Staten Island.

Questions 16 - 20

Answer questions 16 - 20 based on the information contained in the following paragraphs.

Police Officers Elton Young and Mary Long were on patrol in their squad car on November 14, 2016 when at 4:10 p.m. a woman approached them. The woman stated that her parked car, a 2012 black Ford Mondeo had just been struck by a 2010 Chrysler Sebring that was in the process of parking in front of her car. Police Officer Elton Young called the police dispatcher at 4:15 p.m. and reported the traffic accident, which occurred in front of 1744 35th Street, Bronx. Police Officer Mary Long questioned the driver of the Ford Mondeo. Both Police Officers reported to the dispatcher that the driver of the Mondeo and the driver of the damaged Sebring did not sustain any injuries. Also, there were two passengers in the Ford Mondeo, but they also did not sustain any injuries. One of the vehicles, the black Ford Mondeo, was driven and owned by a female, Alice Darwin. It had moderate damage to the front bumper. The other vehicle, the Chrysler Sebring, driven and owned by a female, Barbara Montaine, sustained moderate damage to the rear bumper.

Officer Young examined the vehicle registration certificates and license identification cards. The auto owned by Alice Darwin, age 43, was a 2012 black Ford Mondeo, N.Y. license plate 5687EF. Ms. Darwin's home address was 430 Abermarle Place, N.Y., N.Y. Ms. Darwin's N.Y. driver's license identification number is Y2321 38147 21376 and the expiration date is October 31, 2019.

The owner and driver of the 2010 Chrysler Sebring was Barbara Montaine, age 57, residing at 225 East 39th Street, Brooklyn, N.Y. Ms. Montaine's auto was a black 2010 Chrysler Sebring, NY license plate 5428HMU. Ms. Montaine's driver's license identification number is H3121 2344 2572 and the expiration is November 30, 2019.

Officers Young and Long completed a Vehicle Accident Report at 4:35 p.m. The report number was 224636754229.

-----

16. Select the best answer: The time of the accident is approximately:
A. 4:20 p.m.   C. 4:35 p.m.
B. 4:25 a.m.   D. 4:10 p.m.

----

17. Which of the following cars sustained damage to the front bumper?
A.   2012 black Ford Mondeo, N.Y. license plate 5678EF
B.   2010 Chrysler Sebring, NY license plate 5428KMU
C.   2012 black Ford Mondeo, N.Y. license plate 5687EF
D.   2010 Chrysler Sebring, NY license plate 5428HMU

----

18. At what time was the Vehicle Accident Report completed?
A. 4:35 a.m.   B. 4:10 p.m.   C. 4:05 p.m.   D. 4:35 p.m.

----

19. Which of the following statements is correct?
A. The license plate number of the car owned by Alice Darwin is 5587EF.
B. The vehicle accident report number is 22463675429.
C. Police Officer Elton Young called the police dispatcher at 4:35 p.m.
D. The vehicle driven by Alice Darwin had damage to the front bumper.

----

20. Which of the following statements is correct?
A. Police Officer Mary Long examined the vehicle registration certificates.
B. Police Officer Elton Young called the police dispatcher at 4:15 a.m.
C. Officers Young and Long completed a Vehicle Accident Report at 4:35 a.m.
D. Mr. Montaine's driver's license identification number is H3121 2344 2572.

Questions 21 - 26

Answer questions 21 - 26 based on the information contained in the following paragraphs.

Police Officers Gary Wilks and Helen Dansing were on patrol in their squad car on June 12, 2016 when at 3:25 p.m. a female approached them. The female stated that she had just been involved in a car accident with the white Honda that was now stopped next to her car, a black Ford. Police Officer Gary Wilks called the police dispatcher at 3:30 p.m. and reported the traffic accident (which occurred in front of 2877 West 137th Street, Jamaica). Police Officer Helen Dansing questioned the driver of the white Honda. Both Police Officers reported to the dispatcher that both drivers did not sustain any injuries. Also, there were no passengers in the two cars. One of the vehicles, the black Ford, was driven and owned by a female, Catrina Follins. It had damage to the rear bumper. The other vehicle, driven by a female, Ella Spivitz, had damage to the front bumper.

Officer Dansing examined the driver's licenses, vehicle registration certificates and vehicle insurance identification cards. The auto driven by Catrina Follins, age 45, was a black 2008 Ford, N.Y. license plate 17548TU, owned by the driver, residing at 225 Nolan Road, Brooklyn, N.Y. Ms. Follins' N.Y. driver's license identification number is K2537 68497 62435 and the expiration date is December 31, 2016.

The driver and owner of the other auto was Ella Spivitz, age 25, residing at 297 Jefferson Drive, Bronx, N.Y. Ms. Spivitz's auto was a 2010 white Honda, NY license plate 7451LBM. Ms. Spivitz's driver's license identification number is F545 293 934 and the expiration is November 30, 2016.

Officers Wilks and Dansing completed a Vehicle Accident Report at 3:40 p.m. The report number was 324576764321.

-----

21. Select the best answer: The closest time of the accident is approximately:
A. after 4:15 p.m.
B. after 3:25 p.m.
C. before 3:25 p.m.
D. after 3:40 p.m.

----

22. Which car sustained damage to the front bumper?
A. NY plate #17548TU, black 2008 Ford
B. NY plate #7451LBM, white 2010 Honda
C. NY plate #17548TU, white 2010 Honda
D. NY plate #7451LBM, black 2008 Ford

----

23. What is the total number of persons involved in the accident?
A. 1
B. 2
C. 3
D. none of the above

----

24. The owner of the vehicle with damage to the rear bumper resides at:
A. 225 Nolan Road, Bronx, N.Y.
B. 297 Jefferson Drive, Bronx, N.Y.
C. 225 Nolan Road, Brooklyn, N.Y.
D. 297 Jefferson Drive, Brooklyn, N.Y.

----

25. Which of the following is correct?
A. The report number was 324576764327.
B. Ms. Follins' N.Y. driver's license identification number is K2537 68497 65435
C. The driver and owner of the 2008 black Ford was Ella Spivitz
D. the black Ford, was driven and owned by a female, Catrina Follins.

----

26. Which of the following is not correct?
A. The driver and owner of the 2010 white Honda was Ella Spivitz
B. the black Ford, was driven and owned by a female, Catrina Follins.
C. The report number was 324576764321.
D. Ms. Follins' N.Y. driver's license identification number is K2537 68497 62432.

Questions 27 - 34

27. An officer is reviewing a report he is preparing. It contains the following two drafts. Which of the two drafts are grammatically correct?

1. One of the greatest challenges that a Police Officer faces is the application of broad policies and procedures to specific situations, unlike specific guidelines, broad policies prescribe the boundaries of acceptable behaviors and responses to a wide spectrum of applications.

2. One of the greatest challenges that a Police Officer faces is the application of broad policies and proccedures to specific situations. Unlike specific guidelines, broad policies prescribe the boundaries of acceptable behaviors and responses to a wide spectrum of applications.

A. Only draft 1 is grammatically correct.
B. Only draft 2 is grammatically correct.

C. Both drafts 1 and 2 are grammatically correct.

D. Neither draft 1 nor draft 2 is grammatically correct.

----

28. An officer is asked by his partner to review a report that the officer is preparing. It contains the following two versions of one part of the report. Which versions are grammatically correct?

     1. Certain items carried by persons entering the precinct building must be vouchered by the Police Officer on duty and stored in the main safe. Upon leaving the building, the person who owns the item may at any time during the day present his voucher to the officer who will retrieve the item from the safe and return it to him.

     2. Certain items carried by members of the public entering the precict building must be vouchered by the Police Officer on duty and stored in the main safe. Upon leaving the building, the member of the public who owns the item may at any time during the day present his voucher to the officer who will retrieve the item from the safe and return it to the member of the public.

A. Only version 1 is grammatically correct.
B. Only version 2 is grammatically correct.
C. Both versions 1 and 2 are grammatically correct.
D. Neither version 1 nor version 2 is grammatically correct.

----

29. An officer is preparing a report and has not decided which of two versions he wishes to use. Which of the following two versions are grammatically correct?

     1. Mr. Betancourt and Ms. Spellman has not decided whether to attend the meeting. Both will inform us of their decision before this evening.

     2. Mr. Betancourt and Ms. Spellman has not decided whether to attend the meeting; both will inform us of their decision before this evening.

A. Only version 1 is grammatically correct.
B. Only version 2 is grammatically correct.
C. Both version 1 and 2 are grammatically correct.
D. Neither version 1 nor version 2 is grammatically correct.

----

30. Police Officer George Prior is preparing a speech that he will give at a Community Board meeting. Which of the following two versions are correct?

1. Unattended items, especially bags and luggage, are a main security concerns. If you see an unattended bag or luggage, notify the person at the main desk.

2. If you see an unattended bag or luggage, notify the person at the main desk, unattended items, especially bags and luggage are a main security concern.

A. 1 only is correct.

B. 2 only is correct.

C. Neither 1 nor 2 is correct.

D. Both 1 and 2 are correct.

----

31. Police Officer Janet Ryker is preparing an instruction sheet on how to process reports. Which of the following two versions are correct?

1. Form A must be filled out and submitted within 24 hours. Form B must also be submitted with Form A if an ambulance was used to transport any victim to a medical facility.

2. Form A must be filled out and submitted within 24 hours, Form B must also be submitted with Form A if an ambulance was used to transport any victim to a medical facility.

A. 1 only is correct.

B. 2 only is correct.

C. Neither 1 nor 2 is correct.

D. Both 1 and 2 are correct.

----

32. Police Officer John McGee is checking the correctness of sentences in one of his reports. Which of the following two versions are correct?

1. A Police Officer must always be vigilant. Sometimes small clues lead to important discoveries.

2. Sometimes small clues lead to important discoveries because a Police Officer must always be vigilant.

A. 1 only is correct.   C. Neither 1 nor 2 is correct.

B. 2 only is correct.   D. Both 1 and 2 are correct.

33. Officer Bryer is asked to select the best summary (A, B, C, or D) of the following information: (The best summary is the one that expresses the information in the most clear, accurate and complete manner.)

Place of accident: in front of 245 East 25ᵗʰ Street, Bronx
Time of accident: 3:05 P.M.
Date of accident: July 20, 2016
Vehicle involved: 2008 Camri
Driver: Bella Lugowski
Damage: cracked windshield
Details: A traffic light loosened from its supports and struck the windshield of the 2008 Camri.

A. On July 20, 2016, at 3:05 P.M., in front of 245 East 25ᵗʰ Street, Bronx, a traffic light loosened from its supports and struck the windshield of a 2008 Camri, owned by Bella Lugowski.

B. On July 20, 2016, in front of 245 East 25ᵗʰ Street, Bronx, a traffic light loosened from its supports and struck the windshield of a 2008 Camri, driven by Bella Lugowski.

C. On July 20, 2016, at 3:05 P.M., in front of 245 East 25ᵗʰ Street, Bronx, a traffic light loosened from its supports and struck the windshield of a 2008 Camri.

D. On July 20, 2016, at 3:05 P.M., in front of 245 East 25ᵗʰ Street, Bronx, a traffic light loosened from its supports and cracked the windshield of a 2008 Camri, driven by Bella Lugowski.

----

34. Police Officer Edington collects the following information at the scene of a traffic accident:

Date of accident: September 9, 2016
Time of accident: 1:10 P.M.
Place of accident: intersection of 98ᵗʰ Street and Dwayne Avenue, Staten Island
Vehicles involved: 2008 Nissan and 2012 Buick
Drivers: Ben Morley (2008 Nissan) and Marcia Costa (2012 Buick)
Damage: dent on driver's door of 2012 Buick; no damage to the 2008 Nissan

-----

Police Officer Edington drafts four versions of a report to express the above information. Which of the following four versions is most clear, accurate and complete?

A. On September 9, 2016, at 1:10 P.M., at the intersection of 98th Street and Dwayne Avenue, Staten Island, a 2012 Nissan and a 2008 Buick were involved in a traffic accident. The 2012 Buick, driven by Marcia Costa, sustained a dent on the driver's door. The 2008 Nissan, driven by Ben Morley, did not sustain any damage.

B. On September 9, 2016, at 1:10 P.M., at the intersection of 89th Street and Dwayne Avenue, Staten Island, a 2008 Nissan and a 2012 Buick were involved in a traffic accident. The 2012 Buick, driven by Marcia Costa, sustained a dent on the driver's door. The 2008 Nissan, driven by Ben Morley, did not sustain any damage.

C. On September 9, 2016, at 1:10 P.M., at the intersection of 98th Street and Dwayne Avenue, Staten Island, a 2008 Nissan and a 2012 Buick were involved in a traffic accident. The 2012 Buick, driven by Marcia Costa, sustained a dent on the passenger's front door. The 2008 Nissan, driven by Ben Morley, did not sustain any damage.

D. On September 9, 2016, at 1:10 P.M., at the intersection of 98th Street and Dwayne Avenue, Staten Island, a 2008 Nissan and a 2012 Buick were involved in a traffic accident. The 2012 Buick, driven by Marcia Costa, sustained a dent on the driver's door. The 2008 Nissan, driven by Ben Morley, did not sustain any damage.

Questions 35 – 40

35. While patrolling the area surrounding a shopping mall, Police Officer Marero is informed by a female that she has just discovered that the wallet inside her handbag is missing and that she is not sure whether she left it at home or whether she has just been pickpocketed.

According to the information provided by the female, Police Officer Marero should:

A. question all persons in the nearby area.

B. go into the shopping mall and complain to the security captain.

C. ask the female to check at home and if she does not find the wallet, to report it to the police.

D. question all unescorted females surrounding the mall, as the pickpocket is probably a female working alone.

----

36. Police Officer David Fitzgerald notices that the plastic cover of a traffic light is cracked, but does not pose an immediate danger. He has several traffic cones with him. Police Officer Fitzgerald should:

A. immediately barricade all lanes to stop all traffic and thereby decrease the possibility of an accident.

B. immediately barricade all lanes except one in order to keep traffic moving.

C. report the cracked plastic cover to the proper authority.

D. take no action, as traffic lights are not the responsibility of the police department.

----

37. At midnight, during his patrol, Police Officer William Reese notices that the padlock of the metal roll down gate of a store is on the floor. The contact number for the gate repair company is on a sticker on the gate. Another sticker has a contact number for the owner of the store.

Based on the preceding information, what is the first step that Police Officer Reese should take?

A. He should call for backup since he is on patrol alone.

B. Quickly tape the area to preserve the crime scene.

C. Call the owner and inform him and see if he is aware that the lock is on the floor.

D. Roll up the gate and go inside the store to see if there are any persons in there.

----

38. At 8:00 p.m. your sergeant asks that you patrol a school yard and see if there are any persons there. Because of gang fights, the school yard was posted with a sign that no one should be in there after 7:00 p.m. As you pass by the school yard, you see an elderly man sitting on a bench and feeding pigeons. What is the first step you should take in this situation?

A. Arrest the man, as his age does not give him special privileges.

B. Leave the man alone, as he is elderly and feeding pigeons.

C. Take the man to the precinct for questioning.

D. Ask the man if he is aware that he is not permitted in the school yard after 7:00 p.m.

----

39. Police Officer Tina Barley is on patrol alone when she notices a man comfortably sleeping on a bench, a machete in his hand and his shirt stained with dried blood from a wound on his shoulder. On the floor next to him is an open bottle of vodka.

Based on the preceding information, what should Police Officer Barley do first?

A. Pick up the bottle and taste the liquid to see if it actually is vodka.

B. Gently wake the man and ask him if he needs assistance.

C. Call for backup and medical assistance.

D. Go into a nearby apartment house and investigate the situation.

----

40. Prior to the start of your patrol, your sergeant informs you that a nearby public school has reported that a thin white male was seen trying to entice young children into his red car. What should you do first?

A. Quickly go to the school area and question all thin white males.

B. Quickly go to the school area and question all thin white males in cars.

C. Be vigilant for any white males in a red car lingering near the school.

D. Do nothing as the information provided is not sufficient to take any action.

_____

"Good things come to people who wait, but better things come to those who go out and get them."

- Anonymous

Questions 41 - 43

Answer question 41 based on the following PL 80.05 table.

PL 80.05 FINES FOR MISDEMEANORS AND VIOLATIONS:

Offense	Fine	Alternative Sentence
A misdemeanor	up to $1000.00	Court may sentence the defendant to pay an amount not exceeding double the amount of the defendant's gain.
B misdemeanor	up to $500.00	
Unclassified Misdemeanor	in accordance with law or ordinance that defines the crime	
Violation	up to $250.00	

41. Which of the following statements is correct?

A. Fines for violations can only be $25.00 or less.

B. Fines for all misdemeanors must be over $500.

C. Fines for all B misdemeanors must be $500 or more.

D. Fine for an "A" misdemeanor cannot be greater than $1,000.00

Answer question 42 based on the following CPL 30.30 table.

CPL 30.30 Where a defendant has been committed to the custody of the sheriff, he must be released on bail or his own recognizance where the people are not ready for trial within the following days after commencement of defendant's commitment to the custody of the sheriff:

Offense committed	People must be ready for trial within this period (after the commencement of defendant's commitment to the custody of the sheriff)
felony	90 days
misdemeanor with jail term over 3 months	30 days
misdemeanor with jail term up to 3 months	15 days
petty offense	5 days

42. Based on the above table, where the defendant has been committed to the custody of the sheriff and the charge is a petty offense, the people must be ready for trial within _____ days after the commencement of defendant's commitment to the custody of the sheriff.

A. 15 days

B. 5 days

C. 90 days

D. 30 days

Answer question 43 based on the following section of CPL 110.10

CPL 110.10 How to require defendant's appearance for arraignment in a local criminal court

Prior to the commencement of a criminal action, a person may be compelled to appear in a local criminal court for arraignment upon an accusatory instrument to be filed at or before his appearance by:

  (a) an arrest made without a warrant (CPL 140), or

  (b) issuance and service upon him of an appearance ticket (CPL 150).

-----

43. Based on CPL 110.10, which of the following statements is not correct?

A. A person may be compelled to appear in a Local Criminal Court for arraignment upon an accusatory instrument to be filed at or before his appearance by an arrest made without a warrant (CPL 140), or issuance and service upon him of an appearance ticket (CPL 150).

B. A person cannot be compelled to appear in a criminal court prior to the commencement of a criminal action.

C. A person may be compelled to appear in a Local Criminal Court for arraignment upon an accusatory instrument to be filed at or before his appearance by an arrest made without a warrant.

D. A person may be compelled to appear in a Local Criminal Court for arraignment upon an accusatory instrument to be filed at or before his appearance by the issuance and service upon him of an appearance ticket (CPL 150).

Deductive Reasoning: Question 44

Below is a drawing of a "Revolver" and 4 more drawings of revolvers (A, B, C, and D).

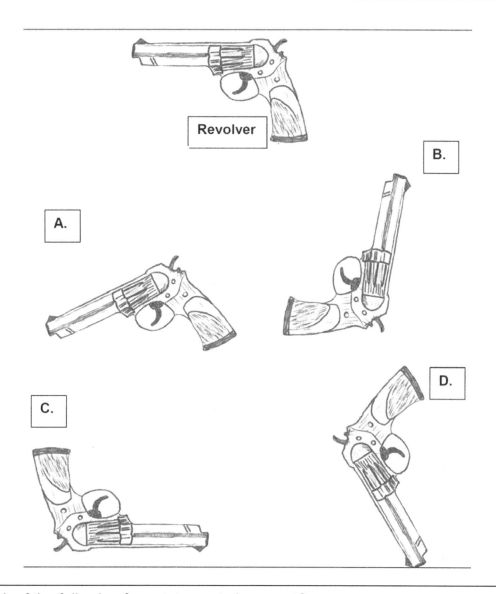

44. Which of the following four statements is correct?

A. Drawing "A" is different from the "Revolver" drawing.

B. Drawing "B" is different from the "Revolver" drawing.

C. Drawing "C" is different from the "Revolver" drawing.

D. Drawings "A", "B", "C," and "D" are the same as the "Revolver" drawing.

Questions 45 - 47

Answer questions 45 - 47 based on the definitions provided in the following summary of Penal Law Section 10.00.

Penal Law (PL) S 10.00

A **Traffic infraction** is an offense defined as a traffic infraction in section 155 of the Vehicle and Traffic Law.

A **Violation** is an offense (other than a traffic infraction) for which a sentence in excess of 15 days cannot be imposed.

A **Misdemeanor** is an offense (other than a traffic infraction) for which a sentence of more than 15 days and up to and including a year can be imposed.

A **Felony** is an offense for which a sentence of more than 1 year can be imposed.

A **Crime** means a misdemeanor or a felony.

Physical injury means impairment of physical condition or substantial pain.

Serious physical injury means physical injury which creates a substantial risk of death, or which causes death or serious and protracted disfigurement, protracted impairment of health or protracted loss or impairment of the function of any bodily organ.

Deadly physical force means physical force which under the circumstances used is readily capable of causing death or other serious physical injury.

Deadly weapon means any loaded weapon from which a shot, readily capable of producing death or other serious physical injury, may be discharged, or any of the following: switchblade knife, gravity knife, pilum ballistic knife, metal knuckle knife, dagger, billy, blackjack, plastic knuckles, metal knuckles.

Dangerous instrument means any instrument, including a vehicle, which is readily capable of causing death or other serious physical injury.

-----

45. Based on the definitions in the above summary of Penal Law 10.00, which of the following statements is not correct?

A. A "dagger' is defined as a deadly weapon.

B. A violation is defined as a "crime."

C. A car is a dangerous instrument.

D. A sentence for a violation may be for 15 days.

46. Based on the definitions in the above summary of Penal Law 10.00, which of the following statements is correct?

A. A sentence of 13 months may be imposed for a misdemeanor.

B. Traffic infractions are defined in the Penal Law.

C. A sentence of 360 days may be imposed for a misdemeanor.

D. Deadly weapons and dangerous instruments have the same definition.

----

47. According to Penal Law (PL) S 10.00, which of the following statements is not correct?

A. Serious physical injury means physical injury which creates a substantial risk of death, or which causes death or serious and protracted disfigurement, protracted impairment of health or protracted loss or impairment of the function of any bodily organ.

B. Deadly physical force means physical force which under the circumstances used is readily capable of causing death or other serious physical injury.

C. Dangerous weapon means any instrument, including a vehicle, which is readily capable of causing death or other serious physical injury.

D. Deadly weapon means any loaded weapon from which a shot, readily capable of producing death or other serious physical injury, may be discharged, or any of the following: switchblade knife, gravity knife, pilum ballistic knife, metal knuckle knife, dagger, billy, blackjack, plastic knuckles, metal knuckles.

Questions 48 - 51 are based on the following map. In answering the questions, follow the flow of traffic, as indicated by the arrows. Names of streets, buildings, public areas, and points 1-9 are indicated on the map.

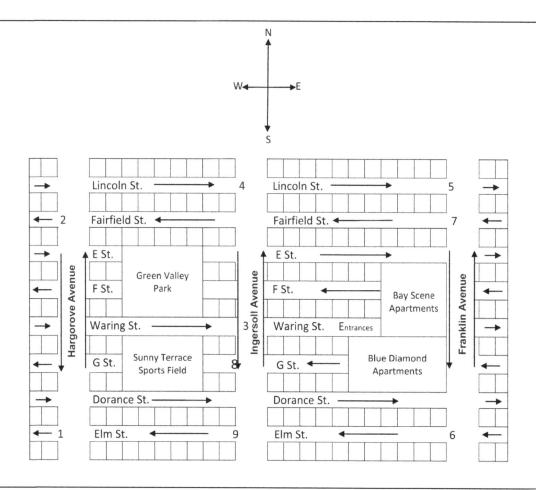

48. Imagine that you are at Dorance Street and Franklin Avenue and then drive north to Fairfield Street, then turn west to Ingersoll Avenue, then travel south to Elm Street, then west to Hargrove Avenue. Near which number location will you be nearest?

A. 6   B. 1   C. 9   D. 8

49. If you start your drive at point number 6, then drive north to Fairfield Street, then drive south to Elm St., then west to Hargrove Avenue, you will be closest to which point?

A. 6   B. 1   C. 9   D. 8

50. You are driving south in your patrol car and are at the intersection of Lincoln St. and Franklin Avenue. You are informed that an auto accident has just occurred at the intersection of Elm Street and Ingersoll Avenue. Assuming that you must obey all traffic signs, which one of the following four choices describes the most direct route?

A. Drive south on Franklin Avenue to Elm Street, then drive east on Elm Street to Ingersoll Avenue.

B. Drive north on Franklin Avenue to Elm Street, then drive west on Elm Street to Ingersoll Avenue.

C. Drive east on Franklin Avenue to Elm Street, then drive west on Elm Street to Ingersoll Avenue.

D. Drive south on Franklin Avenue to Elm Street, then drive west on Elm Street to Ingersoll Avenue.

----

51. You are driving north in your patrol car and are at Ingersoll Avenue and E St. You are informed that there is a fight between two males at the corner of Lincoln Street and Franklin Avenue. Which one of the following four choices describes the most direct route?

A. Drive south to Lincoln St., then west on Lincoln St. to the corner of Lincoln St. and Franklin Avenue.

B. Drive north to Lincoln St., then west on Lincoln St. to the corner of Lincoln St. and Franklin Avenue.

C. Drive north to Fairfield Street, then east to the corner of Lincoln St. and Franklin Avenue.

D. Drive north to Lincoln St. then make a right and continue to the corner of Lincoln St. and Franklin Avenue.

----

52. During the month of September 2016 there were 8 burglaries reported in Police Officer Cohen's precinct. In two of the burglaries, neighbors reported that at the approximate time of the burglaries they witnessed a female white, average height, shoulder length dark hair, "with a small rose tattoo on the left side of her neck." Both times the female was carrying a striped shopping bag out of the residence that had been burglarized. They also reported that at both times she had been wearing a pink T-shirt, dark blue dungarees, and pink sneakers.

During his patrol, Officer Cohen stops four white females for questioning. He had recorded in his memo book the description given by the two witnesses. Which piece of information should Officer Cohen consider the most important and pay careful attention in identifying the suspected burglar?

A. the dark blue dungarees

B. small rose tattoo on the left side of her neck

C. the shoulder length, dark hair

D. the pink T-shirt

53. Officer Marietta James learns at the precinct that a female, 75 years old, had been mugged one hour earlier by a person who the victim described as a "white young female, about twenty years old, with dark hair tied in a shoulder length ponytail, and with a mole at the base of her nose." The victim also described the perpetrator as wearing black pants, a red T-shirt, and black sneakers.

During her patrol, Officer James sees a group of three white females, about 20 – 25 years old, drinking beer in front of a 24-hour store. Officer James stops her patrol car about thirty feet away to get a better look at the three females. Which of the following parts of the description provided by the victim is most important for Officer James to consider in her attempt to identify the possible suspect?

A. the red T-shirt

B. the shoulder length pony tail

C. the black sneakers

D. the mole at the base of her nose

----

54. Police Officer Jenkins is assigned to patrol a shopping area which includes four "99 cent stores." During the last four weeks, crime statistics show that four shoplifters were reported at the Amazing 99 Cent Store, all between the hours of 10:00 a.m. and 4:00 p.m. At the Whacko 99 Cent Store two robberies were reported. At Crown Discount Store three front windows were broken (one in each of three occasions). At the Goody Discount Store three bicycles were stolen from the sidewalk in front of the store. The shoplifters were reported between 9:30 a.m. and 4:30 p.m. The robberies occurred between 9:30 a.m. and 10:30 a.m. The bicycles were all reported stolen in the afternoon and before 5:00 p.m.

Officer Jenkins works the 9:00 a.m. to 5:00 p.m. tour. On Tuesday, his sergeant instructs him to pay careful attention to robberies. To try to reduce the number of robberies, Office Jenkins should patrol the:

A. Amazing 99 Cent Store

B. Goody Discount Store

C. Whacko 99 Cent Store

D. Crown Discount Store

----

55. On Wednesday Officer Jenkins also works the 9:00 a.m. to 5:00 p.m. tour. On Wednesday, his sergeant tells him that three more bicycles were stolen at the same store as in the previous four weeks and instructs him to pay careful attention to bicycle thefts. To try to reduce the number of bicycle thefts, Officer Jenkins should patrol the:

A. Amazing 99 Cent Store

B. Goody Discount Store

C. Whacko 99 Cent Store

D. Crown Discount Store

_____

Questions 56 - 57

Answer questions 56 - 57 based on the following "Enterprise Zone Security Procedure."

_____

A business enterprise zone has been established in Brooklyn. Although private security patrols the area and is primarily responsible for enforcing zone rules, there has been a recent increase in crimes. The Mayor's Office and the management of the enterprise zone have asked for NYPD assistance.

Your sergeant has assigned you to the enterprise zone entrance gate and has directed you to follow the "Enterprise Zone Security Procedure."

Enterprise Zone Security Procedure

1. At the gated entrance to the enterprise zone, you are to randomly check the Enterprise Zone I.D. cards of incoming individuals.

2. Drivers of incoming vehicles must produce a driver's license, registration, and proof of insurance upon your request.

3. If the driver is transporting alcohol, the driver must present identification that proves the driver is of legal age to drink.

4. If proper I.D. is not produced, you are to inform the private security staff.

-----

56. On your first day at the enterprise zone, you question a driver of an incoming vehicle who states that he forgot his Enterprise Zone I.D. at home. Based on the above procedure, which of the following is the most correct action to take?

A. Ask the driver to go home and get his I.D.

B. Deny entry to the driver unless he can produce an official NYS issued I.D.

C. Conduct a thorough search of the vehicle.

D. Contact the private security staff and inform them.

----

57. According to the "Enterprise Zone Security Procedure," which of the following statements is correct?

A. A person who does not have proper I.D. must be detained.

B. Alcohol is not permitted within the enterprise zone.

C. Enterprise Zone I.D. cards cannot be checked by police officers.

D. A driver's license must be produced upon request.

Energy and persistence conquer all things.

- Benjamin Franklin

Questions 58 - 59

Answer questions 58 - 59 on the basis of the following "Building Bomb Search Procedure," received by Police Officer Wells.

Building Bomb Search Procedure

1. Officers will be assigned to search specified areas.

2. If a suspicious object is found:
    a. do not touch the object
    b. keep the area clear of other people
    c. inform security headquarters

3. Be prepared to evacuate all others and yourself.

4. When instructed by security headquarters, evacuate the building according to instructions.

5. Request all persons to take with them all personal belongings when evacuating.

-----

58. Officer Wells is assigned to do a bomb search of the first floor of a three-story paint and household items store. Halfway through his search, he discovers a very suspicious package under a display counter. He listens and hears a distinct ticking sound. There are four other persons on the first floor. Based on the above "Building Bomb Search Procedure," Officer Wells should first:

A. instruct all persons to gather their belongings, as he is about to report the suspicious package and an evacuation may be necessary.
B. issue an evacuation order, as the bomb is ticking and could go off at any second.
C. take the package and put it in an unoccupied section of the store to avoid fatalities.
D. keep the area clear of other people and inform security headquarters.

----

59. According to the preceding "Building Bomb Search Procedure":

A. When a police officer is instructed by security headquarters to evacuate the building, the officer must request that all persons take with them all personal and business belongings when evacuating.

B. An officer shall never evacuate himself or herself from the building.

C. If a suspicious object is found, the police officer must inform security headquarters.

D. All officers are assigned to search all areas of the building.

Questions 60 - 68

60. You and another officer notice a boy crying at the curb. He tells you that a man in a yellow car just tried to pull him into the car. You notice a yellow car heading northbound to the end of the block where it makes a right turn. While your partner stays with the boy, you follow the yellow car and observe the car continuing for two more blocks before turning left.

According to the information in the preceding passage, you would be most correct to radio that you last saw the car heading:

A) north   B) south   C) east   D) west

----

61. While in your patrol car, you notice a car with stolen license plates heading southbound. You follow the car, which after eight blocks makes a right turn and then after two more blocks makes a left turn.

According to the information in the preceding passage, you would be most correct to radio that you last saw the car heading:

A) north   B) south   C) east   D) west

----

62. Your attention is drawn to a taxi cab driver shouting "He robbed me!" and pointing to a man running down the block. You shout for the man to stop, but he continues running westbound. After four blocks, he makes a right turn and runs for three more blocks before making a left turn.

According to the information in the preceding passage, you would be most correct to radio that you last saw the man heading:

A) north   B) south   C) east   D) west

----

63. You and another officer witness a man grab a purse from a baby carriage. You shout for the man to stop, but he runs down the block in a westbound direction. You chase the man for two blocks before he turns right and then for another block, at which point he makes another right.

According to the information in the preceding passage, you would be most correct to radio that the man was running:

A) north   B) south   C) east   D) west

----

64. While in your patrol car, you witness two men run out of a donut shop, each holding a pouch and a revolver. They quickly get into a car and head northbound. You follow. After three blocks, they make a right turn and then after two more blocks they make a left turn.

According to the information in the preceding passage, you would be most correct to radio that you last saw the car heading:

A) north   B) south   C) east   D) west

----

65. Your attention is drawn to a pedestrian shouting, "He just broke the store window!" and pointing to a man running in an eastbound direction. After three blocks, he makes a left turn and runs for two more blocks before making a right turn.

According to the information in the preceding passage, you would be most correct to radio that you last saw the man heading:

A) north   B) south   C) east   D) west

----

66. You and another officer notice a male shouting, "He just robbed me!" and pointing to a male running away from the scene. You notice a man running down the block westbound to the end of the block where he makes a right turn. While your partner stays with the victim, you follow the man and observe him continuing to run for four blocks before turning left.

According to the information in the preceding passage, you would be most correct to radio that you last saw the man running:

A) north   B) south   C) east   D) west

----

67. While in your patrol car, you notice a blue car sideswipe a parked car and then drive off northbound without stopping. You follow the car, which after five blocks makes a right turn and then after two more blocks makes a left turn.

According to the information in the preceding passage, you would be most correct to radio that you last saw the car heading:

A) east   B) south   C) north   D) west

----

68. A gas station employee points down the block and shouts, "That guy just robbed us!" You shout for the man to stop, but he continues running westbound. After four blocks, he makes a left turn and runs for two more blocks before making another left turn.

According to the information in the preceding passage, you would be most correct to radio that you last saw the suspect heading:

A) north   B) south   C) east   D) west

Question 69

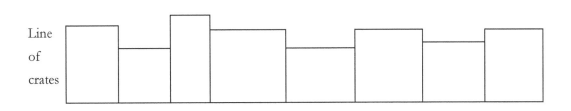

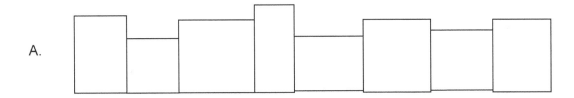

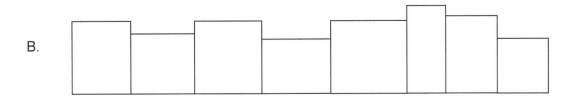

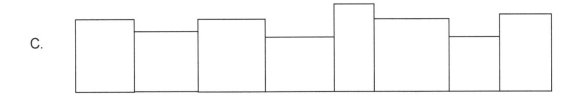

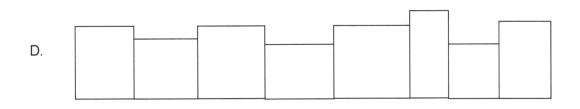

69. The "Line of Crates" when viewed from the back would appear as which of the following choices?

A. Choice A
B. Choice B

C. Choice C
D. Choice D

Questions 70 - 75

Read the following passage, then answer questions 70 – 75 on the basis of the information contained in the passage.

While on patrol, Police Officers Durley and Golan are dispatched to 1492 Brighton Avenue, first floor "Texas AA Prime Meats, Inc." at 9:20 p.m. on November 22, 2016. The owner of "Texas AA Prime Meats" had just called 911 to report a burglary. They arrive at the store at 9:25 p.m. and are greeted by Mr. Marvin West, the owner of the store and Mr. Barnie Leiber, an employee of "Texas AA Prime Meats."

Mr. Marvin West tells the officers that he and Barnie Leiber had closed the store for the day at 7:00 p.m. They had locked the front and back doors and properly rolled down the security gate and padlocked it. Mr. West received a call at 9:01 p.m. from a neighbor who happened to be passing by the store when he saw men trying to enter the building. Mr. West checked his security cameras on his home TV screen. Although security camera #1 showed the outdoor front entrance and security camera #4 showed the outdoor back door area, it was with security cameras #2 and #3 that he saw the burglars. Security camera # 2 covered the outdoor roof skylight and security camera # 3 covered the inside area of the store, including the cashier area.

Two burglars, all dressed in black and wearing grey face masks, had broken the glass in the skylight and with a rope had descended into the store. The smaller of the two persons descended first and the much taller one followed. The person who descended first carried a black garbage bag and the other person held a flash light in the right hand.

The two burglars took all the $139.00 cash and coins that had been left in the cash register, a box of filet mignon steaks valued at $455.00, three identical meat cutting machines worth a total of $1,500.00, two professional electric knives worth $219 each, and six carving boards worth $119.00 each. Mr. West tells the officers that he will prepare a complete list of missing items as soon as possible.

Mr. West tells Officer Golan that he is 55 years old and lives at 1830 Crichton Avenue in Brooklyn. His cell number is 718-555-7928. Barnie Leiber tells Officer Golan that he is 28 years old and lives at 2875 East 27 Street, Brooklyn. His cell number is 718-555-8311.

Police Officers Durley and Golan complete their investigation at 10:15 p.m. Before they completed their crime report, they performed a careful sweep of the store to make certain that the burglars had left.

-----

70. Which of the following security cameras cover the cashier area?

A. 1 and 2 only

B. 2 only

C. 1 and 3 only

D. 3 only

----

71. Which of the following statements is correct?

A. The address of Texas AA Prime Meats is 1495 Brighton Avenue, first floor.

B. The two burglars descended into the store using a chain.

C. The burglars were dressed in grey and wore black face masks.

D. The person who called 911 was Mr. West.

----

72. Which one of the following statements is correct? Among the items stolen were:

A. $193.00 cash and coins

B. three professional electric knives worth $219 each

C. six carving boards worth $119.00 each

D. a box of filet mignon steaks valued at $445.00

----

73. Which of the following statements is correct according to the information provided by Mr. West and Mr. Barnie Leiber?

A. Mr. West tells Officer Golan that he is 55 years old and lives at 1830 Crichton Avenue in Brooklyn. His cell number is 718-555-7982.

B. Mr. Barnie Leiber tells Officer Golan that he is 28 years old and lives at 2875 East 27 Avenue, Brooklyn. His cell number is 718-555-8311.

C. Mr. West tells Officer Golan that he is 55 years old and lives at 1830 Crichton Avenue in Brooklyn. His cell number is 718-555-7928.

D. Mr. Barnie Leiber tells Officer Golan that he is 28 years old and lives at 2857 East 27 Street, Brooklyn. His cell number is 718-555-8311.

----

74. Choose the best answer: The value of each of the meat cutting machines is:

A. $50

B. $500

C. $1,000

D. $1,500

----

75. The total value of all items missing is:

A. $3,027

B. $3,246

C. $2,651

D. $3,540

Question 76

During her patrol, Police Officer Dawn Heller is called to the scene of an accident. The driver/owner of vehicle #2 stated that he was driving on Hart Ave. when car #1 hit his car from behind, causing him to hit vehicle number 3.

Assume that all 3 vehicles were in their proper lanes of traffic.

Which of the following 4 diagrams best matches the statement of the driver of vehicle #2?

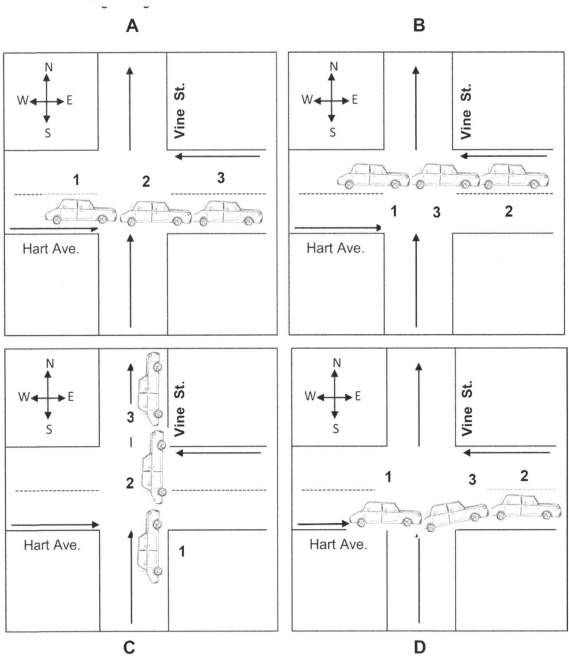

76. The diagram which best matches the statement of driver of vehicle #2 is:

A. diagram "A"

B. diagram "B"

C. diagram "C"

D. diagram "D"

Questions 77 - 79

Answer questions 77 – 79 based on the details provided.

Officer Unger collects the following details at the scene of an auto accident:

Date of Accident: August 16, 2016

Time of accident: 5:02 p.m.

Place of accident: intersection of Ferndale Avenue and Willows Avenue, Bronx

Driver: Fred Bellows

Vehicle: 2007 Toyota Sienna

Damage: damage to front bumper when vehicle struck a bicycle partially parked on the sidewalk, but protruding into the street

-----

77. Officer Unger is preparing a report of the accident and has four drafts of the report. He wishes to use the draft that expresses the information most clearly, accurately and completely. Which draft should he choose?

A. At 5:02 p.m., on August 16, 2016, at the intersection of Ferndale Avenue and Willows Avenue, Bronx, a vehicle driven by Fred Bellows struck a bicycle partially parked on the sidewalk, but protruding into the street.

B. On August 16, 2016, at 5:02 p.m., at the intersection of Ferndale Avenue and Willows Avenue, Bronx, a 2007 Toyota Sienna driven by Fred Belows struck a bicycle partially parked on the sidewalk, but protruding into the street.

C. At the intersection of Ferndale Avenue and Willows Avenue, Bronx, on August 16, 2016, at 2:05 p.m., a 2007 Toyota Sienna driven by Fred Bellows struck a bicycle partially parked on the sidewalk, but protruding into the street.

D. On August 16, 2016, at 5:02 p.m., at the intersection of Ferndale Avenue and Willows Avenue, Bronx, a 2007 Toyota Sienna driven by Fred Bellows sustained damage to the front bumper when it struck a bicycle partially parked on the sidewalk, but protruding into the street.

Officer Able responds to a car theft. She questions the owner of the vehicle who reported the car stolen and obtains the following information:

Suspect: Unidentified

Date of crime: August 15, 2016

Time of crime: between 6:20 p.m. and 11:30 p.m.

Place of crime: driveway in front of 167 28th Street, Staten Island

Crime: theft of car

Vehicle stolen: 2010 Volvo

Victim: owner of car, Charles Williams

-----

78. Officer Able is comparing the information she recorded in her memo pad (at the scene of the accident) to the information in her report. Which of the following choices (A, B, C, or D) has one detail that does not agree with the information in the officer's memo pad?

A. Date of crime: August 12, 2016; Time of crime: between 6:20 p.m. and 11:30 p.m.

B. Crime: theft of car

C. Victim: owner of car, Charles Williams

D. Vehicle stolen: 2010 Volvo

79. Officer Able is preparing a report of the accident and has prepared four drafts of the report. She wishes to use the draft that expresses the information most clearly, accurately and completely. Which of the following drafts should she choose?

A. A car theft of a 2010 Volvo happened at the driveway in front of 167 28th Street, Staten Island where Charles Williams' car was parked for the night. The alleged thief is unidentified, as the theft happened in the evening hours.

B. On August 15, 2016, between 6:20 p.m. and 11:30 p.m., at the driveway in front of 167 28th Street, Staten Island, a 2010 Volvo owned by Charles Williams was stolen by an unidentified suspect.

C. A car was stolen on August 15, 2016, between 6:20 p.m. and 11:30 p.m., at the driveway in front of 167 28th Street, Staten Island, owned by Charles Williams. The suspect is unidentified.

D. On August 15, 2016, at the driveway in front of 167 28th Street, Staten Island, between 6:30 p.m. and 11:30 p.m., a 2010 Volvo owned by Charles Williams was stolen by an unidentified suspect.

Answer question 80 based on the following "Procedure for Contact with Media."

Procedure for Contact with Media

When a criminal case is pending in the courts, the Police Officer who made the arrest is prohibited from discussing the case with any newspaper, magazine, TV reporters and all other media. Exceptions to this are when:

1. a New York court of competent jurisdiction formally orders the Police Officer to discuss one or more particulars of the case.

2. the NYPD orders such discussion.

3. the Police Officer is subpoenaed to testify before an authorized NYC, NYS or federal board.

4. a case is classified as R-16 by the NYPD Case Classification section.

-----

80. Police Officer Janet Peters arrests a person suspected of kidnapping a child who is still missing. The suspect has been indicted and is in jail, waiting for trial. A newspaper reporter, Brian Collins, contacts Officer Janet Peters and asks for information that might help the reporter to investigate the kidnapping and perhaps locate the missing child. He tells her that he checked with the NYPD Case Classification section and that the case is classified as an R-16 case. Officer Janet Peters should:

A. give assistance to Brian Collins by providing information that might help to locate the missing child.

B. give assistance only if the reporter can guarantee that the child will be found.

C. not provide any information until she confirms with the NYPD Case Classification section that the case is classified as an R-16 case.

D. provide only information relating to locating the child, and not any other information.

Questions 81 - 82

Answer questions 81 - 82 based on the following extracts of CPL 500.10.

CPL 500.10 Definitions

1. PRINCIPAL is a defendant in a criminal action, or person adjudged to be a material witness.

2. RELEASE ON OWN RECOGNIZANCE means to allow a principal to be at liberty during pendency of an action.

3. TO FIX BAIL means a court designating a sum of money, the posting of which allows the principal to be at liberty during the pendency of the criminal action.

4. COMMIT TO THE CUSTODY OF THE SHERIFF occurs when a court orders a principal confined and in the custody of the sheriff during the pendency of the criminal action.

5. SECURING ORDER is a court order which:

    1) commits a principal to custody of the sheriff, or

    2) fixes bail, or

    3) releases the principal on his own recognizance.

-----

81. Which of the following statements is correct?

A. A person can be committed to the custody of the sheriff only if he is a defendant in a criminal action.

B. If a defendant posts bail, he cannot be released.

C. A "principal" can only be a defendant in an action.

D. If a person is released on his own recognizance, he can remain at liberty during the pendency of the criminal action.

----

82. According to the definitions in CPL 500.10, which of the following statements is correct?

A. A principal means only a defendant in a criminal action.

B. A securing order cannot order the release of the principal on his own recognizance.

C. A judge cannot designate a sum of money when posting bail.

D. A securing order can order the release of the principal in his own recognizance.

----

83. A female, about 21 years old, reports that she had chained her poodle to a parking meter pole and gone into a beauty supplies store to purchase nail polish, only to discover when she came out of the store that her poodle had been stolen. Four witnesses give you four statements. Which of the following four statements is most likely to be correct?

A. The person who cut the chain and rode away with the bicycle was a male, white, about 30 years old and about five feet five inches tall. He was wearing black sneakers, blue dungarees, a white T-shirt, and a blue denim backpack. He headed south for one block and then made a right turn.

B. The person who cut the chain and rode away with the bicycle was a male, black, about 30 years old and about five feet five inches tall. He was wearing black sneakers, blue dungarees, a white T-shirt, and a blue denim backpack. He headed south for one block and then made a right turn.

C. The person who cut the chain and rode away with the bicycle was a male, white, about 50 years old and about five feet five inches tall. He was wearing black sneakers, blue dungarees, a white T-shirt, and a blue denim backpack. He headed south for one block and then made a right turn.

D. The person who cut the chain and rode away with the bicycle was a male, white, about 30 years old and about five feet five inches tall. He was wearing black sneakers, black dungarees, a white T-shirt, and a grey denim backpack. He headed south for one block and then made a right turn

84. Four witnesses to a hit and run accident tell Police Officer Tumi that they memorized the license plate number of the car that sped away from the accident. Which of the following is the most likely to be correct?

A. 8237AFN

B. 8587AFN

C. 8537AFN

D. 8531AFN

Answer question 85 based on the following table.

Summonses and Desk Appearance Tickets Issued by Police Officer Wooster

Week	Dates	Parking Summonses	Moving Summonses	Desk Appearance Tickets
1	Sept 1 – 7	14	15	3
2	Sept 8 -14	11	3	6
3	Sept 15 -21	16	10	1
4	Sept 22 – 28	9	12	5
5	Sept 29 – Oct 5	18	11	7

85. Police Officer Wooster is adding up the total number of summonses and Desk Appearance Tickets issued by her during the above five-week period. Which of the following four formulas should she use to arrive at the correct number of summonses that she issued?

A. 18+11+7

B. 3+6+1+5+7

C. 14+11+16+9+18+15+3+10+12+11+3+6+1+5+7

D. 1(14+11+16+9+18) + 2(15+3+10+12+11) + 3(3+6+1+5+7)

END OF TEST #2

PRACTICE TEST #2 ANSWERS

Memory Question

Study the photo below for the next ten minutes. Try to remember as many details about the people and objects as you can. During the ten minutes, you are not permitted to take any notes or write anything.

At the end of the ten minutes you will be asked to answer questions 1 – 10 (<u>without</u> looking back at the picture.)

(After ten minutes)

Instructions for questions 1 – 10:

<u>Without</u> looking back at the picture, answer questions 1 – 10 on the following page.

1. The number of people in the picture is:

A. 4   **B. 5**   C. 6   D. 7

2. Choose the best answer.

The person holding the cookie tray in the center of the picture is:

A. male white   B. female white   C. male black   **D. female black**

3. The man holding the wine bottle:

A. is wearing a T-shirt

B. has blonde hair

C. is wearing white pants

D. is wearing short pants

4. The woman on the extreme right is:

A. cutting meat

B. pouring a drink

C. mixing a salad

D. none of the above

5. The number of bottles in the picture is:

A. four

B. two

C. three

D. one

6. In the picture there are:

A. two women and three men

B. three women and three men

C. two men and three women

D. none of the above

7. Choose the best answer. The person on the far right is wearing a _____ shirt.

A. white

B. black

C. plaid

D. none of the above

8. On the back wall there is a:

A. a painting of the New York skyline.

B. a painting of the Eifel Tower.

C. a painting of a beach scene.

D. none of the above

9. The person holding the glass is:

A. a male with dark hair.

B. a male with blonde hair.

C. a female with blonde hair and taller than the person holding the wine bottle.

D. none of the above (a female with dark hair)

10. The person holding the cookie tray is wearing a glove that can be described as:

A. white

B. black

C. checkered

D. none of the above.

_____

Answers 11 - 15

Answer questions 11 - 15 based on the information contained in the following paragraphs.

Police Officers Jack Ellis and Rhonda Cordan were on patrol on November 3, 2016 when at **7:15 p.m.** they witnessed a minor traffic accident (in front of 2455 Elmer Street, in Staten Island). Officer Ellis called the Police Dispatcher at 7:25 p.m. and reported that **the two drivers and four passengers (two in each vehicle)** did not sustain any personal injuries. One of the vehicles, the one driven by a male named Fred Ulmer, did have minor damage to the driver's side door, and the other vehicle, **driven by a male named Oswald Trunger, had minor damage to the front bumper.**

Officer Cordan examined the driver's licenses, vehicle registration certificates and vehicle insurance identification cards. The auto driven by Fred Ulmer, age 49, was a **white 2010 Acura**, N.Y. license plate 2845AB, owned by the driver, residing at 282 Carle Road, New York, N.Y. Mr. Ulmer's N.Y. driver's license identification number is E172 73 561 and the expiration date is December 31, 2016.

The driver of the other auto was Oswald Trunger, age 50, residing at 3857 Elm Street, Brooklyn, N.Y. Mr. Trunger's auto was a **silver 2012 Ford Escape, NY license plate 325DKL**. Mr. Trunger's driver's license identification number is R261 392 142 and the expiration is November 30, 2016.

Officers Ellis and Cordan completed a Vehicle Accident Report at 7:35 p.m. The report number was **28332757362.**

-----

11. What is the time of the accident?

A. 7:25 p.m.

B. 7:15 p.m.
(CORRECT. "Police Officers Jack Ellis and Rhonda Cordan were on patrol on November 3, 2016 when at 7:15 p.m. they witnessed a minor traffic accident.")

C. 7:25 a.m.

D. before 7:10 p.m.

----

12. How many persons were injured as a result of the traffic accident?

A. 1

B. 0
(CORRECT. "…the two drivers, and four passengers (two in each vehicle) did not sustain any personal injuries.")

C. 2

D. 4

----

13. Which car sustained damage to the front bumper?

A.   NY plate #2845AB, white 2010 Acura

B.   NY plate #2845AB, white 2012 Acura

C.   NY plate #325DKL, silver 2012 Ford Escape
(CORRECT. "…the other vehicle, driven by a male named Oswald Trunger, had minor damage to the front bumper… Mr. Trunger's auto was a <u>silver</u> 2012 Ford Escape, NY license plate 325DKL.")

D.   NY plate #325DKL, white 2012 Ford Escape

----

14. Which of the following statements is not correct?

A. The auto driven by Oswald Trunger, age 50, was a silver 2012 Ford Escape.

B. The vehicle Accident Report number was 2832757362.
(The correct number is 283<u>3</u>2757362.)

C. Fred Ulmer, age 49, resides at 282 Carle Road, New York, N.Y.

D. Mr. Trunger's license plate number is 325DKL.

----

15. Which of the following is not correct?

A. The person residing at 282 Carle Road, New York, N.Y., has a N.Y. driver's license
         identification number of E172 73 561, expiration date of December 31, 2016.

B. Mr. Trunger, age 50, resides at 3857 Elm Street, Brooklyn, N.Y.
C. The auto driven by Fred Ulmer was a black 2010 Acura.
(The car was a <u>white</u> 2010 Acura.)

D. The accident occurred in front of 2455 Elmer Street, in Staten Island.

Answers 16 - 20

Answer questions 16 - 20 based on the information contained in the following paragraphs.

Police Officers Elton Young and Mary Long were on patrol in their squad car on November 14, 2016 when at **4:10 p.m.** a woman approached them. The woman stated that her parked car, a 2012 black Ford Mondeo just been struck by a 2010 Chrysler Sebring that was in the process of parking in front of her car. Police Officer Elton Young called the police dispatcher at 4:15 p.m. and reported the traffic accident, which occurred in front of 1744 35th Street, Bronx. Police Officer Mary Long questioned the driver of the Ford Mondeo. Both Police Officers reported to the dispatcher that the driver of the Mondeo and the driver of the damaged Sebring did not sustain any injuries. Also, there were two passengers in the Ford Mondeo, but they also did not sustain any injuries. One of the vehicles, **the black Ford Mondeo, was driven and owned by a female, Alice Darwin. It had moderate damage to the front bumper**. The other vehicle, the Chrysler Sebring, driven and owned by a female, Barbara Montaine, sustained moderate damage to the rear bumper.

Officer Young examined the vehicle registration certificates and license identification cards. The auto owned by Alice Darwin, age 43, was a **2012 black Ford Mondeo, N.Y. license plate 5687EF**. Ms. Darwin's home address was 430 Abermarle Place, N.Y., N.Y. Ms. Darwin's N.Y. driver's license identification number is Y2321 38147 21376 and the expiration date is October 31, 2019.

The owner and driver of the 2010 Chrysler Sebring was Barbara Montaine, age 57, residing at 225 East 39th Street, Brooklyn, N.Y. Ms. Montaine's auto was a black 2010 Chrysler Sebring, NY license plate 5428HMU. Ms. Montaine's driver's license identification number is **H3121 2344 2572** and the expiration is November 30, 2019.

Officers Young and Long completed a Vehicle Accident Report at **4:35 p.m**. The report number was 224636754229.

-----

16. Select the best answer: The time of the accident is approximately:

A. 4:20 p.m.

B. 4:25 a.m.

C. 4:35 p.m.

D. 4:10 p.m.
(CORRECT. "Police Officers Elton Young and Mary Long were on patrol in their squad car on November 14, 2016 when at 4:10 p.m. a woman approached them. The woman stated that her

parked car, a 2012 black Ford Mondeo just been struck by a 2010 Chrysler Sebring that was in the process of parking in front of her car.")

----

17. Which of the following cars sustained damage to the front bumper?

A.   2012 black Ford Mondeo, N.Y. license plate 5678EF

B.   2010 Chrysler Sebring, NY license plate 5428KMU

C.   2012 black Ford Mondeo, N.Y. license plate 5687EF
(CORRECT. "...the black Ford Mondeo, was driven and owned by a female, Alice Darwin. It had moderate damage to the front bumper.... The auto owned by Alice Darwin, age 43, was a 2012 black Ford Mondeo, N.Y. license plate 5687EF.")

D.   2010 Chrysler Sebring, NY license plate 5428HMU

----

18. At what time was the Vehicle Accident Report completed?

A. 4:35 a.m.

B. 4:10 p.m.

C. 4:05 p.m.

D. 4:35 p.m.
(CORRECT. "Officers Young and Long completed a Vehicle Accident Report at 4:35 p.m.")

----

19. Which of the following statements is correct?

A. The license plate number of the car owned by Alice Darwin is 5587EF.
(WRONG. The license plate number is 5687EF.)

B. The vehicle accident report number is 22463675429.
(WRONG. The correct accident report number is 224636754229.)

C. Police Officer Elton Young called the police dispatcher at 4:35 p.m.
(WRONG. Officer Young called the police dispatcher at 4:15 p.m.)

D. The vehicle driven by Alice Darwin had damage to the front bumper.
(CORRECT. "...the black Ford Mondeo, was driven and owned by a female, Alice Darwin. It had moderate damage to the front bumper.")

20. Which of the following statements is correct?

A. Police Officer Mary Long examined the vehicle registration certificates.
(**WRONG**. Police Officer <u>Young</u> examined the vehicle registration certificates.)

B. Police Officer Elton Young called the police dispatcher at 4:15 a.m.
(**WRONG**: Correct time is 4:15 <u>p.m.</u>)

C. Officers Young and Long completed a Vehicle Accident Report at 4:35 a.m.
(**WRONG**. Correct time is 4:35 <u>p.m.</u>)

D. Mr. Montaine's driver's license identification number is H3121 2344 2572.
(**CORRECT.** "Ms. Montaine's driver's license identification number is H3121 2344 2572.")

Answers 21 - 26

Answer questions 21 - 26 based on the information contained in the following paragraphs.

Police Officers Gary Wilks and Helen Dansing were on patrol in their squad car on June 12, 2016 when **at 3:25 p.m. a female approached them. The female stated that she had just been involved in a car accident** with the white Honda that was now stopped next to her car, a black Ford. Police Officer Gary Wilks called the police dispatcher at 3:30 p.m. and reported the traffic accident (which occurred in front of 2877 West 137th Street, Jamaica). Police Officer Helen Dansing questioned the driver of the white Honda. Both Police Officers reported to the dispatcher that both drivers did not sustain any injuries. Also, **there were no passengers in the two cars**. One of the vehicles, the black Ford, was driven and owned by a female, **Catrina Follins. It had damage to the rear bumper. The other vehicle, driven by a female, Ella Spivitz, had damage to the front bumper.**

Officer Dansing examined the driver's licenses, vehicle registration certificates and vehicle insurance identification cards. **The auto driven by Catrina Follins, age 45, was a black 2008 Ford, N.Y. license plate 17548TU, owned by the driver,** residing at **225 Nolan Road, Brooklyn, N.Y.** Ms. Follins' N.Y. driver's license identification number is **K2537 68497 62435** and the expiration date is December 31, 2016.

The driver and owner of the other auto was Ella Spivitz, age 25, residing at 297 Jefferson Drive, Bronx, N.Y. Ms. Spivitz's auto was a **2010 white Honda, NY license plate 7451LBM**. Ms. Spivitz's driver's license identification number is F545 293 934 and the expiration is November 30, 2016.

Officers Wilks and Dansing completed a Vehicle Accident Report at 3:40 p.m. The report number was 324576764321.

-----

21. Select the best answer: The closest time of the accident is approximately:

A. after 4:15 p.m.

B. after 3:25 p.m.

C. before 3:25 p.m.
(CORRECT. "Police Officers Gary Wilks and Helen Dansing were on patrol in their squad car on June 12, 2016 when at 3:25 p.m. a female approached them. The female stated that she had just been involved in a car accident.")

D. after 3:40 p.m.

----

22. Which car sustained damage to the front bumper?

A.   NY plate #17548TU, black 2008 Ford

B.   NY plate #7451LBM, white 2010 Honda
(CORRECT. "The other vehicle, driven by a female, Ella Spivitz, had damage to the front bumper... Ms. Spivitz's auto was a 2010 white Honda, NY license plate 7451LBM.")

C.   NY plate #17548TU, white 2010 Honda

D.   NY plate #7451LBM, black 2008 Ford

----

23. What is the total number of persons involved in the accident?

A. 1

B. 2
(CORRECT. "Both Police Officers reported to the dispatcher that both drivers did not sustain any injuries. Also, there were no passengers in the two cars.")

C. 3

D. none of the above

----

24. The owner of the vehicle with damage to the rear bumper resides at:

A. 225 Nolan Road, Bronx, N.Y.

B. 297 Jefferson Drive, Bronx, N.Y.

C. 225 Nolan Road, Brooklyn, N.Y.
(**CORRECT.** "One of the vehicles, the black Ford, was driven and owned by a female, Catrina Follins. It had damage to the rear bumper… residing at 225 Nolan Road, Brooklyn, N.Y.")

D. 297 Jefferson Drive, Brooklyn, N.Y.

----

25. Which of the following is correct?

A. The report number was 324576764327.
(**WRONG.** Correct report number is 324576764321)

B. Ms. Follins' N.Y. driver's license identification number is K2537 68497 65435
(**WRONG.** Correct number is K25376489762435)

C. The driver and owner of the 2008 black Ford is Ella Spivitz.
(**WRONG.** Driver and owner is Catrina Follins.)

D. the black Ford, was driven and owned by a female, Catrina Follins.
(**CORRECT.** "…the black Ford, was driven and owned by a female, Catrina Follins.")

----

26. Which of the following is not correct?

A. The driver and owner of the 2010 white Honda was Ella Spivitz.

B. the black Ford, was driven and owned by a female, Catrina Follins.

C. The report number was 324576764321.

D. Ms. Follins' N.Y. driver's license identification number is K2537 68497 62432.
(The correct number is K25376849762435.)

Answers 27 - 34

27. An officer is reviewing a report he is preparing. It contains the following two drafts. Which of the two drafts are grammatically correct?

1. One of the greatest challenges that a Police Officer faces is the application of broad policies and procedures to specific <u>situations, unlike</u> specific guidelines, broad policies prescribe the boundaries of acceptable behaviors and responses to a wide spectrum of applications.

2. One of the greatest challenges that a Police Officer faces is the application of broad policies and <u>proccedures</u> to specific situations. Unlike specific guidelines, broad policies prescribe the boundaries of acceptable behaviors and responses to a wide spectrum of applications.

A. Only draft 1 is grammatically correct.

B. Only draft 2 is grammatically correct.

C. Both drafts 1 and 2 are grammatically correct.

D. Neither draft 1 nor draft 2 is grammatically correct.
(Draft 1 is a run-on sentence. It needs a period after "situations," and a second sentence started. In draft 2 the word "procedures" is misspelled "proccedures.")

----

28. An officer is asked by his partner to review a report that the officer is preparing. It contains the following two versions of one part of the report. Which versions are grammatically correct?

1. Certain items carried by persons entering the precinct building must be vouchered by the Police Officer on duty and stored in the main safe. Upon leaving the building, the person who owns the item may at any time during the day present his voucher to the officer who will retrieve the item from the safe and return it to him.

2. Certain items carried by members of the public entering the <u>precict</u> building must be vouchered by the Police Officer on duty and stored in the main safe. Upon leaving the building, the member of the public who owns the item may at any time during the day present his voucher to the officer who will retrieve the item from the safe and return it to the member of the public.

A. Only version 1 is grammatically correct.
(In version two, "precinct" is misspelled "precit.")

B. Only version 2 is grammatically correct.

C. Both versions 1 and 2 are grammatically correct.

D. Neither version 1 nor version 2 is grammatically correct.

----

29. An officer is preparing a report and has not decided which of two versions he wishes to use. Which of the following two versions are grammatically correct?

1. Mr. Betancourt and Ms. Spellman <u>has</u> not decided whether to attend the meeting. Both will inform us of their decision before this evening.

2. Mr. Betancourt and Ms. Spellman <u>has</u> not decided whether to attend the meeting; both will inform us of their decision before this evening.

A. Only version 1 is grammatically correct.

B. Only version 2 is grammatically correct.

C. Both versions 1 and 2 are grammatically correct.

D. Neither version 1 nor version 2 is grammatically correct.
(In both versions the singular word "has" should be the plural "have" in order to agree with the plural subject "Mr. Betancourt and Ms. Spellman.")

----

30. Police Officer George Prior is preparing a speech that he will give at a Community Board meeting. Which of the following two versions are correct?

1. Unattended items, especially bags and luggage, are a main security concern. If you see an unattended bag or luggage, notify the person at the main desk.

2. If you see an unattended bag or luggage, notify the person at the <u>main desk, unattended items,</u> especially bags and luggage are a main security concern.

A. 1 only is correct.
(Sentence 2 is a run-on sentence. A period is needed after "main desk," and a second sentence needs to be started.)

B. 2 only is correct.

C. Neither 1 nor 2 is correct.

D. Both 1 and 2 are correct.

31. Police Officer Janet Ryker is preparing an instruction sheet on how to process reports. Which of the following two versions are correct?

1. Form A must be filled out and submitted within 24 hours. Form B must also be submitted with Form A if an ambulance was used to transport any victim to a medical facility.

2. Form A must be filled out and submitted within 24 <u>hours, Form</u> B must also be submitted with Form A if an ambulance was used to transport any victim to a medical facility.

A. 1 only is correct.
(Sentence 2 is a run-on sentence. A period is needed after after "24 hours," and a second sentence needs to be started.)

B. 2 only is correct.

C. Neither 1 nor 2 is correct.

D. Both 1 and 2 are correct.

----

32. Police Officer John McGee is checking the correctness of sentences in one of his reports. Which of the following two versions are correct?

1. A Police Officer must always be vigilant. Sometimes small clues lead to important discoveries.

2. Sometimes small clues lead to important discoveries because a Police Officer must always be vigilant.

A. 1 only is correct.
(Version 2 is not clear or logical.)

B. 2 only is correct.

C. Neither 1 nor 2 is correct.

D. Both 1 and 2 are correct.

----

33. Officer Bryer is asked to select the best summary (A, B, C, or D) of the following information: (The best summary is the one that expresses the information in the most clear, accurate and complete manner.)

Place of accident: in front of 245 East 25th Street, Bronx

Time of accident: 3:05 P.M.

Date of accident: July 20, 2016

Vehicle involved: 2008 Camri

Driver: Bella Lugowski

Damage: cracked windshield

Details: A traffic light loosened from its supports and struck the windshield of the 2008 Camri.

A. On July 20, 2016, at 3:05 P.M., in front of 245 East 25th Street, Bronx, a traffic light loosened from its supports and struck the windshield of a 2008 Camri, <u>owned</u> by Bella Lugowski.
(**WRONG.** "Owned" should be "<u>driven by</u>.")

B. On July 20, 2016, in front of 245 East 25th Street, Bronx, a traffic light loosened from its supports and struck the windshield of a 2008 Camri, driven by Bella Lugowski.
(**WRONG.** No time is stated.)

C. On July 20, 2016, at 3:05 P.M., in front of 245 East 25th Street, Bronx, a traffic light loosened from its supports and struck the windshield of a 2008 Camri.
(**WRONG.** The name of the driver is not stated.)

D. On July 20, 2016, at 3:05 P.M., in front of 245 East 25th Street, Bronx, a traffic light loosened from its supports and cracked the windshield of a 2008 Camri, driven by Bella Lugowski.
(**CORRECT.** This summary has all the information and is accurate.)

----

34. Police Officer Edington collects the following information at the scene of a traffic accident:

Date of accident: September 9, 2016

Time of accident: 1:10 P.M.

Place of accident: intersection of 98th Street and Dwayne Avenue, Staten Island

Vehicles involved: 2008 Nissan and 2012 Buick

Drivers: Ben Morley (2008 Nissan) and Marcia Costa (2012 Buick)

Damage: dent on driver's door of 2012 Buick; no damage to the 2008 Nissan

Police Officer Edington drafts four versions of a report to express the above information. Which of the following four versions is most clear, accurate and complete?

A. On September 9, 2016, at 1:10 P.M., at the intersection of 98th Street and Dwayne Avenue, Staten Island, <u>a 2012 Nissan and a 2008 Buick</u> were involved in a traffic accident. The 2012 Buick, driven by Marcia Costa, sustained a dent on the driver's door. The 2008 Nissan, driven by Ben Morley, did not sustain any damage.
(**WRONG. "**…a "2012 Nissan" and a "2008 Buick"…." should be "<u>a 2008 Nissan" and "2012 Buick</u>.")

B. On September 9, 2016, at 1:10 P.M., at the intersection of <u>89th Street</u> and Dwayne Avenue, Staten Island, a 2008 Nissan and a 2012 Buick were involved in a traffic accident. The 2012 Buick, driven by Marcia Costa, sustained a dent on the driver's door. The 2008 Nissan, driven by Ben Morley, did not sustain any damage.
(**WRONG.** The street should be <u>98th</u> Street.)

C. On September 9, 2016, at 1:10 P.M., at the intersection of 98th Street and Dwayne Avenue, Staten Island, a 2008 Nissan and a 2012 Buick were involved in a traffic accident. The 2012 Buick, driven by Marcia Costa, sustained a dent on the <u>passenger's front door</u>. The 2008 Nissan, driven by Ben Morley, did not sustain any damage.
(**WRONG.** The "passenger's front door" should be "<u>driver's front door</u>.")

D. On September 9, 2016, at 1:10 P.M., at the intersection of 98th Street and Dwayne Avenue, Staten Island, a 2008 Nissan and a 2012 Buick were involved in a traffic accident. The 2012 Buick, driven by Marcia Costa, sustained a dent on the driver's door. The 2008 Nissan, driven by Ben Morley, did not sustain any damage.
(**CORRECT.** This summary has all the information and is accurate.)

Answers 35 – 40

35. While patrolling the area surrounding a shopping mall, Police Officer Marero is informed by a female that she has just discovered that the wallet inside her handbag is missing and that she is not sure whether she left it at home or whether she has just been pickpocketed.

According to the information provided by the female, Police Officer Marero should:

A. question all persons in the nearby area.

B. go into the shopping mall and complain to the security captain.

C. ask the female to check at home and if she does not find the wallet, to report it to the police.

POLICE OFFICER EXAM NEW YORK CITY

(The female does not know if the wallet is stolen or she forgot it at home. To do any investigation at this point would be premature. Complaining to the security captain is not helpful.)

D. question all unescorted females surrounding the mall, as the pickpocket is probably a female working alone.

----

36. Police Officer David Fitzgerald notices that the plastic cover of a traffic light is cracked, but does not pose an immediate danger. He has several traffic cones with him. Police Officer Fitzgerald should:

A. immediately barricade all lanes to stop all traffic and thereby decrease the possibility of an accident.

B. immediately barricade all lanes except one in order to keep traffic moving.

C. report the cracked plastic cover to the proper authority.

(This does not appear to be a dangerous or an emergency situation. Notifying the proper authority is adequate action.)

D. take no action, as traffic lights are not the responsibility of the police department.

----

37. At midnight, during his patrol, Police Officer William Reese notices that the padlock of the metal roll down gate of a store front entrance is on the floor. The contact number for the gate repair company is on a sticker on the gate. Another sticker has a contact number for the owner of the store.

Based on the preceding information, what is the first step that Police Officer Reese should take?

A. He should call for backup since he is on patrol alone.

B. Quickly tape the area to preserve the crime scene.

C. Call the owner and inform him and see if he is aware that the lock is on the floor.

(Checking with the owner is adequate, as there is no firm sign at this point that there has been any criminal activity.)

D. Roll up the gate and go inside the store to see if there are any persons in there.

----

38. At 8:00 p.m. your sergeant asks that you patrol a school yard and see if there are any persons there. Because of gang fights, the school yard was posted with a sign that no one should be in there after 7:00 p.m. As you pass by the school yard, you see an elderly man sitting on a bench and feeding pigeons. What is the first step you should take in this situation?

A. Arrest the man, as his age does not give him special privileges.

B. Leave the man alone, as he is elderly and feeding pigeons.

C. Take the man to the precinct for questioning.

D. Ask the man if he is aware that he is not permitted in the school yard after 7:00 p.m.

(Indications are that the elderly man perhaps is not aware of the posting. Informing him is the best course of action.)

----

39. Police Officer Tina Barley is on patrol alone when she notices a man comfortably sleeping on a bench, a machete in his hand and his shirt stained with dried blood from a wound on his shoulder. On the floor next to him is an open bottle of vodka.

Based on the preceding information, what should Police Officer Barley do first?

A. Pick up the bottle and taste the liquid to see if it actually is vodka.

B. Gently wake the man and ask him if he needs assistance.

C. Call for backup and medical assistance.

(The man probably needs medical attention. Also, because the man has a machete, calling for backup is advisable. An investigation should then be done.)

D. Go into a nearby apartment house and investigate the situation.

40. Prior to the start of your patrol, your sergeant informs you that a nearby public school has reported that a thin white male was seen trying to entice young children into his red car. What should you do first?

A. Quickly go to the school area and question all thin white males.

B. Quickly go to the school area and question all thin white males in cars.

C. Be vigilant for any white males in a red car lingering near the school.

(Reasonable suspicion must be had before questioning persons. A white male in a red car hanging around the school would probably be enough cause for the officer to question the person.)

D. Do nothing as the information provided is not sufficient to take any action.

———————————

Answers 41- 43

Answer question 41 based on the following PL 80.05 table.

PL 80.05 FINES FOR MISDEMEANORS AND VIOLATIONS:

Offense	Fine	Alternative Sentence
A misdemeanor	up to $1000.00	Court may sentence the defendant to pay an amount not exceeding double the amount of the defendant's gain.
B misdemeanor	up to $500.00	
Unclassified Misdemeanor	in accordance with law or ordinance that defines the crime	
Violation	up to $250.00	

41. Which of the following statements is correct?

A. Fines for violations can only be $25.00 or less.
(WRONG. Fine can be <u>up to $250.00</u>)

B. Fines for all misdemeanors must be over $500.
(WRONG. Fine for B misdemeanor is <u>up to $500.00</u>)

C. Fines for all B misdemeanors must be $500 or more.
(WRONG. Fine for B misdemeanor is <u>up to $500.00</u>)

D. Fine for an "A" misdemeanor cannot be greater than $1,000.00
(CORRECT)

Answer question 42 based on the following CPL 30.30 table.

CPL 30.30 Where a defendant has been committed to the custody of the sheriff, he must be released on bail or his own recognizance where the people are not ready for trial within the following days after commencement of defendant's commitment to the custody of the sheriff:

Offense committed	People must be ready for trial within this period (after the commencement of defendant's commitment to the custody of the sheriff)
felony	90 days
misdemeanor with jail term over 3 months	30 days
misdemeanor with jail term up to 3 months	15 days
petty offense	5 days

42. Based on the above table, where the defendant has been committed to the custody of the sheriff and the charge is a petty offense, the people must be ready for trial within _____ days after the commencement of defendant's commitment to the custody of the sheriff.

A. 15 days

B. 5 days

C. 90 days

D. 30 days

Answer question 43 based on the following section of CPL 110.10

CPL 110.10 How to require defendant's appearance for arraignment in a local criminal court

Prior to the commencement of a criminal action, a person may be compelled to appear in a local criminal court for arraignment upon an accusatory instrument to be filed at or before his appearance by:

(a) an arrest made without a warrant (CPL 140), or

(b) issuance and service upon him of an appearance ticket (CPL 150).

-----

43. Based on CPL 110.10, which of the following statements is not correct?

A. A person may be compelled to appear in a Local Criminal Court for arraignment upon an accusatory instrument to be filed at or before his appearance by an arrest made without a warrant (CPL 140), or issuance and service upon him of an appearance ticket (CPL 150).

B. A person cannot be compelled to appear in a criminal court prior to the commencement of a criminal action.
("Prior to the commencement of a criminal action, a person <u>may</u> be compelled to appear....")

C. A person may be compelled to appear in a Local Criminal Court for arraignment upon an accusatory instrument to be filed at or before his appearance by an arrest made without a warrant.

D. A person may be compelled to appear in a Local Criminal Court for arraignment upon an accusatory instrument to be filed at or before his appearance by the issuance and service upon him of an appearance ticket (CPL 150).

"Our greatest weariness comes from work not done."

\- Eric Hoffer

Answer 44

Below is a drawing of a "Revolver" and 4 more drawings of revolvers (A, B, C, and D).

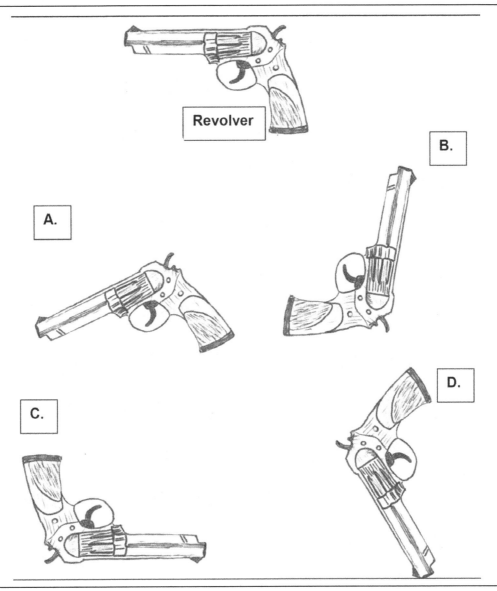

44. Which of the following four statements is correct?

A. Drawing "A" is different from the "Revolver" drawing.

B. Drawing "B" is different from the "Revolver" drawing.

C. Drawing "C" is different from the "Revolver" drawing.

D. Drawings "A", "B", "C," and "D" are the same as the "Revolver" drawing.

Answers 45 - 47

Answer questions 45 - 47 based on the definitions provided in the following summary of Penal Law Section 10.00.

Penal Law (PL) S 10.00

A **Traffic infraction** is an offense defined as a traffic infraction in section 155 of the Vehicle and Traffic Law.

A **Violation** is an offense (other than a traffic infraction) for which a sentence in excess of 15 days cannot be imposed.

A **Misdemeanor** is an offense (other than a traffic infraction) for which a sentence of more than 15 days and up to and including a year can be imposed.

A **Felony** is an offense for which a sentence of more than 1 year can be imposed.

A **Crime** means a misdemeanor or a felony.

Physical injury means impairment of physical condition or substantial pain.

Serious physical injury means physical injury which creates a substantial risk of death, or which causes death or serious and protracted disfigurement, protracted impairment of health or protracted loss or impairment of the function of any bodily organ.

Deadly physical force means physical force which under the circumstances used is readily capable of causing death or other serious physical injury.

Deadly weapon means any loaded weapon from which a shot, readily capable of producing death or other serious physical injury, may be discharged, or any of the following: switchblade knife, gravity knife, pilum ballistic knife, metal knuckle knife, dagger, billy, blackjack, plastic knuckles, metal knuckles.

Dangerous instrument means any instrument, including a vehicle, which is readily capable of causing death or other serious physical injury.

-----

45. Based on the definitions in the above summary of Penal Law Section 10.00, which of the following statements is not correct?

A. A "dagger' is defined as a deadly weapon.

B. A violation is defined as a "crime."

(NOT CORRECT. A "Crime" means a "misdemeanor" or a "felony." Violations are not included in the definition of "crime.")

C. A car is a dangerous instrument.

D. A sentence for a violation may be for 15 days.

----

46. Based on the definitions in the above summary of Penal Law 10.00, which of the following statements is correct?

A. A sentence of 13 months may be imposed for a misdemeanor.
(WRONG. Maximum sentence for a misdemeanor is <u>up to</u> a year.)

B. Traffic infractions are defined in the Penal Law.
(WRONG. Traffic Infractions are defined in the <u>Vehicle and Traffic Law</u>.)

C. A sentence of 360 days may be imposed for a misdemeanor.
(CORRECT. A misdemeanor is an offense (other than a traffic infraction) for which a sentence of more than 15 days and <u>up to and including a year</u> can be imposed. A year is 365 days.)

D. Deadly weapons and dangerous instruments have the same definition.
(WRONG. They have <u>two different definitions</u>.)

----

47. According to Penal Law (PL) S 10.00, which of the following statements is not correct?

A. Serious physical injury means physical injury which creates a substantial risk of death, or which causes death or serious and protracted disfigurement, protracted impairment of health or protracted loss or impairment of the function of any bodily organ.

B. Deadly physical force means physical force which under the circumstances used is readily capable of causing death or other serious physical injury.

C. Dangerous weapon means any instrument, including a vehicle, which is readily capable of causing death or other serious physical injury.
(NOT CORRECT because "A <u>dangerous instrument</u> means any instrument, including a vehicle, which is readily capable of causing death or other serious physical injury.")

D. Deadly weapon means any loaded weapon from which a shot, readily capable of producing death or other serious physical injury, may be discharged, or any of the following: switchblade knife, gravity knife, pilum ballistic knife, metal knuckle knife, dagger, billy, blackjack, plastic knuckles, metal knuckles.

Answer 48

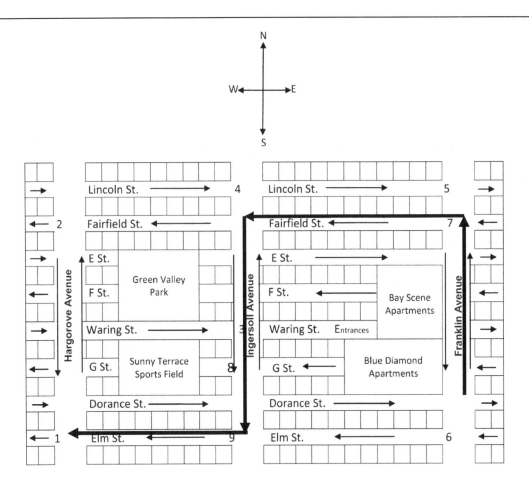

48. Imagine that you are at Dorance Street and Franklin Avenue and then drive north to Fairfield Street, then turn west to Ingersoll Avenue, then travel south to Elm Street, then west to Hargrove Avenue. Near which number location will you be nearest?

A. 6   **B. 1**   C. 9   D. 8

Answer 49

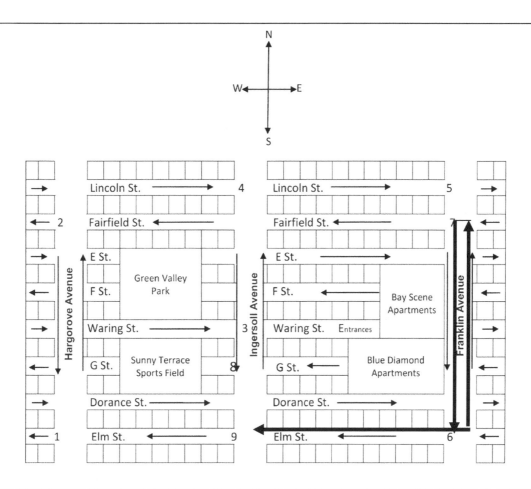

49. If you start your drive at point number 6, then drive north to Fairfield Street, then drive south to Elm St., then west to Hargrove Avenue, you will be closest to which point?

A. 6   B. 1   **C. 9**   D. 8

Answer 50

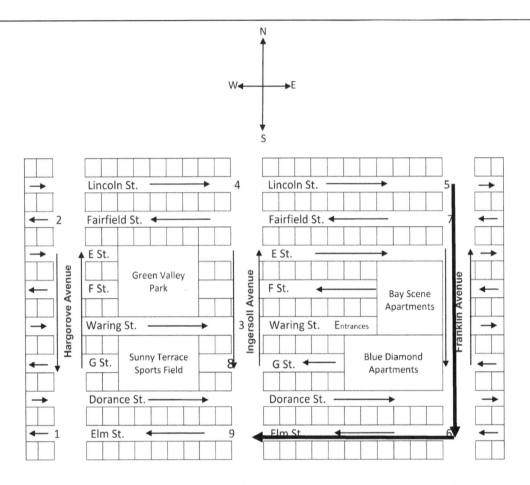

50. You are driving south in your patrol car and are at the intersection of Lincoln St. and Franklin Avenue. You are informed that an auto accident has just occurred at the intersection of Elm Street and Ingersoll Avenue. Assuming that you must obey all traffic signs, which one of the following four choices describes the most direct route?

A. Drive south on Franklin Avenue to Elm Street, then drive east on Elm Street to Ingersoll Avenue.

B. Drive north on Franklin Avenue to Elm Street, then drive west on Elm Street to Ingersoll Avenue.

C. Drive east on Franklin Avenue to Elm Street, then drive west on Elm Street to Ingersoll Avenue.

D. Drive south on Franklin Avenue to Elm Street, then drive west on Elm Street to Ingersoll Avenue.

Answer 51

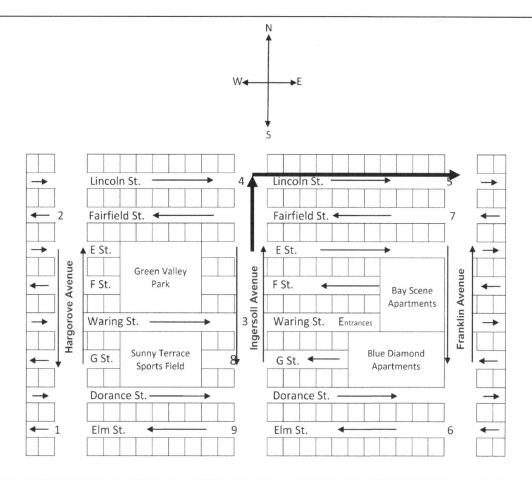

51. You are driving north in your patrol car and are at Ingersoll Avenue and E St. You are informed that there is a fight between two males at the corner of Lincoln Street and Franklin Avenue. Which one of the following four choices describes the most direct route?

A. Drive south to Lincoln St., then west on Lincoln St. to the corner of Lincoln St. and Franklin Avenue.

B. Drive north to Lincoln St., then west on Lincoln St. to the corner of Lincoln St. and Franklin Avenue.

C. Drive north to Fairfield Street, then east to the corner of Lincoln St. and Franklin Avenue.

D. Drive north to Lincoln St. then make a right and continue to the corner of Lincoln St. and Franklin Avenue.

52. During the month of September 2016 there were 8 burglaries reported in Police Officer Cohen's precinct. In two of the burglaries, neighbors reported that at the approximate time of the burglaries they witnessed a female white, average height, shoulder length dark hair, "with a small rose tattoo on the left side of her neck." Both times the female was carrying a striped shopping bag out of the residence that had been burglarized. They also reported that at both times she had been wearing a pink T-shirt, dark blue dungarees, and pink sneakers.

During his patrol, Officer Cohen stops four white females for questioning. He had recorded in his memo book the description given by the two witnesses. Which piece of information should Officer Cohen consider the most important and pay careful attention in identifying the suspected burglar?

A. the dark blue dungarees

B. small rose tattoo on the left side of her neck

(**CORRECT.** This is the one piece of the description that cannot be easily changed or disguised.)

C. the shoulder length, dark hair

D. the pink T-shirt

----

53. Officer Marietta James learns at the precinct that a female, 75 years old, had been mugged one hour earlier by a person who the victim described as a "white young female, about twenty years old, with dark hair tied in a shoulder length ponytail, and with a mole at the base of her nose." The victim also described the perpetrator as wearing black pants, a red T-shirt, and black sneakers.

During her patrol, Officer James sees a group of three white females, about 20 – 25 years old, drinking beer in front of a 24-hour store. Officer James stops her patrol car about thirty feet away to get a better look at the three females. Which of the following parts of the description provided by the victim is most important for Officer James to consider in her attempt to identify the possible suspect?

A. the red T-shirt

B. the shoulder length pony tail

C. the black sneakers

D. the mole at the base of her nose

(CORRECT. This is the one piece of the description that cannot be easily changed or disguised.)

----

54. Police Officer Jenkins is assigned to patrol a shopping area which includes four "99 cent stores." During the last four weeks, crime statistics show that four shoplifters were reported at the Amazing 99 Cent Store, all between the hours of 10:00 a.m. and 4:00 p.m. **At the Whacko 99 Cent Store two robberies were reported.** At Crown Discount Store three front windows were broken (one in each of three occasions). **At the Goody Discount Store three bicycles were stolen from the sidewalk in front of the store.** The shoplifters were reported between 9:30 a.m. and 4:30 p.m. The robberies occurred between 9:30 a.m. and 10:30 a.m. The bicycles were all reported stolen in the afternoon and before 5:00 p.m.

Officer Jenkins works the 9:00 a.m. to 5:00 p.m. tour. On Tuesday, his sergeant instructs him to pay careful attention to robberies. To try to reduce the number of robberies, Office Jenkins should patrol the:

A. Amazing 99 Cent Store

B. Goody Discount Store

C. Whacko 99 Cent Store

(CORRECT. This is the store where <u>robberies</u> occurred the prior weeks.)

D. Crown Discount Store

----

55. On Wednesday Officer Jenkins also works the 9:00 a.m. to 5:00 p.m. tour. On Wednesday, his sergeant tells him that three more bicycles were stolen at the same store as in the previous four weeks and instructs him to pay careful attention to bicycle thefts. To try to reduce the number of bicycle thefts, Officer Jenkins should patrol the:

A. Amazing 99 Cent Store

B. Goody Discount Store

(CORRECT. This is the store where bicycles were stolen the prior weeks.)

C. Whacko 99 Cent Store

D. Crown Discount Store

_____

Answers 56 - 57

Answer questions 56 - 57 based on the following "Enterprise Zone Security Procedure."

_____

A business enterprise zone has been established in Brooklyn. Although private security patrols the area and is primarily responsible for enforcing zone rules, there has been a recent increase in crimes. The Mayor's Office and the management of the enterprise zone have asked for NYPD assistance.

Your sergeant has assigned you to the enterprise zone entrance gate and has directed you to follow the "Enterprise Zone Security Procedure."

Enterprise Zone Security Procedure

1. At the gated entrance to the enterprise zone, you are to randomly check the Enterprise Zone I.D. cards of incoming individuals.

2. Drivers of incoming vehicles must produce a driver's license, registration, and proof of insurance upon your request.

3. If the driver is transporting alcohol, the driver must present identification that proves the driver is of legal age to drink.

4. If proper I.D. is not produced, you are to inform the private security staff.

-----

56. On your first day at the enterprise zone, you question a driver of an incoming vehicle who states that he forgot his Enterprise Zone I.D. at home. Based on the above procedure, which of the following is the most correct action to take?

A. Ask the driver to go home and get his I.D.

B. Deny entry to the driver unless he can produce an official NYS issued I.D.

C. Conduct a thorough search of the vehicle.

D. Contact the private security staff and inform them.

(Item 4 states, "If proper I.D. is not produced, you are to inform the private security staff.")

----

57. According to the "Enterprise Zone Security Procedure," which of the following statements is correct?

A. A person who does not have proper I.D. must be detained.

B. Alcohol is not permitted within the enterprise zone.

C. Enterprise Zone I.D. cards cannot be checked by police officers.

D. A driver's license must be produced upon request.

(CORRECT. Item 2 states, "Drivers of incoming vehicles must produce a driver's license, registration and proof of insurance upon your request." Choices A, B, and C are not prescribed procedures.)

"The man who removes a mountain
begins by carrying away small stones."
- Chinese Proverb

Answers 58 - 59

Answer questions 58 - 59 on the basis of the following "Building Bomb Search Procedure," received by Police Officer Wells.

Building Bomb Search Procedure

1. Officers will be assigned to search specified areas.

2. If a suspicious object is found:
   a. do not touch the object
   b. keep the area clear of other people
   c. inform security headquarters

3. Be prepared to evacuate all others and yourself.

4. When instructed by security headquarters, evacuate the building according to instructions.

5. Request all persons to take with them all personal belongings when evacuating.

-----

58. Officer Wells is assigned to do a bomb search of the first floor of a three-story paint and household items store. Halfway through his search, he discovers a very suspicious package under a display counter. He listens and hears a distinct ticking sound. There are four other persons on the first floor. Based on the above "Building Bomb Search Procedure," Officer Wells should first:

A. instruct all persons to gather their belongings, as he is about to report the suspicious package and an evacuation may be necessary.

B. issue an evacuation order, as the bomb is ticking and could go off at any second.

C. take the package and put it in an unoccupied section of the store to avoid fatalities.

D. keep the area clear of other people and inform security headquarters.

(Steps 2 and 3 state:

"2. If a suspicious object is found:

    a. do not touch the object

    b. keep the area clear of other people

    c. inform security headquarters….")

----

59. According to the preceding "Building Bomb Search Procedure":

A. When a police officer is instructed by security headquarters to evacuate the building, the officer must request that all persons take with them all personal and <u>business</u> belongings when evacuating.

(WRONG. The procedure refers to <u>personal</u> belongings.)

B. An officer shall never evacuate himself or herself from the building.

(WRONG. An officer must do so when instructed.)

C. If a suspicious object is found, the police officer must inform security headquarters.

(CORRECT. Steps 2 states:

"2. If a suspicious object is found:

    a. do not touch the object

    b. keep the area clear of other people

    <u>c. inform security headquarters</u>….")

D. All officers are assigned to search <u>all</u> areas of the building.

(WRONG. Officers are assigned to search <u>specified</u> areas.)

_____

Answers 60 - 68

60. You and another officer notice a boy crying at the curb. He tells you that a man in a yellow car just tried to pull him into the car. You notice a yellow car heading northbound to the end of the block where it makes a right turn. While your partner stays with the boy, you follow the yellow car and observe the car continuing for two more blocks before turning left.

According to the information in the preceding passage, you would be most correct to radio that you last saw the car heading:

A) north

B) south

C) east

D) west

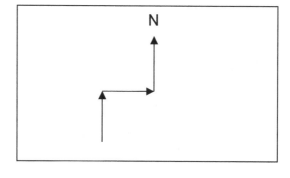

----

61. While in your patrol car, you notice a car with stolen license plates heading southbound. You follow the car, which after eight blocks makes a right turn and then after two more blocks makes a left turn.

According to the information in the preceding passage, you would be most correct to radio that you last saw the car heading:

A) north

B) south

C) east

D) west

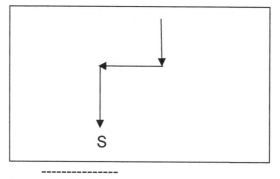

----

62. Your attention is drawn to a taxicab driver shouting "He robbed me!" and pointing to a man running down the block. You shout for the man to stop, but he continues running westbound. After four blocks, he makes a right turn and runs for three more blocks before making a left turn.

According to the information in the preceding passage, you would be most correct to radio that you last saw the man heading:

A) north

B) south

C) east

D) west

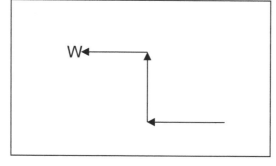

63. You and another officer witness a man grab a purse from a baby carriage. You shout for the man to stop, but he runs down the block in a westbound direction. You chase the man for two blocks before he turns right and then for another block, at which point he makes another right.

According to the information in the preceding passage, you would be most correct to radio that the man was running:

A) north

B) south

C) east

D) west

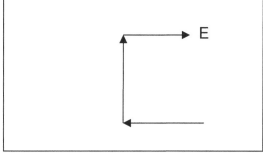

----

64. While in your patrol car, you witness two men run out of a donut shop, each holding a pouch and a revolver. They quickly get into a car and head northbound. You follow. After three blocks, they make a right turn and then after two more blocks they make a left turn.

According to the information in the preceding passage, you would be most correct to radio that you last saw the car heading:

A) north

B) south

C) east

D) west

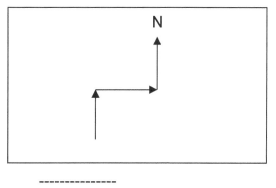

----

65. Your attention is drawn to a pedestrian shouting, "He just broke the store window!" and pointing to a man running in an eastbound direction. After three blocks, he makes a left turn and runs for two more blocks before making a right turn.

According to the information in the preceding passage, you would be most correct to radio that you last saw the man heading:

A) north

B) south

C) east

D) west

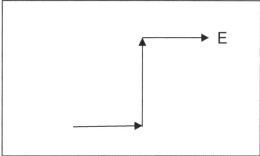

66. You and another officer notice a male shouting, "He just robbed me!" and pointing to a male running away from the scene. You notice a man running down the block westbound to the end of the block where he makes a right turn. While your partner stays with the victim, you follow the man and observe him continuing to run for four blocks before turning left.

According to the information in the preceding passage, you would be most correct to radio that you last saw the man running:

A) north
B) south
C) east
D) west

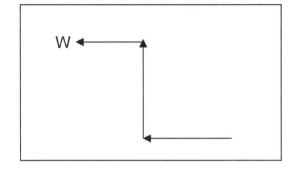

----

67. While in your patrol car, you notice a blue car sideswipe a parked car and then drive off northbound without stopping. You follow the car, which after five blocks makes a right turn and then after two more blocks makes a left turn.

According to the information in the preceding passage, you would be most correct to radio that you last saw the car heading:

A) east
B) south
C) north
D) west

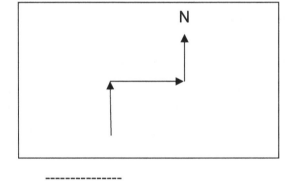

----

68. A gas station employee points down the block and shouts, "That guy just robbed us!" You shout for the man to stop, but he continues running westbound. After four blocks, he makes a left turn and runs for two more blocks before making another left turn.

According to the information in the preceding passage, you would be most correct to radio that you last saw the suspect heading:

A) north
B) south
C) east
D) west

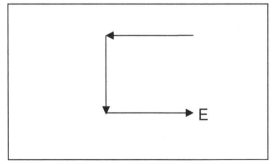

Answer 69

Line
of
crates

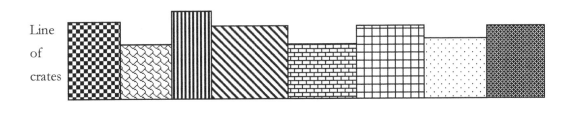

A.

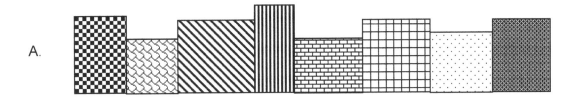

B.

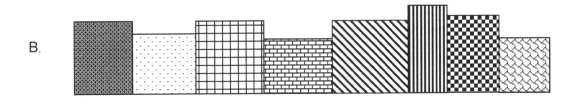

C.

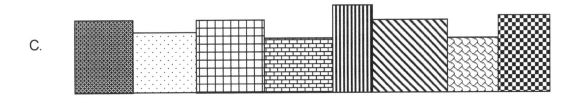

D.

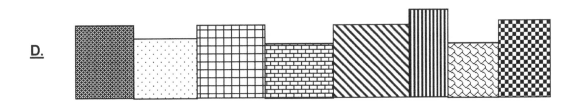

69. The "Line of Crates" when viewed from the back would appear as which of the following choices?

A. Choice A

B. Choice B

C. Choice C

D. Choice D

Answers 70 - 75

Read the following passage, then answer questions 70 – 75 that follow based on the information contained in the passage.

While on patrol, Police Officers Durley and Golan are dispatched to 1492 Brighton Avenue, first floor "Texas AA Prime Meats, Inc." at 9:20 p.m. on November 22, 2016. **The owner of "Texas AA Prime Meats" had just called 911 to report a burglary.** They arrive at the store at 9:25 p.m. and are greeted by Mr. Marvin West, the owner of the store and Mr. Barnie Leiber, an employee of "Texas AA Prime Meats."

Mr. Marvin West tells the officers that he and Barnie Leiber had closed the store for the day at 7:00 p.m. They had locked the front and back doors and also properly rolled down the security gate and padlocked it. Mr. West received a call at 9:01 p.m. from a neighbor who happened to be passing by the store when he saw men trying to enter the building. Mr. West checked his security cameras on his home TV screen. Although security camera #1 showed the outdoor front entrance and security camera #4 showed the outdoor back door area, it was with security cameras #2 and #3 that he saw the burglars. Security camera # 2 covered the outdoor roof skylight and **security camera # 3 covered the inside area of the store, including the cashier area.**

Two burglars, all dressed in black and wearing grey face masks, had broken the glass in the skylight and with a rope had descended into the store. The smaller of the two persons descended first and the much taller one followed. The person who descended first carried a black garbage bag and the other person held a flashlight in the right hand.

The two burglars took all the $139.00 cash and coins that had been left in the cash register, a box of filet mignon steaks valued at $455.00, three identical meat cutting machines worth a total of $1,500.00, two professional electric knives worth $219 each, and **six carving boards worth $119.00 each.** Mr. West tells the officers that he will prepare a complete list of missing items as soon as possible.

Mr. West tells Officer Golan that he is 55 years old and lives at 1830 Crichton Avenue in Brooklyn. His cell number is 718-555-7928. Barnie Leiber tells Officer Golan that he is 28 years old and lives at 2875 East 27 Street, Brooklyn. His cell number is 718-555-8311.

Police Officers Durley and Golan complete their investigation at 10:15 p.m. Before they completed their crime report, they performed a careful sweep of the store to make certain that the burglars had left.

-----

70. Which of the following security cameras covered the cashier area?

A. 1 and 2 only

B. 2 only

C. 1 and 3 only

D. 3 only
("security camera # 3 covered the inside area of the store, including the cashier area.")

---

71. Which of the following statements is correct?

A. The address of Texas AA Prime Meats is 1495 Brighton Avenue, first floor.
(**WRONG.** <u>1492</u> Brighton Avenue.)

B. The two burglars descended into the store using a chain.
(**WRONG.** They used a <u>rope</u>.)

C. The burglars were dressed in grey and wore black face masks.
(**WRONG.** They dressed in <u>black</u> and wore <u>grey</u> face masks)

D. The person who called 911 was Mr. Marvin West.
(**CORRECT**. "The owner of "Texas AA Prime Meats" had just called 911 to report a burglary.")

----

72. Which one of the following statements is correct? Among the items stolen were:

A. $193.00 cash and coins
(**WRONG**. <u>$139.00</u> in cash and coins)

B. three professional electric knives worth $219 each
(**WRONG**. <u>two</u> knives)

C. six carving boards worth $119.00 each
(**CORRECT**. "six carving boards worth $119.00 each.")

D. a box of filet mignon steaks valued at $445.00
(**WRONG**. <u>$455.00</u>)

----

73. Which of the following statements is correct according to the information provided by Mr. Marvin West and Mr. Barnie Leiber?

A. Mr. West tells Officer Golan that he is 55 years old and lives at 1830 Crichton Avenue in Brooklyn. His cell number is 718-555-7982.
(**WRONG.** Correct number is 718-555-79<u>28</u>)

B. Mr. Barnie Leiber tells Officer Golan that he is 28 years old and lives at 2875 East 27 Avenue, Brooklyn. His cell number is 718-555-8311.

(**WRONG.** The address is East 27 <u>Street</u>.)

C. Mr. West tells Officer Golan that he is 55 years old and lives at 1830 Crichton Avenue in Brooklyn.

(**CORRECT**. "Mr. West tells Officer Golan that he is 55 years old and lives at 1830 Crichton Avenue in Brooklyn.)

D. Mr. Barnie Leiber tells Officer Golan that he is 28 years old and lives at 2857 East 27 Street, Brooklyn. His cell number is 718-555-8311.

(**WRONG.** Barnie Leiber is 28 years old and lives at <u>2875</u> East 27 Street, Brooklyn)

----

74. Choose the best answer: The value of each of the meat cutting machines is:

A. $50

B. $500
(**CORRECT**. "…three identical meat cutting machines worth a total of $1,500.00.")

C. $1,000

D. $1,500

----

75. The total value of all items missing is:

A. $3,027

B. $3,246

C. $2,651

D. $3,540

$ 139	cash and coins
455	filet mignon
1500	3 cutting machines ($500 each)
438	2 knives, $219 each
714	6 carving boards, $119 each
$ 3246	**Total**

Answer 76

During her patrol, Police Officer Dawn Heller is called to the scene of an accident. The driver/owner of vehicle #2 stated that he was driving on Hart Ave. when car #1 hit his car from behind, causing him to hit vehicle number 3.

Assume that all 3 vehicles were in their proper lanes of traffic.

Which of the following 4 diagrams best matches the statement of the driver of vehicle #2?

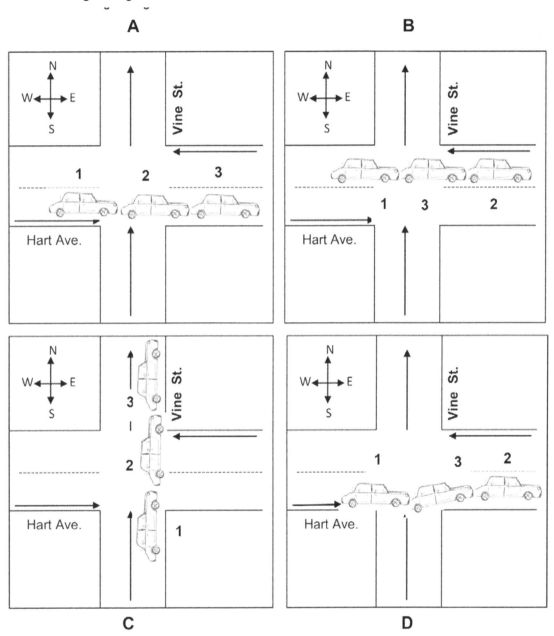

76. The diagram which best matches the statement of driver of vehicle #2 is:

A. diagram "A"

C. diagram "C"

B. diagram "B"

D. diagram "D"

(The correct accident sequence is Car 1>Car 2>Car 3, on Hart Avenue and in the proper lane.)

Answers 77 - 79

Answer questions 77 - 79 based on the details provided.

Officer Unger collects the following details at the scene of an auto accident:

Date of Accident: August 16, 2016

Time of accident: 5:02 p.m.

Place of accident: intersection of Ferndale Avenue and Willows Avenue, Bronx

Driver: Fred Bellows

Vehicle: 2007 Toyota Sienna

Damage: damage to front bumper when vehicle struck a bicycle partially parked on the sidewalk, but protruding into the street

-----

77. Officer Unger is preparing a report of the accident and has four drafts of the report. He wishes to use the draft that expresses the information most clearly, accurately and completely. Which draft should he choose?

A. At 5:02 p.m., on August 16, 2016, at the intersection of Ferndale Avenue and Willows Avenue, Bronx, a vehicle driven by Fred Bellows struck a bicycle partially parked on the sidewalk, but protruding into the street.

(WRONG. Type of vehicle, a "2007 Toyota Sienna", is not stated.)

B. On August 16, 2016, at 5:02 p.m., at the intersection of Ferndale Avenue and Willows Avenue, Bronx, a 2007 Toyota Sienna driven by Fred <u>Belows</u> struck a bicycle partially parked on the sidewalk, but protruding into the street.

(WRONG. Bellows is misspelled <u>Belows</u>.)

C. At the intersection of Ferndale Avenue and Willows Avenue, Bronx, on August 16, 2016, at <u>2:05 p.m.</u>, a 2007 Toyota Sienna driven by Fred Bellows struck a bicycle partially parked on the sidewalk, but protruding into the street.

(WRONG. Correct time is <u>5:02 p.m.</u>)

D. On August 16, 2016, at 5:02 p.m., at the intersection of Ferndale Avenue and Willows Avenue, Bronx, a 2007 Toyota Sienna driven by Fred Bellows sustained damage to the front bumper when it struck a bicycle partially parked on the sidewalk, but protruding into the street.

(CORRECT. This has all the information and no errors.)

Officer Able responds to a car theft. She questions the owner of the vehicle who reported the car stolen and obtains the following information:

Suspect: Unidentified

Date of crime: August 15, 2016

Time of crime: between 6:20 p.m. and 11:30 p.m.

Place of crime: driveway in front of 167 28th Street, Staten Island

Crime: theft of car

Vehicle stolen: 2010 Volvo

Victim: owner of car, Charles Williams

-----

78. Officer Able is comparing the information she recorded in her memo pad (at the scene of the accident) to the information in her report. Which of the following choices (A, B, C, or D) has one detail that does not agree with the information in the officer's memo pad?

A. Date of crime: August 12, 2016; Time of crime: between 6:20 p.m. and 11:30 p.m.

(The correct date is August 15.)

B. Crime: theft of car

C. Victim: owner of car, Charles Williams

D. Vehicle stolen: 2010 Volvo

----

79. Officer Able is preparing a report of the accident and has prepared four drafts of the report. She wishes to use the draft that expresses the information most clearly, accurately and completely. Which of the following drafts should she choose?

A. A car theft of a 2010 Volvo happened at the driveway in front of 167 28th Street, Staten Island where Charles Williams' car was parked for the night. The alleged thief is unidentified, as the theft happened in the evening hours.

(WRONG. Date is missing. Time is missing. Language and grammar are sloppy.)

B. On August 15, 2016, between 6:20 p.m. and 11:30 p.m., at the driveway in front of 167 28th Street, Staten Island, a 2010 Volvo owned by Charles Williams was stolen by an unidentified suspect.
(**CORRECT.** It contains all the information and is accurate.)

C. A car was stolen on August 15, 2016, between 6:20 p.m. and 11:30 p.m., at the driveway in front of 167 28th Street, Staten Island, owned by Charles Williams. The suspect is unidentified.
(**WRONG.** The type of car, a "2010 Volvo", is not stated.)

D. On August 15, 2016, at the driveway in front of 167 28th Street, Staten Island, between 6:30 p.m. and 11:30 p.m., a 2010 Volvo owned by Charles Williams was stolen by an unidentified suspect.
(**WRONG.** Correct time is "6:20 p.m. and 11:30 p.m.")

Answer question 80 based on the following "Procedure for Contact with Media."

Procedure for Contact with Media

When a criminal case is pending in the courts, the Police Officer who made the arrest is prohibited from discussing the case with any newspaper, magazine, TV reporters and all other media. Exceptions to this are when:

1. a New York court of competent jurisdiction formally orders the Police Officer to discuss one or more particulars of the case.

2. the NYPD orders such discussion.

3. the Police Officer is subpoenaed to testify before an authorized NYC, NYS or federal board.

4. a case is classified as R-16 by the NYPD Case Classification section.

-----

80. Police Officer Janet Peters arrests a person suspected of kidnapping a child who is still missing. The suspect has been indicted and is in jail, waiting for trial. A newspaper reporter, Brian Collins, contacts Officer Janet Peters and asks for information that might help the reporter to investigate the kidnapping and perhaps locate the missing child. He tells her that he checked with the NYPD Case Classification section and that the case is classified as an R-16 case. Officer Janet Peters should:

A. give assistance to Brian Collins by providing information that might help to locate the missing child.

B. give assistance only if the reporter can guarantee that the child will be found.

C. not provide any information until she confirms with the NYPD Case Classification section that the case is classified as an R-16 case.

(CORRECT. One exception to the prohibition of contact with media is where a case is classified as R-16 by the NYPD Case Classification section. A, B, and D do not qualify as exceptions.)

D. provide only information relating to locating the child, and not any other information.

Answers 81 - 82

Answer questions 81 - 82 based on the following extracts of CPL 500.10.

CPL 500.10 Definitions

1. PRINCIPAL is a defendant in a criminal action, or person adjudged to be a material witness.

2. RELEASE ON OWN RECOGNIZANCE means to allow a principal to be at liberty during the pendency of an action.

3. TO FIX BAIL means a court designating a sum of money, the posting of which allows the principal to be at liberty during the pendency of the criminal action.

4. COMMIT TO THE CUSTODY OF THE SHERIFF occurs when a court orders a principal confined and in the custody of the sheriff during the pendency of the criminal action.

5. SECURING ORDER is a court order which:

      1) commits a principal to custody of the sheriff, or

      2) fixes bail, or

      3) releases the principal on his own recognizance.

-----

81. Which of the following statements is correct?

A. A person can be committed to the custody of the sheriff only if he is a defendant in a criminal action.

(WRONG. A person can also be committed to the custody of the sheriff if he is adjudged to be a <u>material witness</u>.)

B. If a defendant posts bail, he cannot be released.

(**WRONG.** If a defendant posts bail, he <u>must</u> be released.)

C. A "principal" can only be a defendant in an action.

(**WRONG.** A "principal" can be a <u>material witness.</u>)

D. If a person is released on his own recognizance, he can remain at liberty during the pendency of the criminal action.

(**CORRECT.** "2. RELEASE ON OWN RECOGNIZANCE means to allow a principal to be at liberty during the pendency of an action.")

-----

82. According to the definitions in CPL 500.10, which of the following statements is correct?

A. A principal means only a defendant in a criminal action.

(**WRONG**. A principal can also be a person who is a <u>material witness</u>.)

B. A securing order cannot order the release of the principal on his own recognizance.

(**WRONG**. A securing order <u>can</u> order the release of the principal on his own recognizance.)

C. A judge cannot designate a sum of money when posting bail.

(**WRONG.** The <u>judge designates the sum of money</u> to be posted as bail.)

D. A securing order can order the release of the principal in his own recognizance.

(**CORRECT.** "5. SECURING ORDER is a court order which:

    1) commits a principal to custody of the sheriff, or

    2) fixes bail, or

    3) <u>releases the principal on his own recognizance.</u>")

----

83. A female, about 21 years old, reports that she had chained her poodle to a parking meter pole and gone into a beauty supplies store to purchase nail polish, only to discover when she

came out of the store that her poodle had been stolen. Four witnesses give you four statements. Which of the following four statements is most likely to be correct?

A. The person who cut the chain and rode away with the bicycle was a male, white, about 30 years old and about five feet five inches tall. He was wearing black sneakers, blue dungarees, a white T-shirt, and a blue denim back pack. He headed south for one block and then made a right turn.
(MOST LIKELY TO BE CORRECT.)

B. The person who cut the chain and rode away with the bicycle was a male, <u>black</u>, about <u>30</u> years old and about five feet five inches tall. He was wearing black sneakers, blue dungarees, a white T-shirt, and a blue denim backpack. He headed south for one block and then made a right turn.

C. The person who cut the chain and rode away with the bicycle was a male, white, about <u>50</u> years old and about five feet five inches tall. He was wearing black sneakers, <u>blue</u> dungarees, a white T-shirt, and a blue denim backpack. He headed south for one block and then made a right turn.

D. The person who cut the chain and rode away with the bicycle was a male, white, about <u>30</u> years old and about five feet five inches tall. He was wearing black sneakers, <u>black</u> dungarees, a white T-shirt, and a grey denim backpack. He headed south for one block and then made a right turn.

One way to tackle this question is to determine which details provided by a witness differ from the accounts of other witnesses, thereby making the account of this witness less reliable.

In this example, statement "B" describes the alleged robber as "black." All the other statements describe him as "white." Therefore, statement "B" is not reliable.

Of the remaining three statements ("A", "C", and "D"), statement "C" describes the alleged robber as "50 years old." However, "A," "B," and "D" describe him as "30 years old." Because of this we can eliminate statement "C." We are left with statements "A" and "D."

Which of the two is more reliable?

Statements "A", "B" and "C" describe the dungarees worn by the robber as "blue." However, statement "D" describes them as "black."

Because of this, we are left with statement "A" as being the most reliable statement.

----

84. Four witnesses to a hit and run accident tell Police Officer Tumi that they memorized the license plate number of the car that sped away from the accident. Which of the following is the most likely to be correct?

A. 8237AFN

B. 8587AFN

C. 8537AFN

D. 8531AFN

Explanation:

The first digit "8" is the same in all choices.

Choice "A" differs from all others in that the second digit is "2" instead of "5." We can eliminate "A".

Choice "B" differs from the remaining by having an "8" as the third digit instead of "3." This leaves choices "C" and" D."

Choice "D" differs from the other choices in that the fourth digit is "1" instead of "7."

The best choice is therefore **"C."**

"I came, I saw, I conquered."

- Julius Caesar

Answer question 85 based on the following table:

Summonses and Desk Appearance Tickets Issued by Police Officer Wooster

Week	Dates	Parking Summonses	Moving Summonses	Desk Appearance Tickets
1	Sept 1 – 7	14	15	3
2	Sept 8 -14	11	3	6
3	Sept 15 – 21	16	10	1
4	Sept 22 – 28	9	12	5
5	Sept 29 – Oct 5	18	11	7

85. Police Officer Wooster is adding up the total number of summonses and Desk Appearance Tickets issued by her during the above five-week period. Which of the following four formulas should she use to arrive at the correct number of summonses that she issued?

A. 18+11+7

(**WRONG** because this totals only the summonses issued Sept 29 – Oct 5.)

B. 3+6+1+5+7

(**WRONG** because this only totals the Desk Appearance Tickets issued.)

C. 14+11+16+9+18+15+3+10+12+11+3+6+1+5+7

(**CORRECT.** This correctly includes all the summonses and Desk Appearance Tickets, a total of 141.)

D. 1(14+11+16+9+18) + 2(15+3+10+12+11) + 3(3+6+1+5+7)

(**WRONG** because this is a mathematical formula which multiplies each parenthetical group of summonses and Desk Appearance Tickets issued by the number preceding the parenthesis. The total would be 236.)

<u>**ANSWER KEY- PRACTICE TEST #1**</u>

1. A	26. B	51. D	76. D
2. C	27. C	52. C	77. D
3. B	28. D	53. D	78. D
4. D	29. B	54. C	79. B
5. A	30. A	55. B	80. D
6. D	31. D	56. D	81. D
7. B	32. A	57. D	82. C
8. D	33. D	58. C	83. D
9. A	34. D	59. C	84. C
10. B	35. D	60. A	85. C
11. C	36. C	61. A	
12. B	37. B	62. C	
13. D	38. B	63. D	
14. B	39. C	64. B	
15. C	40. A	65. D	
16. D	41. D	66. B	
17. C	42. A	67. C	
18. C	43. D	68. A	
19. B	44. B	69. C	
20. D	45. D	70. B	
21. C	46. C	71. D	
22. D	47. C	72. D	
23. B	48. D	73. D	
24. C	49. C	74. A	
25. D	50. D	75. D	

POLICE OFFICER EXAM NEW YORK CITY

<u>ANSWER KEY- PRACTICE TEST #2</u>

1. B	26. D	51. D	76. A
2. D	27. D	52. B	77. D
3. A	28. A	53. D	78. A
4. C	29. D	54. C	79. B
5. B	30. A	55. B	80. C
6. C	31. A	56. D	81. D
7. C	32. A	57. D	82. D
8. D	33. D	58. D	83. A
9. D	34. D	59. C	84. C
10. C	35. C	60. A	85. C
11. B	36. C	61. B	
12. B	37. C	62. D	
13. C	38. D	63. C	
14. B	39. C	64. A	
15. C	40. C	65. C	
16. D	41. D	66. D	
17. C	42. B	67. C	
18. D	43. B	68. C	
19. D	44. D	69. D	
20. D	45. B	70. D	
21. C	46. C	71. D	
22. B	47. C	72. C	
23. B	48. B	73. C	
24. C	49. C	74. B	
25. D	50. D	75. B	

VOCABULARY AND SPELLING | 17

The following are important <u>spelling</u> and <u>vocabulary</u> words for police officers. Understanding the spelling and meaning of these words is helpful in answering Written Expression passages. Try to review this list during brief study sessions (as opposed to a few long study sessions.) There is a theory of learning which states that students remember most when they study for short periods instead of one long period. Therefore, seven study periods during the week are more effective than one long period during the weekend.

• abide	• aggression	• atheist
• absence	• aggressive	• assassination
• acceptable	• alias	• assailant
• accessory	• alibi	• assassination
• accident	• allegation	• August
• accidentally	• alleged	• autopsy
• accommodate	• allegiance	• awful
• accomplice	• amateur	• battery
• achieve	• ambulance	• because
• acknowledge	• analysis	• becoming
• acquaintance	• angle	• beginning
• acquainted	• annotate	• believe
• acquire	• annually	• belligerent
• acquit	• apparent	• bellwether
• address	• apparently	• benevolent
• adjacent	• apprised	• bicycle
• admonish	• approach	• boisterous
• adultery	• arctic	• burglary
• adversary	• argument	• business
• advisable	• arraign	• calendar
• affect	• arrest	• caliber
• affidavit	• arson	• camouflage
• aggravated	• asphalt	• capitol

- Caribbean
- category
- Caucasian
- caught
- cemetery
- changeable
- chief
- coerce
- colleague
- collectible
- collision
- column
- coming
- commit
- committed
- concealed
- concede
- congratulate
- conscientious
- conscious
- consensus
- consideration
- contempt
- continuing
- controlling
- controversy
- contusion
- conviction
- coolly
- coroner
- corroborate
- countenance
- counterfeit
- credulity

- culprit
- cumbersome
- curfew
- deceive
- defamation
- definitely
- delinquent
- derision
- desist
- desperate
- detain
- deterrent
- difference
- dilapidated
- dilemma
- disappear
- disappoint
- disastrous
- discernable
- disheveled
- disorderly
- disperse
- disturbance
- drown
- drunkenness
- dumbbell
- embarrass
- embezzlement
- emulate
- enamored
- enigma
- epilepsy
- equipment
- erratic

- exceed
- exhaust
- exhibit
- exhilarate
- existence
- exonerate
- experience
- extort
- extradition
- extreme
- famished
- farthest
- fascinating
- February
- felonious
- fictitious
- fiery
- flippant
- fluorescent
- fondle
- forcible
- foreign
- forgery
- formidable
- friend
- fugitive
- fulfil
- gauge
- government
- grateful
- guarantee
- guidance
- handicapped
- harass

- harassed
- height
- heroin
- hierarchy
- hindrance
- homicide
- humorous
- hygiene
- hypodermic
- hysterical
- ignorance
- illicit
- illiterate
- imaginary
- imbued
- imitate
- immediately
- impetuous
- incessant
- incidentally
- incoherent
- incriminating
- incursion
- independent
- indictment
- indispensable
- informant
- inhabited
- innocence
- inoculate
- insidious
- intelligence
- interfering
- interrogation

- intruder
- irrational
- jewelry
- judgment
- jurisdiction
- kernel
- laboratory
- laceration
- leisure
- lethal
- lethargic
- liaison
- library
- license
- lightning
- lose
- maintain
- maintenance
- malicious
- manslaughter
- memento
- militant
- millennium
- miniature
- minuscule
- miscellaneous
- mischief
- mischievous
- misdemeanor
- misspell
- necessary
- negligent
- neighbor
- niece

- noticeable
- notify
- obscene
- obstruct
- obvious
- occasion
- occasionally
- occurred
- occurrence
- occurrence
- offender
- omission
- opinion
- opium
- original
- outrageous
- pallid
- pamphlet
- paralyze
- parliament
- pastime
- perceive
- perjury
- perpetrator
- perseverance
- persistent
- personnel
- plagiarize
- playwright
- plead
- possession
- potatoes
- precede
- precedent

- prescription
- presence
- prevalent
- principle
- privilege
- probable cause
- prodigious
- professor
- prolific
- promise
- pronunciation
- proof
- prosecute
- protruding
- publicly
- puncture
- pursuit
- quarantine
- quarrel
- questionnaire
- readable
- really
- receipt
- receive
- recollection
- recommend
- reconciliation
- recurrence
- refer
- reference
- referred
- refrigerator
- registration

- regress
- relevant
- religious
- rendezvous
- repetition
- repudiate
- respiration
- restaurant
- restitution
- resuscitation
- rhyme
- rhythm
- ridiculous
- scarcely
- schedule
- secretary
- seize
- seizure
- separate
- sergeant
- sergeant
- siege
- significance
- silhouette
- similar
- simultaneous
- sparse
- specimen
- speech
- straighten
- strength
- subpoena
- subsidiary

- successful
- suicide
- summons
- superstitious
- suppress
- surprise
- surprised
- surveillance
- suspicious
- swerve
- syringe
- tattoo
- testify
- tetanus
- thieve
- thirtieth
- thorough
- Thursday
- tomatoes
- tomorrow
- transient
- traumatic
- Tuesday
- turbulent
- turmoil
- twelfth
- tyranny
- unconscious
- underrate
- unequivocal
- unforeseen
- until
- upholstery

- vacuum • vandalize • vehicle • vehicular • vicinity • vicious • visible • warrant • weather
- Wednesday • weird • welfare • whether • withhold

TEST-TAKING SUGGESTIONS

1. Get a good night's sleep! The night before the exam is not the time to go to a party or to a sports game. Scientific studies have shown that sleep deprivation dulls the mind.

2. If at all possible, try not to cram. If you can, review the exercises, suggestions and hints, and practice tests. If you have been studying correctly, you owe it to yourself to rest. Cramming often hurts instead of helping. Pace yourself each day and you won't feel the need to sprint at the last moment.

3. Pay careful attention to the time and location of the test site. Plan to get there in comfort and without having to rush. For more than thirty years I have heard many horror stories of candidates not arriving at the test site on time.

4. Do <u>not</u> go into the test hungry. Eat and drink enough to last you through the test.

5. At the test site, listen attentively and don't take anything for granted. Follow directions carefully. Make sure that you don't miss any information that might help you get a higher score.

6. If you have time, familiarize yourself with the computer you will be using. Check to see if it is working properly. If there are any problems, bring them to the attention of the proctor as soon as possible.

7. Crystallize in your mind how many questions you have to answer - and the types of questions.

8. Quickly develop a time budget - and during the exam check the time <u>on your watch</u> to make sure you are not falling behind. Do not rely on the proctor to keep you informed of the time. Remember that you are not allowed to use a cell phone.

9. Usually every question is worth the same as the other questions. Don't spend too much time on any one question (unless you have finished all the other questions and are satisfied with your answers).

10. If you find during the test that there are questions for which you believe there is more than one valid answer, do not lose time thinking about it. Select the best answer that you can - and go on.

11. Finally - and very important - if you finish early, do <u>not</u> get up and go home. If allowed, review the exam and your answers.

<u>GOOD LUCK !!!</u>

Fotolia images: check mark, scales, hand with books

Books by Angelo Tropea
Non-Fiction

Florida Law Enforcement Basic Abilities Test (BAT) Exam Guide

School Safety Agent New York City

Police Officer Exam New York City
Police Officer Exam New York City Speed-Prep
MTA Police Officer Exam

Sanitation Worker Exam New York City
Sanitation Worker New York City Speed-Study Guide

Bridge and Tunnel Officer Exam New York City

Traffic Enforcement Agent

Court Office Assistant

Pass the New York Notary Public Exam
Pass the New York Notary Public Exam (Questions and Answers)
Notary Public Journal of Notarial Acts
Notary Public Journal 600 Entries
Notary Public Journal Large Entries
Notary Public Journal Two-Page Entries
New York Notary Public Exam Speed-Study Guide
New York Notary Public Reference Guide

California Notary Public Exam

Pass the New Postal Test 2010 Edition
Pass the New Postal Test Second Edition
Postal Test 473E Study Guide

Pass the New Citizenship Test 2012 Edition
Pass the New Citizenship Test Third Edition
Pass the New Citizenship Test Questions and Answers (English, Spanish and Chinese Editions)

Examen de Ciudadania Americana Español Y Inglés

Pass the New Citizenship Test Quick Civics Lessons
Quick Civics Lessons from USICS and Civics Cards for Cut-Out

Canadian Citizenship Test

Goldmine of Baby Names Boys and Girls
Goldmine of Baby Names Boys
Goldmine of Baby Names Girls

Aliens and UFOs: Case Closed
Zombie Pocket Guide

Cruise Fan Tips and Tricks How to Get the Most Out of Your Cruise Adventure
Cruise Fan Cruising With Norwegian
Cruise Fan Bermuda Cruise

NYS Surrogate's Court Procedure Act Vol. 1
NYS Surrogate's Court Procedure Act Vol. 2
NYS Surrogate's Court Procedure Act Vol. 3
NYS Surrogate's Court Procedure Act Vol. 4

Amazing Science News and Facts No. 1

Arizona Civics Test
North Dakota Civics Test
Utah Civics Test
Idaho Civics Test

Fiction
Pinocchio and the Dragons of Martoon (age 12 and up)

The following two pages are for recording important information as you go through the testing and hiring process. All of these categories are listed on the "Notice of Examination" for the Police Officer Exam.

NOTES AND REMINDERS

Salary:

Application for Exam:

Education Requirement:

Character and Background:

Medical and Psychological Assessment:

Physical Testing:

Drug Testing:

License Requirement:

Residency Requirement:

English Requirement:

New York City Residency Credit:

Selective Certification for Foreign Language.

Test Results:

Investigation:

Special Test Accommodations:

Made in the USA
Columbia, SC
15 February 2018